Anything is possible—when you know your own mind! *Mindworks* will show you how to:

- Communicate more precisely with yourself and others
- Identify and access your resources
- Create a map for action by asking yourself a few simple questions
- Recycle mistakes, setbacks, and failures into resourceful experiences
- Replace destructive behaviors with constructive ones
- Open yourself to new perspectives
- Define your choices

Mindworks shows you all of the astonishing and wonderful ways to take full advantage of your full potential, to accomplish all that you set out to do!

Unlock the Promise Within

MINDWORKS

*NLP Tools for
Building a Better Life*

Anné Linden

with Kathrin Perutz

BERKLEY BOOKS, NEW YORK

MINDWORKS

A Berkley Book / published by arrangement with
Andrews McMeel Publishing

PRINTING HISTORY
Andrews McMeel Publishing edition / 1997
Berkley edition / November 1998

The Penguin Putnam Inc. World Wide Web site address is
http://www.penguinputnam.com

ISBN: 0-425-16624-4

BERKLEY®
Berkley Books are published by The Berkley Publishing Group,
a member of Penguin Putnam Inc.,
375 Hudson Street, New York, New York 10014.
BERKLEY and the "B" design
are trademarks belonging to Penguin Putnam Inc.

PRINTED IN THE UNITED STATES OF AMERICA

10   9   8   7   6   5   4   3   2

For my beloved children,
Edward, Melissa, and Raven-Wolf,
who taught me about love,
joy, pain, and change.

Contents

Contents

Preface

Mindworks is an unusual self-help book in that it tells you what you already know. The main point of reading it isn't so much to get new information, as to learn how to use the information you already have but don't know about or have access to.

This book is for and about *you*. Its aim is to help you achieve *your* goals, whatever they are—to open up *your* particular choices.

Don't just read this book, *use it!* The skills outlined here are of no use at all unless you practice them. These are not intellectual propositions; this is not about intellectual solutions. Even if you are accustomed to solving problems through logic and reasoning, suspend that way of thinking for the space of this book. Let it work its magic. Let it work *your* magic.

When you do the exercises—actually *do* them instead of thinking about them—you effect the changes, conscious and unconscious, that lead to choice.

Read the book through systematically, from beginning to end, and then go back and concentrate on a particular section or skill or technique. Bring your own abilities, resources, fears, and habits to this book. Make it your own, and at the end you will discover that your mind is the most interesting place you know.

Acknowledgments

I wish to acknowledge with appreciation and respect Richard Bandler and John Grinder, the creators of Neuro Linguistic Programming, who were my original teachers. This book is based on their work. Some of the exercises and processes were developed from their training sessions. I especially want to express my deep appreciation to the memory of Milton H. Erickson, one of the most influential "ancestors" of NLP, with whom I had the privilege to study and whose wisdom continues to inform and energize my life and my work. I also want to recognize Robert Dilts from whom the idea of shifting perspectives came. I thank my dear friends Murray Spalding, who helped give birth to this book; Susan James, whose ongoing support and enthusiasm has always sustained and encouraged me; and Joanne Fabris, who brought me together with Kathy, without whom this book would not have been written. Last, many thanks to Jane Dystel, who helped make this book a reality.

Introduction: Turning on the Magic

Everyone has dreams, big and little dreams, impossible dreams, and close-at-hand ones. Dreams of adventure, love, and success of every kind: daring to stand up to someone who's always had a hold on you, cooking an unforgettable meal, writing a book, winning the gold, wearing purple, learning French, making responsible choices, taking control of your life.

Make a picture in your mind of a dream you have, something you want to accomplish, a promise made to yourself, a goal you hope to reach. Make that picture small and dark and far away. Hold it in your mind's eye a few seconds. Notice the feelings you have. Let it go.

Now make the picture big and bright and bring it closer to you. See it projected on your mental inner screen. Notice the feelings you have. Let it go.

Which way of representing your dream makes you feel more motivated to go after it? Which of the images makes you believe more strongly in the possibility of achieving it?

Your brain is a magic place. It may take awhile before you can turn on the sights and sounds and feelings of experience with the ease of adjusting your TV or VCR, but it will come much more quickly than you now think possible.

All of us are making pictures inside our heads and playing tapes and talking to ourselves; it's the way our brains represent experience. When you think about something that has happened, something that might happen, or something you want to happen, you see and hear and feel it through your senses. This is the way we think, though most of the time we're unaware of how we do it.

In order to achieve our goals, resolve problems, or sort out our values, we have to be able to get in touch with the part of ourselves that controls most of what we do: walking, talking, breathing, moving, and all the hundreds of automatic behaviors that get us through the course of a day. I'm talking about the unconscious mind.

To make changes in our lives, we need to access this part of ourselves, to open up the connections between our conscious and unconscious thoughts.

Much has been written about communication, particularly about the difficulties in communicating across gaps of age, gender, expectations, ethnicity, or education. *Interpersonal communication*—communication between people, between yourself and someone else—is extremely important for our daily social interactions. You have to make sure that the message you're trying to send is received and understood. You also have to insure that you understand what someone else is trying to tell you. In many jobs, being able to communicate with others is crucial, and certainly few if any relationships can survive without it.

But at least as important as the ability to communicate clearly with others is the ability to communicate with yourself. *Intrapersonal communication* means doing within yourself what you do to establish understanding and *rapport* with others: listening, paying close attention, and creating an atmosphere of trust and safety.

Unless you trust yourself, you can't communicate. And only by communicating with yourself can you discover the way you think. Then you can change your way of thinking to resolve problems and obstacles, and to break out of unprofitable or limiting habits and patterns.

You start this process of change by discovering what's already there, the resources and abilities you possess, the things you do to motivate yourself or hold yourself back. You start by thinking out loud.

How do you represent your goals or dreams to yourself? Can you actually picture them? If you can't see your dream out in front of you, how will you follow it? If you don't know what you're looking for, how will you know when you've found it?

Once you've imagined (literally, "made an image of") what you hope to accomplish or where you're going, you are already that much closer to fulfillment. In all probability that's what you're doing now. That's what we all do, whether or not we're aware of it. If you're lucky, you're already making a big bright colorful picture of whatever you want to achieve, even without knowing it. Or you're talking to yourself, cheering yourself on with "You can do it!" and other words of encouragement, like the Little Engine That Could.

But maybe you're doing the opposite—again, whether or not you're aware of it. Maybe you're telling yourself "I'll never be able to do this" or "I'm stupid" or "Everyone else is better than I am." You may have been telling yourself this so often you've come to believe it.

Try this: Take the message you send yourself that keeps you from accomplishing the great or small things you hope to do, and play it over in your mind. Repeat the words you tell yourself: "I'll never finish that" or "I'm not smart enough" or whatever you say.

Turn that message down until it's very quiet, and make it come from very far away.

Now turn up the volume. Make the message loud and close.

Put circus music underneath it.

What happens?

The words remain the same, but the meaning will alter. *How* you do or think or feel something determines its impact. You can change how you feel by changing how you think. You can take conscious control over your unconscious behavior.

Within your brain right now are thousands of choices you might not have a clue about. You didn't notice all the alternatives that have been available to you. Maybe you've taken a backseat, until now, and let yourself be driven along the road or tracks of your life.

It's time to take control. By learning how to direct your mind, you can do just about anything: change direction, go backward or forward, accomplish what you dream of, resolve difficulties, alter your habits, get on a new track. You can be in charge, in the driver's seat, the captain of your ship.

This doesn't mean you can always get what you want when you want it. But it does mean you have choices about how you think and feel. It means you can make your brain actively work for you instead of leaving it on automatic pilot.

If you can pinpoint what, specifically, you need to change and have the tools at hand to change it, the results can be magical. In an instant you can go from a feeling of limits to a feeling of strength and freedom, as the new associations flow together like quicksilver.

Each of us is unique. We experience the world in our own way. We each have our own content, the result of our personal histories of sensations, people, events, behavior, and emotions. Yet we're able to communicate to and with another person. How do we do that? How can I be sure that if I say something is beautiful you will know what I mean? Or what about love? Each person conjures up different images and associations when we hear the word *love*, and yet each of us expects to be understood when we say "I love you."

Interpersonal communication is the way we connect with each other. It's what's going on between you and me across this page. I'm bouncing my thoughts off you; you react or respond with your own thoughts and sensations. Maybe you're arguing with me in your mind; or you're forming a picture of what this book is about or how it will affect you.

Mindworks is an owner's manual for the mind. It will show you a number of techniques, all very simple, for allowing you to make maximum use of the strengths and resources you already have.

If you have a flashlight but no batteries, you won't find your way in the dark. If you have batteries but don't know the correct way to insert them, you still won't have any illumination. To shine the light along your path, you'll need your flashlight, batteries, and a few instructions. This book provides the instructions. You already have the rest.

Mindworks is based on the principles of Neuro Linguistic Programming, or NLP. It's what I have been teaching and practicing for close to twenty years, as founder and director of the New York Training Institute for NLP. Now I am bringing the principles and techniques of this extraordinary methodology directly to you, to each reader of this book. Here are the skills or tools to open up your own choices, within the contents and contexts of your own lives.

NLP was founded in the mid 1970s by Richard Bandler and John Grinder (my teachers and colleagues) and incorporates the work of many seminal thinkers in the fields of linguistics, psychology, and anthropology, among others. Essentially, NLP offers practical techniques for changing behavior by means of clear communication, both with ourselves and others. As the name implies (*neuro* refers to the brain, *linguistic* to language, *programming* to habitual patterns of behavior, like thought, created by the impact of language on the brain), NLP shows us how to "reprogram" ourselves. This means first bringing to consciousness the patterns and behaviors that we're constantly engaged in without being aware of them. Then we can challenge the assumptions we hold and don't think about, access the resources we don't even know we have, and finally, by "changing" our minds, we can alter our behavior, thoughts, and feelings.

NLP is concerned with *how* our minds work—the patterns we use to organize information, the ways we motivate (or inhibit) ourselves—*how* we can modify automatic patterns of response to allow new choices, new behaviors, new ways of thinking and feeling. Because NLP concentrates on immediate trouble spots instead of raking over the past, the results are quick, sometimes immediate.

NLP is expressed through specific mental tools that we'll be discussing throughout this book, tools for change so effective and instantaneous they seem like magic. The tools come in the form of simple instructions, often couched as questions, about how to control the workings of your mind.

We've all experienced some of the magic: a mind that can summon up the blue edging on a coat in the long-ago past or remember a melody heard only once; a mind that can step into the future, invent poems, solve mathematical problems, fall in love, understand another person's need. Our minds are more complicated than any other thing in the universe, and yet we can adjust them, fine-tune them, alter their patterns with something as simple as a pointed question.

Mindworks is a user's guide, providing instructions on how to make these tools and techniques work. The names of some of these skills may be unfamiliar to you, though you'll recognize most of them as familiar processes. Like the character in Molière's play who discovers that what he's been speaking all his life is prose, you will discover that you've been doing NLP in some form or other all along.

Mindworks is divided into seven parts, each representing one of the fundamental principles of NLP, which we refer to as presuppositions. In linguistic terms, a presupposition is everything you must assume to be true in order for the statement to make sense. If I say, "The cat jumped from the table," the presupposition behind my statement is that the cat was *on* the table. If I say, "Close the window," that presupposes the window was open.

The basic NLP presuppositions outline what we assume to be true, and the specific skills and techniques follow from that. In using this book, you'll discover it's most effective if you accept the presuppositions. You don't have to believe them (at least not yet; I'm trusting that you'll believe them by the time you come to the end), but they'll have the greatest effect if you act as if they were true. ("As if" is an NLP skill we use in formulating outcomes.) Act as if the presuppositions are true, and you'll discover how this affects your thinking, your attitudes to others and yourself.

These are the presuppositions in the order we'll be discussing them:

1. The meaning of your communication is the response you get

2. You have all the resources you need

3. Success is the ability to achieve intended results

4. You can turn failure into feedback

5. The map is not the territory

6. There is a positive intention behind every behavior

7. There are always more choices

Learning NLP is, for many people, a new way of coming to terms with what you already know. It's a guide to your own programs, a systematic way of making use of your resources, of harnessing your abilities and strengths and being able to communicate freely and clearly to yourself and others. If you'd like more information about any of the patterns, skills, or concepts presented in this book, please contact Anné Linden, 145 Avenue of the Americas, fifth floor, New York, NY 10013. Phone or fax: 212-674-3192.

PART ONE

*The Meaning of Your Communication
Is the Response You Get*

1

Saying What You Mean

> "You should say what you mean," the March Hare went on.
>
> "I do," Alice hastily replied; "at least—at least I mean what I say."
>
> —Lewis Carroll
> *Alice in Wonderland*

Do you know what you're saying?

Of course you do. Otherwise you wouldn't be saying it, right?

Maybe.

What you're saying and what the other person understands may be two different things. The way to know if what you say gets across is by paying attention to the response. Your communication is made up of both the message you intend to send out and the message you receive.

Communication between people, like magnetism, requires two poles: you and me. The message passes between us, and what you say is what I understand you to say, just as much as it is what you think you are saying.

The Meaning of Your Communication Is the Response You Get to What You Say or Do.

Interpersonal communication: an exchange between people. Sounds straightforward, doesn't it? Yet the number one problem that sends people to therapists is lack of communication, people who can't hear what the other person is saying. Husband and wife, parent and child, boss and employee, doctor and patient, partner and client—the problem is the same. They can't get their message across.

With all the emphasis that's usually placed on being a good speaker, one half of the equation has been forgotten. You can't have magnetism with only one pole, and you can't have communication without someone to receive what's being conveyed: a listener for the speaker, audience for the actor, observer for the doer. Without a listener, there's no dialogue. And that means no effective communication.

If you can't listen well, you'll never know if your point gets across. A good listener *watches* as closely as he or she listens. I learned that as a young actress: To be convincing onstage, you have to respond to cues; not only to the lines of another actor or a prompter but to everything that goes on around you.

As in the theater, so in life: All the world's a stage, and how effective you are, how believable, depends on how easily you convey your meaning. If I'm doing a great dramatic role, a Lady Macbeth, and the audience is laughing, I can be absolutely sure I'm not coming across. The response tells me that the meaning of my communication— the meaning I intend—is not being delivered.

I have to stop and examine my behavior. Is it the tonality I'm using? Is it in my movements? Am I overdoing my gestures, talking so quickly that I sound like an organ grinder? The words remain the same, no matter who is saying them—"Out, damned spot"—but the message is contained as much in *how* it's said as in *what* is said. What Shakespeare intends in Lady Macbeth's speech is to illuminate her state of mind as she tries to wash away the guilt of the murder she's just committed. If the words are spoken as if the owner of a Dalmatian is ordering her dog out of the kitchen, the meaning is lost.

Knowing *how* is as important as knowing *what*. That's why there are great actors and mediocre ones. And that's why some people are able to communicate easily or brilliantly, while others can't ever seem to get their meaning across.

Those who can't, generally confuse intention and result. They believe that when they've said what they've meant to say the communication is finished.

If Bill tells Susan "I love you," meaning that he really *loves* her, and Susan goes "Yeah, sure, I love you too," in a tone of voice that would be equally appropriate for "Pass the mustard," it's pretty obvious Susan isn't getting the message that Bill is trying to send her.

Now what usually happens is, the person who feels he's not being understood starts blaming the other. "What's the matter with you? Why don't you ever listen when I talk to you?"—things like that.

Or it's this scenario: Bill comes home, says "I love you" to Susan, who doesn't respond at all. Fifteen minutes later she says, "You never express any affection for me."

He blows up. "I just told you," he insists, "the moment I came into the house. What more do you want?"

She hadn't heard him, not consciously. She was involved in chopping onions, her eyes were tearing, and all she noticed when Bill came in the door was that he seemed to be feeling very pleased with himself. What he said and what she heard were not the same. The feeling he meant to convey was not received. The love he offered wasn't accepted—wasn't even acknowledged.

2

Getting the Message Out:
Other-Orientation and Rapport

"How do I love thee? Let me count the ways," wrote Elizabeth Barrett Browning to her husband, Robert Browning. In a quiet moment, listening to the rain play a soft percussion on the roof, or watching the green and blood orange of flames playing in a winter's fireplace, Susan and Bill might talk of love like poets, billing and cooing, speaking with their lips and words and hands.

But on a late-summer afternoon, in a hot kitchen, preparing a meal she doesn't particularly want to make for an old schoolmate of Bill's, Susan doesn't feel especially loving. She didn't hear or respond to the love Bill is trying to convey.

"I told you I love you," he repeats, "the moment I came in. Didn't you hear me? Why don't you listen when I talk to you?"

"That doesn't mean anything," Susan tells him. "You were saying it only because you were feeling good about yourself. I don't feel you reaching out to me at all. You don't seem to grasp what goes on around here."

Bill is indignant. "That's not true, and you know it! I came over, I gave you a kiss. You must be deaf. I'm always telling you; you just never listen. I'm really trying to tune in to you."

She hadn't heard. Or if she did, it was a nuisance like static, coming between her and the onions she had to chop.

"That doesn't mean anything," she tells him. "My feet are aching, it feels like I've been working in this damn kitchen forever, the air's heavy as molasses, and I certainly don't have the sense that you're on my wavelength or that you care about *me*. All you talk about is your own feelings."

What Susan is telling Bill is that the message he thought he was sending her never got through, though she's not aware she's saying this—and he isn't getting *her* gut message either. They're speaking along different sensory pathways, passing and bypassing without noticing what the other is trying to say.

The Meaning of Your Communication Is the Response You Get, Independent of Your Intention.

For all of us, there's a limited amount of attention we can consciously control.

The word *consciously* is key. We hear, see, feel, respond to a multitude of stimuli without being *consciously* aware of doing it.

Remember when you were a child, wrapped up in whatever game you were playing while your mother kept calling you to come in or come down or come to dinner, until she finally went and got you—demanding "Why don't you answer when I call you?"—and you told her, truthfully it seemed, "I didn't hear you"?

Technically speaking, you probably did hear her. Your ears probably registered the vibrations and frequencies of her voice. But it didn't mean anything to you. It wasn't part of your game; it had nothing to do with whatever you were paying attention to. You were attuned to something else and had no part of your attention left over for your mother's call. Your brain didn't process this particular information because the processing center was already fully utilized with something you considered more important at the time.

As we get older, many things change. We gain a greater degree of conscious control over ourselves in many ways, but we still can take in only a limited amount of information at any given moment.

Our attention span is restricted—*span* by definition is the distance from thumb to pinky in an outspread hand; it refers literally to what we're able to grasp.

The conscious mind can pay attention to only seven pieces of information, plus or minus two, at any given moment. That's a maximum of nine bits of information you can juggle at a time. Imagine taking a drink of water. You need to position each of your fingers on the glass, bring the glass to your lips, open your lips, make the necessary muscular adjustments for swallowing—all in all, a task much too complicated for anyone who would be required to do each part of it consciously.

Or think of learning to drive, particularly on a shift car. You're cruising along in high gear, coming up a hill—and you see there's a stop sign at the crest. Or maybe it's a red light. It doesn't matter; either of them can trigger a panic attack. You try to remember—the brakes, the clutch, something released, something pressed down, the gear to be shifted—and if it doesn't happen to you when you're slowing to a stop, it's bound to happen when you try moving forward again: Inevitably, you're going to stall.

A few weeks or months later you've learned how to do it and you no longer "think" about driving at all. The motions become automatic (even on a manual shift); your attention is freed to focus on something else.

Though our conscious attention is restricted to a minimal amount of information at any given moment, we still have a choice about which bits of information we select. We can choose where to aim our attention, directing it outward, toward another person, like the spotlight that picks out a dancer or an actor onstage, or we can shine the light of our attention back on ourselves. Our conscious mind is not set on automatic. We always have the choice of where we focus our attention, out toward others or inwardly.

When we're sending out a message to another person (remember, this is *interpersonal* communication in contrast to intrapersonal, which is communication with oneself), the most effective direction to aim our conscious attention is on the other. We look and listen for specific indicators that tell us if, when, and sometimes how our message is being received.

In NLP, we call this other-orientation.

Other-orientation means paying attention to the other person, and to the signs and indications that person gives out, behavioral indicators that signify the message is received. Is he or she understanding your communication? Are you presenting what you have to say in a way that makes sense? How do you know? Does the other person give signs of *seeing* what you mean? Being *in tune* with what you're saying? *Grasping* your argument? The emphasized words represent different sensory pathways through which people gather, organize, and store information: visual, auditory, and kinesthetic. We'll be discussing this more a little later.

The information you get by paying close attention to how the other person responds tells you what part of the message was received and what wasn't; it opens up a new range of choices in how to present or reframe your communication so it will be understood. To communicate most effectively, you need continually to reassess what you say in terms of how it is received. Communication, once started, is like a loop—between the message that's sent out and the message that's received. Each influences the other; each proceeds from the other. But before that can happen, you need to open the pathways between yourself and the other person and establish a foundation for communicating. That means you must first get the other's attention. Unless the person you're talking to is willing to listen, it doesn't matter how brilliant or dazzling or amusing or even shocking you are. Like the child playing hopscotch at supper time, that person won't hear you.

This doesn't apply only to people with whom you have formal dealings; it applies to all types of communication, even with those close to you. The initial rule for communicating effectively is to get the other person's attention.

And to do that, you must first establish rapport.

Rapport is the ability to hold someone's attention and create a sense of trust. It means implanting the feeling that you understand each other; that you have the other's best interests at heart and that you can be trusted to do whatever they've come to you for.

One way to establish rapport, something you've probably been doing anyway but without thinking about it, is *behavioral matching*. That means doing what the other person is doing—or something very similar. If the other person is sitting, you take a seat instead of standing. If the other is speaking with a soft voice, you modulate your own. It's what we do unconsciously, particularly in new situations: following the other person's lead, a modified form of Simon Says, without being aware that we're doing it.

By becoming aware, which means making the choice to focus our *conscious* attention on matching another person, we can draw the other into a sense of rapport. You do something similar to what the other person is doing in order to create in him or her the feeling that you're kindred beings, that you understand. Behavioral matching actually increases your understanding of the other person because you've aligned yourself with the other, literally put yourself in his or her position, and the increased understanding isn't a pretense; it's real.

This is not the same as mimicking, however, which would almost certainly have the opposite effect and break the rapport. Mimicking someone, copying the exact tonality or gait or repeating the words back verbatim is a way of teasing or making fun. Above all, it conveys disrespect. Instead, you want to create an environment of respect and understanding with the other person.

Specifically, you match posture, volume, and tempo. If the person you're talking to is sitting, you won't be standing because you don't want to be placed at a higher level; it gives the impression that you're speaking down, and that would not be the best way of relating, to put it mildly. In business, with personal relationships, or even with new, still undefined contacts, you want to start out at eye level. If the other person speaks slowly, it makes sense (and increases rapport) for you to slow down your own speech; you'll speak softer or louder, depending on the cues you're getting. Matching is like dancing, following someone else's lead.

Matching creates the experience of being on the same wavelength. I'm reflecting back what you're doing so we can dance together; my movements suggest yours; we're in tune and in step with each other, seeing eye to eye, aligned with each other.

When you're *mismatching* the behavior of the other, you're out of sync, moving to a different drummer. You're using a different tempo—or volume or posture—and it's almost guaranteed to antagonize the other person so much that your communication has no real chance of getting through.

For example: You're a Realtor, trying to convince someone to buy a house. They're leaning forward and speaking slowly, and you're leaning back and speaking fast. No rapport. No sale. No way.

You, the Realtor, are a city person, used to a hurried pace and to the distance city folk might like to put between themselves. Your clients are country people, used to slower ways, more time, intimacy. If you move your upper body forward, giving the impression that you're really interested and that you have lots of time to hear them out, and speak in a slow, deliberative way, chances are good they'll want to buy from you. If not this property, for sure the next.

◆

RAPPORT EXERCISE

1. Pick someone with whom you sometimes have trouble in getting your message across.

2. Spend a couple of minutes watching his or her posture and listening to the tempo and tonality of his or her voice.

3. Try matching (approximating) his or her posture, tempo, tonality.

4. Notice how it helps get your message across.

If you really want to play with this, try first mismatching the other's posture, tempo, and tonality. Notice the person's response. Then match the other's posture, tempo, and tonality. Notice the response. Ask the person what his or her experience was.

Which way was more helpful in getting across the message you wanted to send?

◆

3

Directing Consciousness:
Uptime

To communicate effectively, we need to establish rapport with the other person. We do this by paying attention to behavioral clues the other person gives out. And to do that we need to be other-oriented, focusing our attention outward.

All of this we can do automatically. We're often attuned to someone; rapport seems to happen naturally; communication sometimes just flows. Other times, none of this happens, and though we need to communicate for the sake of our livelihood, health, happiness, or simple equilibrium, we just can't manage. At that point we need tools or techniques we can call up. We need to make our automatic actions conscious in order to understand what they're composed of. Then we can apply these actions or behaviors to new situations, until they become automatic again. In other words, we have to reverse our learning, taking something we know how to do and learning how we do it so we can do it again in future without thinking about it.

In order to focus our communication skills so we can make use of them whenever we need them, we have to know *how* we think, how we direct our conscious attention. Tools are helpful only if they're available at the right time and if we know how to use them. Having skills we can rely on means being able to direct our conscious attention toward some object or objective and not toward another.

Directing consciousness goes back to the concept that our conscious minds can pay attention only to between five and nine pieces of information at any given moment. Even if we stretch this to the maximum, to the full nine pieces, that doesn't give us enough information to walk across the room. We couldn't get from the door to the window if we had to pay conscious attention to everything we have to expand and contract, shift and do to move our body.

We have a very limited conscious mind, paired with an unlimited unconscious mind. Consciousness refers to what we're aware of at any particular moment. The unconscious mind is made up of all our memories, knowledge, experiences—and the ways we've categorized all this information and experience, and labeled it, and given it meaning. All that is our unconsciousness, wide and deep as the sea.

Our conscious mind sails over it like a small boat, a speck by comparison to the vastness below. But we can control our conscious mind; we can take the small number of items of information we have at any given moment and use them to guide the ship wherever we want it—meaning ourselves—to go.

It's precisely *because* our conscious mind is so limited that we can control which way it's directed.

Most people are not aware that they have this choice. They don't realize their consciousness is limited and therefore accessible. Usually, they're in a mixed state, with three or four pieces of information (at best!) directed *outside* themselves and the remaining five or six pieces of information directed *inside*.

In other words, most of the time we're primarily focused

on ourselves (even if we're not aware of it): on what we feel or think, what we're saying to ourselves ("I can do this, I can't do that"), what we're remembering in the way of images, sounds, words, sensations, feelings. Usually, when we're not consciously directing our attention—when we're floating over the great sea of our consciousness, letting our thoughts drift, carried by whatever current—we are more focused on ourselves than on others.

When consciousness is directed inward in this way, we call it *downtime*. Downtime can be useful for many forms of creative work and for meditation and reflection, and it can be a conscious choice—a freeing of the imagination— that expands your sense of self. It is, however, a private place, where you communicate with yourself, not with others.

When your consciousness is focused externally, on what you see, hear, and touch, you are in *uptime*. This is the place for meeting others. This supports and allows other-orientation, the place to be mentally when you are observing another person's response to something you've said, when you are measuring the other's reaction to ascertain what they've heard of what you've said, to see if the message you meant to send out is the same as the one that was received.

Uptime is the best vantage point for people-watching, for noticing all the small changes and shades of response in gestures, words, and posture, in the tiny movements of an eyebrow or the drumming of fingertips. It sweeps away the inner agenda for a while, the secret messages you're constantly bringing to mind in images and words, talking to yourself. It creates what's essentially an "ego-less" state.

Your consciousness is directed toward what you see and hear *outside* yourself. The ego has been placed on hold like a boat on automatic pilot; the censorship coming from the conscious mind has been silenced. In uptime, there's an open channel between your conscious and unconscious mind: words rise to the surface; your thoughts are spoken.

Uptime is a way of freeing the self from self. You're not preoccupied with how you're doing, but instead you take your functioning for granted and turn your attention to the world around you.

How do you do this? How do you get into uptime?

It's the easiest thing in the world, like turning on the flashlight of consciousness or using words to capture a thought. But often the easiest is the most difficult—like taking the first step.

Focus on something outside yourself. Observe that somebody or something carefully. Pay close attention to what you see; use your eyes and your ears. Get the details.

Give yourself a simple observation task. Look at somebody closely: see what the person is wearing, the colors of the clothes, hairstyle, way of walking, sound of voice, taking note of the details but making no inference from them and coming to no conclusions. From this you begin to direct your attention outward, falling naturally into uptime.

You become aware of the person's facial expressions, changes in posture, gestures—a nodding of the head or the pumping of a foot at the end of a crossed leg—and you listen, to the words and tempo and tonality, and pay attention to whatever else you might be able to notice, leaving all value judgments and interpretations aside, *observing*, not judging. Even this short list is more than the consciousness can handle at any one moment; it's meant only as a little push, a way of getting into uptime, a movement of the conscious mind out of self-absorption and toward the external world by way of focusing on a particular object, thing, or person.

Getting into uptime is a way of energizing yourself, turning on to the world, shining your flashlight ahead of you. Get yourself out of the place you're in, emotionally and physically. Go out; look and listen and sense with your body. Come alive! It just means pitching your attention in front of you. Notice the trees on the street, the gait of people walking, the wind or sun or rain against your skin, the sounds of traffic or water rushing or people talking. When you're shopping for food, go over to the fruit and vegetables and find a beautiful color, an unusual shape: Hold it, look at it, maybe even smell it. Take in the beauty of that object. Uptime increases your pleasure in the world.

Try these exercises to move into uptime.

◆

UPTIME EXERCISE I

1. Go out for a short walk, ten minutes or so.

2. Find as many of these as possible:

   · A flower
   · The color orange/purple/yellow
   · A triangle, a square, a circle
   · An unusually shaped building
   · Something with a smooth, silky texture
   · Something rough-textured
   · Birdsong—can you hear the birds?
   · The wind in the trees
   · Sounds of children playing and laughing

3. Make your own list. You can even send yourself off on a treasure hunt, looking for very specific items (a black stone, a coin) that you can bring back.

4. Repeat this exercise every day until it becomes natural. When you go out for a walk, look and listen to the world outside yourself.

◆

UPTIME EXERCISE II

1. Pretend you're a Martian, a being from another planet. This being has two switches: INSIDE and OUTSIDE. When the INSIDE switch is on, you have access only to *internal* information and experience. When the OUTSIDE switch is on, you have access only to *external* information and experience.

2. The switches are located on either side of your head at your temples. Left controls INSIDE, right controls OUTSIDE.

3. Touch your left temple and walk around the room. Remember that you are aware of *internal* experience: sensations, images, thoughts, sounds, words you say to yourself. Circle the room a few times.

4. Now touch your right temple and repeat the exercise, walking around the room. This time you are aware only of *external* experiences: the colors and shapes of the objects in the room, the textures of furniture, the shapes of windows, temperature, breezes, the sounds coming from outside yourself. Circle the room a few times.

5. When you have each "switch" under control, practice going back and forth: from *internal* to *external* and back again. Get it down so that a light touch

moves you instantaneously from one world of experience into the other.

6. Recognize that the ability to go from downtime to
   uptime is under your control and available to you at
   all times.

◆

4

Calibration

Measurement began our might.

—W. B. Yeats

Anyone who's sat at a sidewalk café or on a park bench for hours, watching the minidramas of everyday life going on all around, knows the endless fascination of observing human behavior. In a restaurant or airport lounge or across a hotel lobby; sitting on a bus, in a car, in traffic; gazing out the window from your office or study; waiting on line—anywhere at all, people-watching has got to be human-kind's favorite sport.

Everybody has a streak of the anthropologist. Or maybe it's just natural curiosity. We want to know what's going on with other people: What is she thinking? What is he feeling? What's *happening*? Sometimes we make up stories about the people we observe—this one's in love, that one has just been through tragedy. It's fun, it's imaginative, but it's hardly reliable.

If you want to know what's actually going on, what state another person is in, and how you can best engage the other's interest, you have to pay attention to certain behavioral indicators. You *calibrate* behavior for consistencies and differences.

To calibrate is to measure, to determine the degree of deviation from a standard or norm. Humans have an amazing capacity for this; we can detect the slightest deviations, the minutest changes in someone's tone of voice or facial expression or way of walking; we can recognize a mood on the telephone in an instant or see it half a block away in the gait of a person moving toward us.

But how do you measure thought? Feelings? Is there any way I can look at you and recognize where your thoughts are directed? Is there a measurement that tells me if you're receptive to what I have to say? If you're listening to me? If you're understanding what I mean?

I can't read your mind, but I *can* have a good idea of what kind of mood or state you're in, or which way your thoughts are tending, by looking and listening for certain behavioral indicators. I observe what you do—with your body, your voice, the movement of your eyes, all the minutiae of your behavior that you may not be aware of. These indicators send out a message for anyone to see and hear, if they know what to look and listen for.

Calibration is knowing how to read another person— what to pay attention to, which specific behaviors reveal a person's state of mind or feeling. It's a way of looking for clues. Calibration indicates a state of alertness, like the cat's tensed posture, measuring the movements of a bird in the leaves, or the dog's vigilant nose sniffing out the direction of the prey. It's a focusing of the conscious mind on another person (other-orientation) and a willingness or curiosity to take in all the clues, signs, and data that the other person gives out, without making interpretations or judgments—simply observing, getting information. This in turn gives you the information you need to become more flexible, and more persuasive, in your communication.

Fine. But what is it, specifically, that we mean by *behavioral indicators*? How do you know where to look, what to listen for?

Picture a pond. Place it in the woods, in summer. Lots

of frogs are living in that pond. Maybe you've heard their deep, musical belches or their piping chorus. But where do you look for them?

The bubbles on the surface of the water can tell you. You take notice of the tops of the lily pads, and then of the small branches lying alongside the pond. Hundreds of frogs come to life. All of a sudden they're in front of you. How could you have missed them?

It's the same with reading people, with seeing the multitude of signs and indicators that tell you what's going on inside a person. It's like bubbles on the surface: a sudden change in tempo as a person speaks, a more rapid breathing, a tensing of facial muscles.

Be aware of changes, mainly. Look for changes in posture, in gestures, in the depth or rate of breathing (deep breath to shallow breath, fast to slow), in facial expressions (muscle tension or relaxation, the deepening or shallowness of facial lines, changes in color), in tonality of voice—changes in pitch from high to low, changes in volume—and in tempo of speech (the rate altering between fast and slow). Beware of interpretations—seeing what looks like a frown and interpreting it to mean that the person is critical; hearing someone speak loudly and interpreting this as anger. These are not useful and probably not accurate.

For specific changes in posture, pay attention to the positioning of shoulders, head, and spine. When you're calibrating gestures, it's particularly important to note their onset and ending. Most people have characteristic gestures that define them as much as does the sound of their voice or their way of speaking. The gestures accompany them like shadows, pointing to the substance. This one drums the tabletop with her nails; that one combs his hair with his fingers; so-and-so presses down invisible pedals with his feet; someone else seems to be shooing away imaginary flies. But beyond the characteristic or individualistic gestures are those that dramatize a person's speech. If you watch for it, you can often see the speaker actually underline certain words by stabbing the space in front with a forefinger or slicing the air with the side of the palm.

Speakers may also snap their fingers, pull an earlobe, jab at their temples; people show you what's important in what they're saying. Gestures emphasize specific words, or else they may try to obscure or even erase them. You've seen people cover their mouths, as if to prevent the words from getting out.

Turn on your TV but leave the sound off. See how much you understand. I bet it's a lot. People can literally *see* what someone else is saying.

Look for facial cues: a furrowing between the eyebrows, a tenseness around the jaw, changes or blotching in color, lips tightening or falling slack, or any other change you notice. Remember, the key is *change*. Change is the marker that indicates something is happening in addition to the words that are being used. Sometimes this means simply an accord or agreement with the words—or it may signal an emphasis or even a contradiction.

Now try turning the sound on and blackening or fading the image.

Are you getting more or less information than before? What cues are you listening for? What changes can you identify in the quality of the voices? Listen to the rise and fall of words indicating emphasis, onset of volume (loudness), or a sudden drop into whispering; the pace of speech; and how two or more voices might match each other, flowing together, as they speak, into a kind of auditory dance.

Or think of listening to a film in a foreign language, without subtitles. You can make out a lot more than you might think; once you get accustomed to the flow or rhythm of the language you'll be able to pick out changes, sudden shifts of pitch, loudness, and whispers, and though you're listening to words you'll be getting the meaning through the nonverbal "dance" of sounds.

Of course, the larger gestures, sudden movements of the body, the pursing of lips, and changes in facial expressions will be giving you many clues also, and you might discover that even without subtitles you understand a lot that's going on. Humans are humans, and though we're used to communicating with each other through a particular language, we can say a lot even without words, or in addition to them.

We speak to each other in many ways beside words, often unconsciously. Words account for less than 20 percent of communication. The rest of communication is through other, nonverbal channels. Each of us has characteristic gestures, gestures that reveal ourselves and are part of our individuality, like markers that identify each of us and set us off from all others.

Reading these markers—these behavioral indicators—is a quick way of getting closer to another person, having a sense of what he or she is about. That leads to rapport, which in turn makes communication easier and more effective.

Here are a few specifics to look and listen for when you're calibrating someone:

LOOK FOR CHANGES IN:	LISTEN FOR CHANGES IN:
Gestures	Volume
Posture	Pitch
Facial lines	Tempo
Color of face and neck	Pauses
Muscle tension and relaxation	Rhythm

LOOK FOR	LISTEN FOR
CHANGES IN:	CHANGES IN:
Widening and narrowing of eyes	

Expansion or contraction of lips,
  color changes in outline of lips

Breathing (faster/slower; deeper/
  shallower)

When you're looking and listening for this type of information, you are aiming your attention outward. You move into uptime and become other-oriented.

Calibrating people is not only one of the most fascinating and totally absorbing things you can do, it's also the most effective means for establishing the groundwork of communication. Unless you can pay close attention to the other person without automatic judgments of what certain things mean, it's unlikely that you'll get that person to pay attention to you. One of the primary requirements of an actor is the ability to listen to others, to observe what goes on. Even if it's the thousandth performance, the actor must make it seem new each time. Only then does it seem real to the audience.

As on the stage, so it is in the world. To make others listen and notice, you have to open your own eyes and ears. By calibrating the other's responses, you discover where and how to step in to make sure your message is getting through.

Here's how it works in everyday situations. A salesman is trying to close a deal on a sporty new convertible. He chats with the customer about this and that, casting about for a topic of interest. "Do you like the Red Sox? Do you think they'll win the pennant this year?" "Are you taking a summer vacation?" "Do you have children?" All these are yes-or-no questions. As the potential customer answers, the salesman calibrates each response. He notices that when the customer answers yes, his eyebrows lift, the color of his face gets more pink, and his voice increases in volume. By calibrating this, the salesman knows how to measure the customer's affirmative mood, and he brings home his closing pitch for the convertible when the customer is feeling most positive.

How about this: A woman who is applying for an executive position with a large corporation is being interviewed by the president. She notices that he frowns a lot—however, immediately after the frown he takes a deep breath and lets his shoulders relax. Moreover, she notices that he frowns whenever she is asking a question. She concludes that what she has interpreted as a frown is actually a sign of concentration on the president's part, not disapproval. Realizing this, she continues with the interview feeling confident about herself and the interaction between the two of them.

Or try this: Let's say you're out with a friend who doesn't always let you know what she really wants to do, and she gets in a cranky mood. It's happened before, and she won't or can't let you know what's wrong. But today you calibrate her. You notice—over time—that when she really wants to do something, her breathing becomes faster, her head nods up and down very subtly, and her voice deepens in pitch. However, when she says yes to something that she ends up really not wanting to do, her breathing becomes slower and irregular, her voice is higher pitched, and she becomes totally still, with no discernible movement at all. Calibrating this, you're able to tell from now on if she means yes when she says it or if she doesn't.

Calibration is measure; it means observing the small changes that take place in another person during interpersonal communication. These changes indicate a way of responding; they tell you how the other person is thinking and feeling. Calibration is simply looking at and listening to what's already there, right in front of you. Like bubbles on the surface of the pond, these behaviors are obvious if you care to notice them. All you have to do is pay attention long enough—and suddenly there it is; obvious as billboards, the person seems to be telling and showing you what he or she is thinking behind the words.

5

Representational Systems

Each of us is unique. We respond to our surroundings, other people, and the world each in our own way, and yet we're all made up of the same bits of matter. Each individual is a different arrangement, a particular organization, a one-of-a-kind solution to the same basic predicament.

One of the chief ways we differ individually is through our *representational systems*. These are the sensory perceptors we rely on to make sense of the world—to think, feel, remember—and to organize the information we take in so we can have access to it at another time.

Representational systems are the channels through which we process experience and by which we represent the world to ourselves. They are the sensory and perceptual filters (seeing, hearing, feeling, smelling, tasting) we use to re-create or literally represent the world within our own minds. Since we can consciously process only a very limited amount of information at a time (nine pieces, tops), these perceptual filters serve to streamline the way we take in experience.

Primarily, we think in pictures, sounds, and sensations through our visual, auditory, and kinesthetic senses. (Occasionally, smell and taste may be powerful filters for some people, but that's relatively rare and needn't concern us here.) The perceptual filters we use to understand and interact with the world are like other filters, in the kitchen, the chemistry lab, or the photography studio.

Filters let you take in certain information selectively; they also let you screen out what is not needed or wanted at that particular moment. As a photographer, you might choose a lens to provide greater contrast, emphasizing the blacks and whites, removing the grays. Or you can choose a lens to blur the photographic image, bring the colors and intensities together in an impressionistic effect, and omit any sharp contrast at all. A cheesecloth filter in the kitchen catches little particles of food in its web and lets soup or other liquid run off clear. A coffee filter does the same with grinds. Filters remove some aspects of the event or experience in order to enhance others.

Our perceptual filters allow us to process new information without becoming overwhelmed. You can think of them as having different-sized openings—some large, others medium, some tiny. The visual filters, which have the largest openings, take in mostly what you see, auditory filters mostly what you hear, and kinesthetic filters mostly what you feel (sensations). This doesn't mean that none of the other sensory systems will affect you; it's simply a question of degree. Each of us has a set of these perceptual filters, ranging from large to tiny. The filter with the largest opening lets in the most information and therefore is the one we tend to rely on. Of course we use other filters at times for different types of information (even the most visual person relies on auditory filters at a concert or poetry reading), but most of us favor one of our senses most of the time. Some of us are more visual, some auditory, others kinesthetic, like the speaker in Theodore Roethke's poem "The Waking" who represents the world in terms of sensations: "We think by feeling."

We enter an experience through a particular sensory pathway and then code and store the experience in terms of that modality, or filter, through images, sounds, words, and feelings. These sensory data become our memories, the stored bank of information we rely on for everyday thinking and decision-making: the ability to determine what's a good experience and what's bad, which kinds of experience to increase and which to avoid, how to motivate ourselves, how to learn. Representational systems are the pathways of our thinking, and our primary representational system is whichever we are most aware of in a particular situation.

So how do you get your message across to someone who doesn't seem to hear you or who can't seem to see what you're saying?

You translate into that person's sensory language. You express yourself in the sensory terms, along the particular sensory channel, that the other will respond to most strongly (whether or not the person is aware of doing so). If someone is using visual language, you don't respond with auditory or kinesthetic words. You stay within the same language. What that means is this:

If someone asks "Are you clear about it?" ("clear" being a visual word), instead of answering "I can get in touch with that" ("touch" is kinesthetic), you would join the other person's representational pathway and say, "I see (visual) what you mean."

Or if someone says, "I hear you" (auditory), instead of replying "I'm glad you get the picture" (visual), you would harmonize with the auditory mode and reply, "I'm happy we're in tune."

Or someone asks "Can you grasp my point?" This indicates kinesthetic thinking. Instead of answering "I see (visual) what you mean" or "I hear you" (auditory), as an effective communicator you would answer along the lines of "I can get a handle on it."

Next time you're in a restaurant, try this very simple experiment: When the server comes over for your order, say you'll have two cups of coffee, hold up three fingers, and see what you get. Did the server respond to what you said (auditory) or what you signaled (visual)?

Or you could observe the same kind of phenomenon in a class at your health club. When the instructor is facing the class and says "Lift your right leg," notice how many people do what they've been told and how many simply mirror the movement of the instructor (in which case they'd be lifting the left leg).

Here's a sample chart to help you recognize sensory words and translate from one representational (sensory) system to another.

You can also use the word list as a guide to help you listen for clues about what someone's primary system is. Or make your own list of words that are sensory-specific, words that refer to seeing, hearing, and feeling. (You may add words that refer to taste and smell also, but keep in mind these are not the primary systems that most people use.) And keep adding words and phrases as they come to you; it will help you remain aware of the subtleties and differences in how each of us understands the world and one another.

VISUAL	AUDITORY	KINESTHETIC
see	*hear*	*feel*
look	*listen*	*touch*
image	*sound*	*grasp*
imagine	*tell yourself*	*place yourself*
symmetry	*harmony*	*balance*
eye-to-eye	*in tune*	*solid*
brilliant	*blaring*	*grating*
sights	*sounds*	*vibrations*
bright	*loud*	*hard*
light	*clear*	*sharp*

clear	*resonant*	*smooth*
flash/lightning	*thunder (clap)*	*punch*
murky	*static*	*rough/bumpy*
perceptive	*good ear*	*intuitive/grip*
glaring	*booming*	*weighty*
focus	*tune in*	*go with the flow*
glimpse	*whisper*	*brush*
shadow	*echo*	*footprint*
blur	*soft*	*soft*
blank	*silence*	*untextured*
blind	*deaf*	*mute*

Whenever you hear people use one set of sensory words like these you can be sure that, for the present anyway, they are thinking with or through one particular representational system. And when you use the same type of sensory language, you give them a strong sense of rapport—that you are following and understanding what they're saying. This is hardly surprising. You are, after all, using the same kind of words in speech that the other person is using to think with. As though you were a mind reader!

6

Expressions of Representational Systems:
Sensory Language

We know that body language is important in communication. As we discussed in chapter 4, Calibration, gestures and nuances of speech are extremely meaningful. You can understand a lot of social interaction without knowing the particular language a person speaks.

That's on a broad scale. In a foreign movie, we can make a very good guess about a person's mood, whether the scene is violent or tender, a dream sequence or actuality. But for precision, to get a specific meaning across, we need words. Words are, after all, important units for transmitting meaning. And the kind of words we use is highly significant in effective communication.

Let's go back to Bill and Susan for a moment. We left them in the kitchen, Susan accusing Bill of not really caring how she feels, Bill arguing that she never listens to him.

"Get a grip," she says now. "Stop feeling sorry for yourself."

"Me?" Bill answers. "Me sorry for myself? Am I hearing this correctly?" He looks around the room in an exaggerated fashion. "There must be an echo in here. Just listen to yourself!"

"I'm not going to stand for this, you know."

"You're the one making a racket about how difficult things are, and getting all weepy and emotional."

"I'm not getting emotional!" she shouts at him.

It could be comedy, except that most of us have been in situations like this one, and what we remember isn't funny at all. We each have a tendency to blame the other for not getting the message, without considering how that person is receiving what we say. We simply ignore the response we're getting. We're wrapped up in our own script, in our own agenda, and go on doing the same thing without taking any account of its impact. Like a man who keeps raising his voice when he speaks to a person who doesn't understand the language, we keep repeating the same words, louder and louder, as if the mere fact of doing it over and over would somehow (miraculously!) produce different results.

You don't keep raising your voice if someone doesn't speak English. Instead, you might try to find a language in common, or show your meaning through gestures and acting, in the form of charades. Or you could look for a translator.

But when you're both speaking English and you say, "I love you" and get the response, "Yeah, right, I love you too," you know something is not happening in the communication. It's as though—for the moment at least—you each have a special language of your own. To get the other one to understand the intention behind the message, you need to translate or to find a language in common.

Wherever you are—at the office of a doctor you've been referred to, trying to arrange a loan at the bank, talking to new clients, students, teachers, or prospective in-laws—careful calibration of the other person's behavior will help you form an estimate of whether and how your message is coming across. But to know what kind of sensory world the other person is most at home with, you need to pay attention to the kind of words the other person is using.

The kind of words a person uses will tell you how that person perceives the world. Is he or she seeing pictures, hearing sounds or words, or having physical sensations? How does that person assimilate an experience? Through what sensory filter are the thoughts primarily being channeled? Which of the three major filters—visual (eye), auditory (ear), kinesthetic (sensation/movement)—does this person rely on most heavily?

Let's say I'm trying to get a bank loan to expand my business. Because I'm primarily visual, I can see my expectations for this business in my mind's eye. My goal is clear as day—to me, anyway.

However, the bank manager may not be the visual type. If he's primarily auditory, he'll respond much more sympathetically if I could make my words ring a bell or click or resonate with him.

Or, if he's kinesthetic, I could solicit his interest by suggesting that this expansion could be a hot opportunity, and I might try convincing him that the project has a good feeling.

What I'm doing here is using the same language as the other person—staying with my content, my story, but changing my language.

Here's how it might work.

At the beginning of this chapter, Bill and Susan were squabbling, each of them wrapped up in his or her own system, speaking his or her particular sensory language.

He insisted he'd told her he loved her.

She argued that she didn't feel he cared about her. Her feet were aching, she said, she was stuck in the kitchen all day, the air in there thick as molasses, and all he could think was how pleased he was feeling with himself.

Susan is using kinesthetic language. Bill, who insists that she won't listen to him, that she's deaf or something, is using auditory language. If they go on as they've been doing, they're headed for the disaster of noncommunication.

Susan: I've been chopping these onions for a decade, it feels like. I'm hot, my head hurts, I can barely breathe—and you don't feel any concern for me, you're completely out of touch.

Bill: OK, if you're going to cover your ears and not hear a thing I'm saying, OK. I'm telling you I love you. I'm saying, here I am, I'm trying to tune in to you, and you're acting like I'm just talking to myself.

Susan: That's how it feels. You send out these vibes of "Me, Me, Me." You're only in touch with your own feelings—you just don't grasp what goes on with me.

Bill: Because you're deaf. You refuse to hear what's said to you. You tune me out.

Now let's assume that Bill has read this chapter and learned about other-orientation and the language of the senses:

Bill: I'm sorry you're down. I know it's been a drag to be making dinner tonight, especially in this heat. You must be real tired of it by now—so how about I get a handle on those onions, then I give you my number one soothing neck massage? I really want to make you feel better.

Susan: (relenting a little): *You do? Well, maybe I'm being a little cranky. It's the heat, you know, and these damn onions, making my eyes smart.*

Bill: I know how you're feeling, hot and bothered. Things are crowding you in. You need some different vibes.

Susan: Yes.

Bill: How about we get a move on? Maybe I could whisk you off your feet. Waltz you right out of here.

Susan: (nodding) *Why not?—except you never learned to waltz.*

Bill: Let's shimmy, then. (Susan laughs.) *You know how I feel about you, honey. I've felt this way since that first moment you danced into my life.*

Susan: Stomped is more like it. Remember? I nearly ran you down the day we met.

Bill: Same thing. Honey, I love you. (They kiss. He has successfully communicated his message.)

Let's take a look at a different kind of scenario. The manager of a hardware company is trying to convince his boss, the president, that it would be a good idea to expand the business and open another office in another city.

Manager: Fred, look. Business is really brightening up.

President: Yeah, right. So I've heard. But our quarterly report is certainly not worth shouting about.

Manager: It's the big picture I'm talking about. I can see our opportunities really coming into focus. It's

*time to expand. It's clear to me that now is the time
to open up our horizons.*

President: *I don't know, it sounds risky at this point.
There's a lot of static out there. Our earnings are
down, and I'm not hearing the sounds of an improving
economy.*

The proposal seems to have reached a dead end. But if
the manager picks up the auditory cues from the president's
dialogue, he might be able to change the outcome:

Manager: *OK, Fred. I hear what you're saying. And
I know there are people making noises about playing
it safe, waiting for change. But listen to me, there's
no way you're going to get the applause you deserve
for having built up this company unless you call for a
bigger venture. You've got to amplify, increase your
volume, tune in to the possibilities.*

President: *You know, I'm beginning to like the sound
of this.*

◆

SENSORY LANGUAGE EXERCISE

1. Pick a person you regularly communicate with, someone with whom you'd like to improve your communication.

2. Listen to this person talk for several minutes. Identify
   the language being used the most.

3. Use a different language. Notice the response.

4. Use the same language. Notice the response.

◆

SENSORY EXERCISE TO DO BY YOURSELF

1. Pay attention to which language you use the most.

2. Notice which language is most foreign to you.

3. Spend ten minutes using that language. What have you noticed by using a different filter?

◆

7

Expressions of Representational Systems:
Eye Movements

You can tell what representational system people are using by listening to their words. You can also read which system a person is using to think with by tracking the eye movements.

When people are thinking—not looking around at things in their external environment but going inside their minds to remember, to figure something out, to make a decision— they move their eyes. The eye movements are connected to our neurology. They indicate *how* someone is thinking, in what form the thoughts are being presented to the brain, whether as pictures, sounds, words, or feelings.

It's as simple as this: When people's eyes go up, they're visualizing. Side to side means auditory; they're hearing words, music, possibly other sounds, though words are the most likely. When people look down to their left, they're having a conversation with themselves, or more likely an argument. (''Do it—Don't do it'';''Get out, run!—Stay put and fight!'') When they look down to their right it means they're getting in touch with their feelings.

You can learn how to map a face to chart the way someone's thoughts are going and then join them in that direction, along that representational path. If someone's eyes keep moving up, you know that person is making images, and you can capture his or her interest by using visual language. If the eyes are moving up in one direction (usually to the person's right), it means he or she is imagining something, a scene, a picture: constructing an image. Eyes moving up in the other direction (usually left) means the person is remembering an image, a visual event, something he or she has seen before.

Pupils dilated (eyes not focused) means the person is making a mental picture, either remembered or constructed, and may be seeing it in the space between the two of you, or behind you, or in place of you.

Eyes moving from side to side indicate auditory images—to one side (right, in people who are typically organized) it's being constructed; the person is thinking of what to say or maybe (more rarely) composing a melody. Eyes to the left means auditory memories—something someone said, a remembered voice, a favorite song.

Looking down to the left is auditory digital, which means the person is talking to himself or herself, going back and forth, possibly arguing both sides of a question. Looking down to the right is a sign that someone is using kinesthetic filters, and that means feelings, sensations, emotions. Unlike visual or auditory, the kinesthetic eye movement doesn't distinguish between remembered or constructed; it's all feeling.

Being able to see *how* people are thinking—knowing where their heads are at by observing how their eyes are moving—means you can help guide them to someplace else, take them from the past to the future, from auditory to visual; or, if you want someone to grasp new information, you might first have to get that person out of his or her feelings.

Let's say you're teaching a class in statistics. One of your students seems to have a lot of difficulty comprehending the material, and you notice that her eyes are often cast down and to her right. That's kinesthetic, you realize, and to help her get out of her feelings, to be able to process the figures she has to learn in your course, you direct her gaze upward. You do this by pointing to something high up on the blackboard, or by raising your own eyes, or lifting your hands—whatever will make her move her eyes up and get her into a visual frame, where she has a much better chance of understanding statistics than in the kinesthetic frame.

Or you're coaching a Little League game. One of the kids, a little guy who has serious problems making contact with the ball whenever he's up at bat, stands there moving his eyes side to side and then looking down to his left. He's talking to himself, and you know he's probably telling himself something on the order of "I can't do it; I'll miss the ball; I'm no good; Everybody knows I can't play; I'll make a fool of myself." As long as he goes on talking to himself that way, he's almost pushing himself to fail. His chances of hitting the ball are negligible.

But now you, the coach, tell him to look up, to see in his mind's eye where the ball is going to go, to imagine how he's going to hit it. You bring him out of the slump, out from hearing his own negative prediction, to seeing an image of success.

The funny face below shows you how to "read" some basic eye movements to know what tracks someone is thinking along.

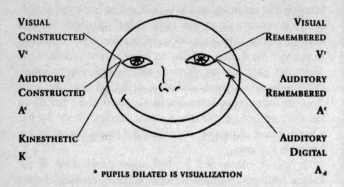

V^c = Visual constructed: imagining something you've never actually seen—your dream house, being on a remote tropical island, receiving the Nobel Prize or Olympic gold; making up pictures.

V^r = Visual remembered: picturing something from the past—your mother's face, a tie you used to own, a movie, your former office; recalling images you've seen before.

A^c = Auditory constructed: making up what you're going to say—or play or sing; inventing sounds or dialogue.

A^r = Auditory remembered: hearing something again—your father asking you to stand tall, a teacher calling your name, a slogan you're familiar with, a song, whether in your own voice or someone else's.

K = Kinesthetic: being aware of bodily sensations—temperature, pressure, movement—or emotions—fear, anger, excitement.

A_d = Auditory digital (words): "Maybe he likes me," "I'll never be good enough," "I wonder what they're saying about me."

* = Dilated pupils: the person is engaged in visualization.

This diagram represents what we call "typical organization" and is accurate for the majority of right-handed people. Left-handed people are often reversed, a mirror image of the typical organization.

By watching people's eyes, you can read their minds: not the content of their thoughts but how they are thinking. Adapt your language to this, and you can also guide someone from a nonproductive state of mind to a more helpful one. Since the person usually is completely unaware of giving himself or herself away, you appear to be something of a mind reader, simply by responding to the clues you've been given. "You read me like a book," they say, surprised and gratified to find a kindred spirit.

If you talk to people in the way they're talking to themselves, you will be listened to, trusted, and probably respected as well.

But when two people are using different representational systems—different languages—each may have the sense that the other is either being contradictory or else not listening or paying attention. It might not be conscious, but either or both may get the impression that they're missing each other, they're not being understood, they're on different wavelengths.

Recognizing where the other is "coming from," through

which filter he or she is perceiving the world, is the basis for establishing rapport, a feeling of mutual trust and understanding.

◆

COMMUNICATION EXERCISE

1. Pick someone important to you.

2. Have a conversation and watch the person's eye movements.

3. Notice which movements he or she does the most.

4. Ask about it.

   • "What are you seeing or imagining?"
   • "What are you saying to yourself?"
   • "What are you feeling?"

Notice how the person responds to your questions.

◆

8

Noticing Sameness or Difference

We code and store information through our sensory systems, each of us favoring one particular sense over the others. The kind of filter we most often rely on (visual, auditory, or kinesthetic) determines the kind of experience we get. Walking into a big party held in a Soho loft, the visual person sees the bustle of color, bright lights, shiny clothes, cherry lipstick and emerald eye shadow, the bar with its setups, the arrangement of dishes holding food. The auditory person notices the excitement of noise, the music and the talk, the sounds of laughter, a jangle of bracelets, the cars passing underneath the window, a distant siren, the refrigerator door being opened and closed in the kitchen. The kinesthetic person feels the closeness of the crowd, the dancing couples, the hardness or smoothness of the floor, the warmth of the bodies as people move together, gesturing as they talk, and so on. This is how the brain sorts information through filters of the representational system.

The brain processes information into one of two categories: sameness or difference. That means you will either notice that something is the same as, or similar to, something else, or you notice that it's different from the others.

Again, as with the perceptual filters (visual, auditory, and kinesthetic) and the sensory language that you use most often, this process is not conscious. You don't decide to notice sameness or difference; this is an automatic cognitive process, one of the ways of organizing information. Is the glass half empty or half full? Is the day partly sunny or partly cloudy? Do you pay attention to what's missing or what's there? Coming into someone's living room, do you notice the windows (spaces) or the walls?

Bill and Susan arrive at the party in the Soho loft. To Bill the noise of the crowd, the happy hubbub of people mingling, the upbeat music, people smiling—everything indicates success. He thinks of other great parties he's been to and he feels wonderful, a sense of being at the center of where it's happening. "Terrific party," he says to Susan.

"Probably," she says, without much conviction. First thing she noticed coming into the building was that it didn't have an elevator. Walking into the party, she realizes that the music isn't live, the lights are not bright enough to see clearly by, the temperature isn't comfortable, and she doesn't know many people. Right now she almost wishes she'd stayed home, in familiar surroundings. She feels like a stranger.

Bill notices what reminds him of other parties where he's enjoyed himself—sameness; Susan notices how this party is not like others—difference.

Later in the evening they go home in a taxi they're sharing with some old friends who were also at the party, Amanda and Felix. Amanda says, "That was some party! Wasn't it terrific?"

"Not bad," says Felix.

"Not bad! What do you mean? It was terrific!" Amanda repeats. Bill nods his agreement.

"I *said* it wasn't bad," says Felix.

"Didn't you enjoy yourself?" Bill asks.

Felix looks at Bill in surprise. "I've just *told* you. It wasn't bad."

No matter how much Bill prods him (Amanda's used to

Felix by now; she leaves him alone when he gets "that way"), Felix can't say the party was terrific or wonderful.

Susan understands; she's much the same way herself. It's not that she's trying to be contrary. What's happening is that as she organizes information into categories (without being aware that she's doing it), she notices which categories *don't* fit with the others. She notices what is different.

Bill and Amanda, on the other hand, also organize information into categories. But they notice what goes with what, what fits, what's the same as or similar to something else.

These different processes—sameness and difference—are not done consciously, and they have nothing to do with pessimism or optimism, with being agreeable or disagreeable. Is the glass half empty or half full? Are you nearly dressed or practically naked? Was that a great movie? "Yes," says Bill. "The acting was great, but the script could have been a little clearer," says Susan.

Being aware of these cognitive differences in processing information can help you avoid many predictable failures of communication. Sometimes, couples who've been together as long as Bill and Susan or Amanda and Felix will continue to have arguments about things they actually agree on. They haven't learned to watch out for certain linguistic indicators, little words and turns of phrase that indicate if the other is a "sameness" type or a "difference" type.

Is the person making sense of an experience by noticing how it's similar to something he's experienced before? Is she noticing what's different about it?

Clarissa is a graphic artist who frequently has run-ins with her boss. Though she admires his critical abilities, she feels he doesn't give her enough credit; he doesn't really appreciate her work. Whenever Clarissa brings in a new design, her boss will invariably find fault with something.

"It's fine," he'll say, "except that this part in the corner is too light; the colors aren't defined clearly enough." Clarissa comes away from their conferences feeling dejected and unappreciated.

One day she complained to Susan who, being a "difference" person herself (though she didn't know it), immediately saw where the trouble lay. "Your boss isn't putting you down," she told her friend. "I'm sure of it. What he wants is for you to do the absolute best design possible. And when he looks at your design, what he sees is how you could improve on it, what's missing. Next time," she suggested, "why don't *you* take the initiative and try pointing out some details that you think *he* might suggest improving?"

The next time Clarissa brought in her design, she said, "Here it is, and on the whole I'm pleased with it, although"—her boss looked up, surprised by a hesitancy in her voice—"in the lower left, the blending of the outline isn't quite resolved, and here"—she pointed—"the blue drops off a little too quickly, and you probably won't think much of the small line drawing at the back, where—"

He was poring over it eagerly. "No," he said, "it's fine the way it is. Don't touch a thing."

Because Clarissa already pointed out what was different (and possibly not up to the standard of the rest of the design), her boss didn't have to. Susan was right: He didn't intend to be critical in any personal way, and he thought very highly of Clarissa's work. His nit-picking, as Clarissa had interpreted it, was simply a way of checking every part of the design very closely. In fact, it was this ability to keep refining, to continually adapt and make improvements, that made Clarissa's boss so successful at his job.

Understanding this fundamental cognitive difference between people can be crucial in all forms of communication, personal or professional. But it's probably most dramatic with people who have lived or worked together for years and never realized that what seems to be a difference of opinion is simply a different way of understanding information and expressing it.

"That's a great-looking shirt you have on," Bill says to Keith.

"You should have seen the one I was wearing yesterday," he answers.

He's a difference person. Tell him that his chicken stew is delicious, and he'll probably let you know that it could use more thyme. When he comes from the barber and you mention his excellent haircut, he'll point out that it'll look even better when it's a week old. He's not disagreeing, only noticing difference.

But tell Clarissa how pretty her hair looks tonight, and she'll smile and thank you. Comment on the intelligent question she asked the speaker at last week's forum, and she'll let you know how happy that makes her. She's a sameness person. She notices how things fit together. When Clarissa puts on an outfit, she'll always wear the same accessories with it. This scarf, these shoes, that bag. This top goes with that skirt.

If someone takes it personally when another person notices difference, this can cause serious misunderstandings that are, however, completely avoidable and without actual substance. The difference person isn't launching a personal attack, it's only his or her other way of perceiving the world. The comment isn't meant to criticize you or put you down, it's merely an observation. It's a way of organizing information.

You can probably tell sameness from difference people by what they say; do they notice similarities or differences? You can also narrow it down to the use of certain key words like these:

SAMENESS	DIFFERENCE
like	yes, but
like this	different
the same	sort of
similar	an example of
fits	I don't know
equal	not bad
as well	probably
	missing

Ask someone "How was your day?" and pay attention to the answer: "It was great, I didn't get caught in traffic, and my boss was not in a bad mood" or "It was great, my commute was easy and fast, and my boss was in a good mood."

People who notice difference are easy to motivate. All you need to say is something like "I don't suppose you'd be able to . . ." or "You probably won't like . . ." In other words, present them with a kind of reverse image—what's missing instead of what's there—for them to fill in.

When you're trying to cheer up a friend or make people feel better, you usually try to get them to remember a time when they were happier or else to think ahead about something they're looking forward to.

With a difference person, if you say, "Remember when . . . ?" and give a specific example—"Remember when you got that contract from your new client?"—the person will answer you with something that didn't work out or something that was different. "Yes, sure I remember, but I didn't end up making enough money on that one."

But if you leave these people free to come up with their own examples, you might get a very different (and I use that word intentionally) answer. If, instead of supplying the example yourself, you say, "There's probably been a time or times when you've felt good about your work; I don't know whether you can remember an example of feeling really positive,'' your difference person will start the wheels churning and come up with, ''Sure. There was that time I made a deadline everyone thought was impossible, and with one of the best proposals I've ever put together.''

With a sameness person you are more direct. ''This is the same as last year, when you felt similar to the way you're feeling now and you ended up surprising yourself with how well you handled things.''

The person will probably light up with, ''That's right, I did overcome all those obstacles. I had the confidence, and I'll do it again.''

The sameness person needs direction in finding specific memories or thoughts, using words such as like, similar, the same as. The difference person needs to be offered options—using words like maybe, probably, an example of, I don't know.

The important thing is to recognize that people either notice what's the same or what's different, what fits or what doesn't, and not to take it personally. A difference or sameness person is not disagreeing or agreeing with you. If you say, ''Wasn't that great!'' and your friend says, ''Not bad,'' leave it alone; you probably agree. Or say, ''You probably didn't like that, did you?'' and your friend will reply, ''No, no—it was great!''

❖

SAMENESS OR DIFFERENCE EXERCISE

1. Pick someone you work with and pay attention to whether he or she notices similarities or differences.

2. Once you've identified which it is, play with the

sameness/difference words (same as, like, fits, versus sort of, probably, different; see text list).

3. Notice the responses. Which type of words makes it easier to get the kind of response you want?

◆

9

Backtracking

You know what you're saying. You know how to get your message across. You have learned to expand your means of communicating by matching posture, tonality, language. You have understood that the meaning of your words is in how they are received, regardless of what was intended.

Excellent. But what about communication in the other direction? Are you sure that *you* are getting the message?

The simplest and most direct way of checking whether or not you've understood what the other person said or meant to say is by *backtracking*. It is also the easiest way to check whether your own communication has been understood. Backtracking is so simple, really, that people often forget how effective and powerful it can be.

It is the frame within which to use the techniques of effective communication that we've discussed so far. Backtracking provides the opportunity for checking tone, tempo, and posture, evaluating sensory language, and using the words of sameness and difference.

Backtracking is summarizing what the other has said in your own words, but using the other's key words and phrases. This doesn't mean repeating word for word or parroting the message; it means doing a recap as if you were using a verbal highlighter, marking out the essential ideas by illuminating the important words and phrases.

For example, the marketing director of an upscale beauty products and fragrances company comes to an ad agency to talk about the new product they're about to launch. It's a perfume, and the client wants the agency to create a brand-new kind of campaign, unlike anything they've done for the company before.

The client explains, "What's important to me is that when people see the ad they should get an experience, a feeling, of faraway places. Unusual, rare, something out of the ordinary. Let's say mysterious. Not scary, but mysterious and different. Something beautiful, exciting, different—way out there. I want people to get the feeling that this is something very different, even unique: something they never experienced before. Something amazing."

To this, the agency person says, "Great idea. I know just what you mean. Leave it to me." They shake hands. A few weeks later the client comes back to see the proposed project, the mock-up or storyboard.

The theme is science fiction, outer space in cyberspace, done in beautiful geometric shapes, cubes, and squares, strings and fiberglass, an ultratechnical display of exciting and mysterious galactic goings-on.

"What is this? This is terrible, I hate it," says the client, staring in disbelief. "That's not what I said. This has nothing whatever to do with what we were talking about. How could you go so wrong?"

"You said something far out, mysterious, and unique," the agency rep argues. "Something different, unusual."

"It's awful," the client responds (though more likely she unleashes a torrent of unprintable rage against the unfortunate rep). "When I said unusual, I was thinking Tahiti: exotic flowers, birds, a kingdom by the sea, shimmering sands, desert islands. . . . Not this outer-space odyssey idiocy. How could you do this?" And so on until the client ends her tirade and takes her business elsewhere.

It could have been prevented so easily. If the agency rep had simply backtracked what the client said, the misunderstanding would have been cleared up instantly.

Look at the client's original presentation. If the rep had backtracked, it might have sounded something like this:

Agency Rep: *If I understand you correctly, you want a sense of mystery in the ads. Far out and different.*

Client: *That's right.*

Agency Rep: *Unusual surroundings, mysterious . . . other-world experience . . . maybe outer space.*

Client: *No. Nothing like outer space. Scratch that. I can't stand sci-fi. What I want is something exotic— maybe primitive—strange and very beautiful. Like the South Seas. Orchids. Flowers opening up. Or the Sahara, rare animals, shimmering sands? . . .*

Agency Rep: *So what you want is something exotic and primitive. Another culture. Mysterious. Like the sands of the Sahara. The desert, an oasis . . . a shimmering mirage. Strange, far out? . . .*

Client: *That's it, those are the lines I'm thinking along.*

In backtracking, you listen for words that are repeated often or are marked by a shift in tonality, tempo, posture, or gesture, including facial expressions. Remember that people will *show* you what to listen for. They'll stab the air or circle their fingers along narrowing rings of a spiral until they touch down on the table or armrest. They'll press their hands together, open their eyes wide, jiggle their feet, or breathe deeply and then suddenly speed up their breathing and make it shallow, like a diver coming up from the depths. Whatever the particular behavior, you'll notice when something is being underlined by sudden shifts in action, tonality, and tempo.

This means you must be paying close attention to the other person, looking and listening for the important cues. When you feel that a substantial amount of information has been given and you want to check that you have understood it, stop the person who's talking and begin the backtrack with the words, "If I understand you correctly."

You may also use a slightly different phrase: "So what you mean is" or "What you're getting at is" or something like that. You don't have to stick with a strict formula, though for most people "If I understand you correctly" is the one that works best.

Remember, the point of backtracking is to make sure you understand what the other is saying to you. It has nothing to do with right or wrong or with what you believe to be true or false. You just summarize briefly what you think the other is talking about, using what you judge to be the key words. You also deepen rapport through backtracking, especially when you match the person's language as well as tone, tempo, and posture.

And then you pay attention to the response you get. The other person may simply agree: "Yes, that's it, that's right." Or he or she might change it somehow, disagree or add to it or edit it in some way, bringing out a new or alternate meaning: "Well, maybe there's some of that in it, but what I also meant was . . ." or "That's only true some of the time" or even "Not really, what's a lot *more* important is . . ."

This doesn't mean your backtrack has failed. On the contrary, it could lead to the opening up of communication, establishing an excellent pattern and foundation for enjoyable, effective communication and deepening rapport.

◆

BACKTRACKING EXERCISE

1. Pick someone you communicate with frequently but have some trouble understanding.

2. Listen to what he or she is saying, paying attention to the key words. Stop the person at intervals and summarize in your own words what your understanding is. Be sure to use his or her key words.

3. Pay attention to the other's response. Keep doing the backtrack until you get a response that shows you are getting the message.

◆

10

Pacing and Leading

When you see two little girls skipping along together down the street, their skips matching and mirroring each other, you know the girls are very much in tune—best friends, probably—if only for today.

Or watch a pair of lovers strolling toward a golden dawn somewhere, their steps synchronized, moving like a single engine with four legs.

A mother and her baby son are having a picnic together in a city park. The child is only a few months old, but he's trying to speak, his little mouth opening and closing, his eyes serious, focused on the object of his all-encompassing love, and she, his mother, is following his movements, opening and closing her own mouth in synchrony with him.

In each case, the two are matching each other, joining forces as if they alone were their own tiny world.

This is *pacing*.

Pacing refers to meeting the other person where he or she is, or happens to be, at that moment. It means aligning yourself with the other, joining that person in his or her particular way of understanding the world (not agreeing with it, necessarily, but respecting it). You're following, getting into the same rhythms, speaking the same language, talking about the same topics, joining the mood.

This creates and maintains a strong sense of rapport. The

skills you use to pace are other-orientation, calibration, matching tone, tempo, posture, language, and backtracking.

The little girls come to the end of the street, to the large road they're not yet allowed to cross by themselves. They turn back and resume their skipping; then one of them starts changing the pattern of the skipping, interspersing little jogs between the skips. Her friend follows suit, and soon the jogs have taken over. The girls are no longer skipping but running.

The mother moves her lips in approximation of the baby's movement. Then she says, "Ma-ma," bringing her lips tightly together, exploding them open on the vowel. The baby watches, trying to emulate her. "Mmm," he says. "Mmm."

What's happening here is what we call *leading*. Leading is moving the person to another topic, perspective, language, rhythm, mood, tempo, or posture.

Once you've paced the person you're ready to serve as guide toward something or somewhere else, to another thought or behavior. Moving someone into a different language or posture or tempo can change his or her perspective. And the new perspective can bring new choices, possibilities, and creativity.

Specifically, what you're doing is altering the pattern that the other person is using. You can pace (match) the other's experience through language, posture, tone, and tempo. Then you can lead the person into a different awareness by shifting your language, posture, or voice, thereby transforming the experience.

If you want something from someone else—to have your boss give you a raise, to get your husband or friend to plan a vacation with you—you first must join the other person in whatever he or she is involved with at the moment. You won't get anywhere by blundering in on someone, trying to impose what *you* want no matter what he or she may be doing, thinking, or feeling.

You do it leisurely. At first you enter into the other person's concerns, his enthusiasm or frustration, her worry or pleasure. You listen, you talk about whatever it is (all this is pacing), and only then do you begin gradually to lead the person to the behavior you have in mind. You shift language, tempo, perspective, or any of the other behavioral markers we've talked about, and you do this respectfully, showing that you have respect for the other's concerns.

Let's say you're trying to talk your workaholic husband into taking a vacation. You've been picturing it on your way home from work, the two of you lying on a beach, the sun shining. . . . You walk in the door. He's on the phone, smiling, and as soon as he hangs up he starts telling you about the exciting new project he's working on. He talks so fast his words run together: "I'm getting a tremendous charge out of this work for a change; this project is *hot*."

"Fine," you say. "Excellent." You speak slowly, drawing out the sounds. "And what I'm seeing when you're finished with it is the two of us on a white sandy beach."

Obviously, that's not going to work. There's no rapport, no connection that makes him receptive to what you're saying. You're on different planets, using different kinds of words.

His language is kinesthetic, yours is visual. His tempo is very fast, yours slow. You can't get him to move to the topic you want to talk about (leading) if you don't start on common ground (pacing).

Here's a more effective way.

> **He:** *This project is the most exciting thing in years. It really gets my blood up, I can feel a thousand ideas bombarding me.*

She: It's wonderful that you're so excited. I can just feel the energy coming off you. I'm sure this project is going to have a real impact. And later on, when you're finished, just picture how great it would be to take some time off and run along a beach somewhere, watch the waves come in.

He: Yeah, that would be terrific.

She: It's great that you're excited about all these ideas, and I know the project will be a success. And then you'll be ready for a vacation. Can't you just see the two of us running with the tide?

He: (laughing) Perfect picture.

She: What do you really feel like doing when you're ready to take off and relax? Where do you see us playing?

She has led him to imagining the vacation, making him look forward to it, first by matching his sensory language (kinesthetic) and his tempo (fast) and then by moving him into visual language and a slower tempo. She moves back and forth, pacing and leading in an interactive loop between input and feedback. She paces him, then moves into leading, goes back to pacing and once again leading.

Or consider this. You want to ask your boss for a raise, but when you come into his office he's worrying about making a deadline.

Boss: I can't get tuned in to what I have to get done. It doesn't sound like I'll make the deadline. I can hear the doors closing.

You: You'll be fine. You always make it. Don't worry.
The reason I'm here is I'm feeling really down about
the money I make here. I feel that what I make doesn't
fit the amount of work I do.

Boss: I can't believe what I'm hearing! They're getting ready to blow the whistle on me if I don't finish
in time and you want a raise? What's the matter with
you? You know I can't listen to this stuff now.

You are not getting your point across, to put it mildly.
But if you try it again, being aware that your boss uses
auditory language and notices difference, while you use
kinesthetic language and notice sameness, it might go
something like this:

You: I know it sounds to you as if you're not going
to meet the deadline, that you won't be able to strike
the right chord for this proposal. And it's true, you
might not make it before the bell. But you've done it
in the past, so you'll probably tune in to what needs
to be done at the last minute, like you usually do.
   And listen. This is probably a bad time, but I've
been hearing some grumbles from the staff about their
paychecks and I felt that maybe, if you want them on
their feet, doing their best to help you meet that deadline, you could tell them you're going to hand them a
bonus or raise next month.
   And fitting in with that, doesn't it sound to you as
if it's time for me to get the raise we mentioned?

Boss: I hear you. I suppose it's not a good time, as
you say, but whenever is it a good time? And maybe
you're right. I'd get less static from the staff. OK, now

*be quiet about money and help me sound out my ideas
for this proposal.*

Unless you are really oriented toward the other person,
the one you're intending to lead into doing something that
you want, it won't work. All communication is cybernetic—
a give and take and give in a dynamic loop of intercon-
nection—and it depends on rapport. Without respect for the
other person and real interest in whatever concerns him or
her, your rapport is as flimsy as smoke, and whatever you
build on it will quickly vanish.

◆

PACING AND LEADING EXERCISE I

When you're with someone who isn't in the same mood as
you—he's quiet while you're bouncy; you're serious, she's
playful—try joining the other person by matching his or
her tempo and posture.

Do this for five minutes. Now begin slowly to change
your tempo and posture, still paying attention to them and
backtracking them, but retaining the change(s). Be sincere;
you want the best for them.

Do this for three minutes. Notice what happens.

◆

PACING AND LEADING EXERCISE II

1. When you want someone to do something, first observe the person for a while. Listen to the type of
   language he or she is using and the tempo (fast or
   slow) of the words. Watch posture, gestures, and eye
   movements. Pay close attention. Think of how what-

ever you want from this person could also benefit him or her.

2. Backtrack the person, matching language, posture, and tempo. You are now pacing the person. Do this for five minutes.

3. Begin leading the other. Add on to your backtrack whatever it is you want the person to do, using a different language or tempo or posture. Choose the language, tempo, or posture that most accords with your outcome.

4. Talk about how what you want would also benefit the other. Be sincere and respectful.

◆

11

Communication Is Flexibility

Imagine an enormous room, high and wide, filled with mazes of all kinds. Place yourself into it. You are walking through a maze, and you have no idea where the path will lead.

Lights flash on. They are pretty lights (imagine them in whichever way pleases you most). They spell out:

CHOICES

Someone hands you a piece of paper. It's a map or maybe a set of written instructions for how to get through the maze. You follow it. You step out into sunshine like the burst of technicolor that announces Dorothy and Toto's arrival in Oz.

Coming out of this first maze, you have learned how to convey what you mean to another person and how to extract the meaning of another's communication. You say what you mean and mean what you say; you can communicate freely between your thoughts and the other's understanding. The key word here is *flexibility*.

Flexibility means having many choices. If you have only one way of doing (thinking, feeling) something, no matter how successful it's been, you have no choice. If you have two ways of doing it, you have a dilemma. Three ways, and you have a choice. You have the choice to match posture or tone or tempo or language; you can direct your consciousness outward, use the clues given by eye movements, or by words of sameness or difference, and put everything together in backtracking.

What you've learned in this labyrinth of neural pathways and sensory trails are the many ways to establish rapport, the ability to capture and hold the attention of another person and to create an environment of understanding and trust. Rapport is the single most essential element in successful communication, the link between self and other.

Communication between people depends on the ability to calibrate and make quick changes. It means responding to the response you're getting—and if it isn't what you want, if the other person isn't getting the message, you adapt your behavior, adjust the way in which you're communicating, to increase your chances of being understood.

By doing this, you learn something about the other person and something new about yourself. Communication is process. Flexibility is essential for learning, for changing habits of thought and feeling, gaining more choices, and allowing possibilities to open up to you. Flexibility lets you break through the tight frames of mind and behavior that have kept you doing the same things in the same ways. You become conscious of alternatives and are able to change.

COMMUNICATION RECAP

RAPPORT: Getting the other's attention and creating an environment of trust.

OTHER-ORIENTATION: Paying attention to the other; your intention is for the other's benefit.

UPTIME: Directing your conscious attention outward toward the external world, especially toward the people with whom you're interacting.

CALIBRATION: Observing sensory data and measuring consistency and difference.

Watching for changes and consistencies in posture, facial expressions, muscle tension/relaxation, gestures, and eye movements.

Listening for changes and consistencies in pitch, volume, and tempo, the rate of speech, and sensory language.

REPRESENTATIONAL SYSTEMS: The perceptual filters used to control external input and the sensory systems people use to re-present their experience.

Sensory language, visual, auditory, or kinesthetic, an indication of how a person is thinking.

Eye movements, another indication of how another person is thinking.

BEHAVIORAL MATCHING: Using the same tonality, volume, or tempo, posture, or sensory language as the other person is using (this increases rapport).

SAMENESS OR DIFFERENCE: A cognitive process that prompts people to notice things that are similar to what they've known or experienced and to notice what's different.

BACKTRACKING: Summarizing in your own words what the other person has said, but using the other's key words and phrases, starting with, "If I understand you correctly . . ."

PACING AND LEADING: Using the skills of rapport to align with another (pacing), and moving the other person to another awareness, thought, or behavior by changing your language, tempo, tone, gestures, or posture (leading).

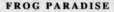

FROG PARADISE

Once upon a time there was a pond full of frogs in the middle of paradise. It was paradise for the frogs because there were no people for miles around, just plenty of food and clear water. The frogs lived here in perfect harmony and happiness, except for one problem.

This problem was caused by one particular frog. Now, as everyone knows, all frogs leap and all frogs say rribbet. *But this particular young frog went* chirp *and flapped his front legs out to the sides. The younger frogs tried to show him how to behave like a proper frog. He listened, but he continued doing things his own way.*

Finally the older and wiser frogs approached this young rebel and tried explaining to him, patiently at first, how unfroglike his behavior was. They demonstrated precisely how he was to leap and say rribbet. *When this had no effect, they became angry and threatened to ostracize him. But nothing seemed to work. The frogs were very upset about this situation, but there didn't seem to be anything they could do about it.*

One day at noon three large shadows appeared over the pond. They circled several times, and then one by one they swooped down and each grabbed a poor terrified frog, which disappeared forever out of sight of the rest of the community. The frogs were distraught. The next day, exactly at noon, the three large shadows flew over the pond again. After making several circles they dove down and each grabbed a frog and flew off with it. Now the whole frog community was truly panicked. They called a meeting to decide what to do. But no one could agree, and at the end they were all frightened and at a loss, with no plan for tomorrow.

This kept happening for many days. The frogs' paradise seemed to have been destroyed, and the frogs didn't know what to do to protect themselves. At the following meeting a young frog spoke up and said she'd noticed that the little frog that flapped his legs and went chirp was never bothered. Perhaps they should all flap their front legs and go chirp, she suggested.

The older and wiser frogs were outraged that anyone should suggest such unfroglike behavior. They decided to try harder to hide—under branches, lily pads, behind tree trunks. But no matter what they did, the shadows returned day after day and stole more members of their community.

Finally in desperation, the oldest and wisest frog asked the young frog who had suggested that they all imitate the frog who went chirp what she thought they all should do. "We could all learn how he does his leg-flapping and how he says chirp and then, just before noon every day, we would all go chirp and flap our legs."

Now the oldest and wisest were very distressed about this behavior; however, they felt their very existence was threatened. *So at noon the entire frog community chirped and flapped.*

When the three large shadows appeared, they circled the pond and then circled again and again. After circling many times, they flew away without stealing any of the frogs. The community was overjoyed, but they still worried about tomorrow. At noon the next day the three large shadows returned again, and all the frogs chirped and flapped for dear life. The shadows circled the pond many times and then left. Again, on the third day they returned, circling lower and lower as the frogs chirped and flapped. Finally, after a very long time, the three hawks flew off, never to return.

The frogs have their paradise back again and a little more flexibility about what "proper" froglike behavior is.

◆   ◆   ◆

PART TWO

You Have All the Resources You Need

12

Hidden Treasures

Communication is part of learning—about others, about the world you live in, about yourself. In communication with others (*inter*personal communication), your greatest asset is flexibility. In communication with yourself (*intra*personal communication), you need first and foremost a willingness to explore: a sense of adventure, curiosity, and a readiness to let your imagination lead you.

You need to listen to yourself: What are you saying— what messages do you give yourself over and over again— unaware that you're doing so? Are you saying things like "I can't do this, I'd make a fool of myself, I'm not smart enough, I'm too old," or "I'm boring: nobody wants to talk to me"? Do you jinx yourself? Or, on the other hand, do you tell yourself you can succeed despite the odds, that you have the ability, that you will win?

It's as easy to say the one as it is the other. But how are you going to get yourself to believe it?

You begin by recognizing that you have resources you haven't begun to appreciate. In fact, you probably don't even know you have them!

But now you are about to start the exploration, treasure map in hand, along the paths of your own accomplishments and abilities, the things you do without thinking about them, the hidden treasures you've kept under wraps for so long you've forgotten (or never known) they were there.

Remember playing Treasure Hunt as a child? It's a pirate game you might have enjoyed at a birthday party or with a little pal of yours, exploring a beach or cave or path through the woods. Maybe you searched for treasure in someone's attic or looked for hidden prizes with adults to tell you when you were "warmer" or "colder."

The search for hidden treasure is part of nearly everyone's life, if not in memory, then in fantasy. It's one of the oldest of stories—searching for the prize, for buried gold, a lost kingdom—and is a favorite theme of fairy tales and legends because it mirrors a quest that most of us understand. Whatever the hidden treasure is for any one of us—becoming beautiful, finding love, coming upon a cache of riches—the magic of the story is that the dreams you hardly dared to dream suddenly do come true.

The other part of the story is that these treasures are *hidden*. You find something that's been there all the time, but you either overlooked it or didn't know where to go to hunt for it. Maybe you never even knew there *was* a treasure you could search for.

To translate this into terms of the human psyche, treasures are resources that are hidden within us and that, when brought to light and utilized, allow us to accomplish whatever it is we hope or intend to do.

In other words, you already have what you need in order to do what you want to do, to make the choices and changes that put you in charge of your life and let you go in whatever direction you choose. What you have are resources, a whole treasure chest full, a deep storage of unexplored possibilities, hidden strengths, unknown powers. The presupposition of Neuro Linguistic Programming is:

You Have All the Resources You Need to Accomplish Whatever You Want.

OK, you say, great, but how come I don't know it? Why can't I accomplish what I want to do? Why can't I find these resources to help myself?

For the same reasons that most other people are not utilizing their resources either. First, you haven't identified them; second, you don't know how to access them, and third, even when you're able to access them, it may not be at the times or in the situations when and where and with whom you really need and want them.

All right. Let's start our exploration by asking, What is a resource?

Our own resources, human or personal, are very much like the natural resources of this planet. Hundreds upon thousands of years ago, this planet had all the uranium, gold, silver, oil, tin, copper, platinum, rubies, and emeralds that it has now. In fact, it had more, much more. But who knew about it? Who knew that this black flowing viscous liquid was useful, that it would fuel engines and keep people warm? Who knew about the unimaginable wealth of South Africa before the Kimberley diamond fields were discovered in 1871?

Before we had labeled oil or coal or diamonds as a resource, they didn't exist for us on this earth. We didn't know we had them. And even after we knew they were there and had labeled them, we were often unable to get to them. We didn't have the technology to coax oil from the ocean floor or extract veins of gold from rocks. The resource was there and we knew what it was, but we didn't know how to reach it.

Even now, when we have the means to access so many of the earth's hidden treasures, we often still ignore some of our most valuable natural resources. We take them for granted until they become polluted.

Nobody labeled air as a resource until fresh air was depleted from industrial centers through factory smoke and car fumes and waste disposal and all the other ingredients that make up the smog of cities.

And water—whoever could have thought, in the days of Huck Finn and Tom Sawyer, that the time was fast approaching when people would be *paying* for their water, in glass or plastic bottles, because what came out of the tap could cause cancer and other diseases?

Air to breathe and water to drink: We took these resources for granted and didn't pay attention to their worth. And as with the planet, the same is also true for human beings. Many of our most important resources are those things we take for granted about ourselves.

One of the most fundamental resources we have is the ability to make pictures in our mind. Another is talking to ourselves. These resources enable us to have a memory, to travel through time, to have an imagination.

We make pictures, we talk to ourselves. These are our most basic resources, so basic, so essential to our sense of who we are, that we never think about them—like the earth's light and darkness, or water and land. Another of our primary resources is the ability to have sensations, feel things: their weight, size, texture, temperature, and the sense of movement.

To see, hear, feel—these resources are like the earth's elements, which combine to create every bit of matter. Our elemental resources allow us to sweep through time and place, to create what never existed before, to see with an inner eye and hear with an inner ear.

Our minds supply us with riches all the time in the form of pictures, signs, words, phrases, sounds, and feelings. We can take these inner representations and adjust them, make them louder or clearer or stronger or more distant. By changing them in little ways, we can have a powerful impact on how we view something and on what meaning it has for us. We take a negative memory and make the image brighter, make it larger, put soft music under it, add some warmth or softness, and transform it into something that no longer holds us back. The memory that hindered us becomes something that motivates us for the future. We flip negative to positive, reverse to forward. Magic.

We do that by learning to adjust the controls of our inner representations. You can change the way you perceive things just as you change the tuning of your TV.

13

Submodalities

Our brains code and store experience instantaneously and without any conscious effort, like magic—except that this sleight of mind is one of our most fundamental traits. The way we capture, filter, and process our experiences and thoughts is an essential human resource. But, as in magic, we don't see how these connections are done.

When we make our resources conscious, we're able to control them. And when we control the resources, we can change the quality and direction of our lives. Submodalities are the specific units of our sensory or representational systems by which we break down experience for storage and future use. They are the units that provide the fine tuning beyond the on-off button of consciousness.

Our primary filters of perception or representational systems are the modalities. Submodalities are the smaller specific and adjustable aspects of these modalities. By manipulating the submodalities, we can quickly and easily change the way we think, feel, and do things.

Through submodalities we can change memory and experience. We rearrange the past in order to have more choice about the future. But what we're changing is the *form* of the memory, not the *content*.

The book in Braille that you read with your fingers is the same as the book in print you read with your eyes. How the book is set up—in print or in Braille—provides the *form*. The book itself is *content*. How you perceive the book will depend on whether you're reading it with your sight or your touch, but the words don't change; only your experience of them changes.

Content is the story; form is the way the story is told. I can write it down, tell it to you, tape it, film it, dance it, sing it, make cartoons of it, paint it. In each version the story remains the same, but the medium is different and changes the impact of the story. Think of how different the same story appears when you see it on a large movie screen instead of on your TV at home. Form changes meaning.

How we think—by images, words, sensations, sounds, and other sensory means—is form. *What* we think—our thoughts, ideas, memories—is content.

If you're planning to buy a new car, you might see it in your mind's eye in a particular way: large and close, colorful, bright, and clear. Buying the car is content; the bright big pictures are form. If you keep telling yourself "I'll never be able to afford a new car," the message is the content; the tone and tempo of your voice as you talk to yourself are the form.

Form is the vehicle, content is the traveler. I can get from Chicago to Detroit by air, rail, bus, car, bike, foot, and possibly even Rollerblades—and though each of these journeys covers the same route, the experience of each will be different from all the others.

It's important to be clear on the distinction. Experience (thoughts, memories) provides content. What you make of it (how you interpret it) comes about through changing or manipulating the form in which your experience is stored. By working on form you can change the meaning or effect of the content. You break out of habitual patterns of behavior and thought by altering the way (form) you recall the experiences that have shaped these patterns. Using the images and sounds that your brain is constantly supplying, you can change the form of a memory or of a future possibility.

Try it now: Remember (call up in your mind) something pleasant that happened to you fairly recently—say within the last year or two.

As you remember it, you'll be aware of an image or a cluster of images connected to that experience—maybe you're walking along a beach, the sand warm between your toes, birds circling overhead, waves rushing to shore; or it's a city street on a winter night, unusually silent, long pale shadows from streetlamps stretching across the snow.

Or you remember a woman's face, the clothes she was wearing, the color of her lipstick, her long vermilion fingernails, the polished black tabletop, portraits hanging on the wall.

Or you're aware of the sounds that made up the experience: a tune you were dancing to, the song of a bird coming in your bedroom window early in the morning, people laughing, a murmuring stream. Maybe you're saying something to yourself in the memory: "I can still see the time when I was in Paris and Jean-Pierre brought over the wine" or "That was on Election Day, and the train was just pulling into Grand Central Station."

Maybe you're reliving feelings you had, pleasant sensations connected with that experience. If you are, you can be sure those feelings are being generated by specific images, pictures, sounds, words: something concrete, something you can describe whether or not you're conscious of it. Like a television that's on: Even though the picture is dark and the volume turned down, the sounds and pictures are all still there. It's just that you haven't adjusted the knobs yet. Our brain works the same way, and if you're not consciously tuned in, you'll miss seeing and hearing a lot of the wonderful programs playing out in your mind.

Let's turn up the picture. Look at the image you're getting of your pleasant memory. (If you're not getting an image, ask yourself, If I *could see* an image connected with this memory, what would it be? What would I be seeing?)

Make that image black and white. Make it small. Make it dark. What kind of impact does this have on you?

Take the same image. Make it large, bright, full of color. What impact does this have?

Which way of representing it brings up more of the original pleasant emotion of this experience?

Take another image. (Imagine switching channels or, even more simply, looking through a photograph album of pleasant scenes. Pick any picture you see.) Move the image away from you. Even farther, very far away.

Now bring it closer, very close, face-to-face.

Which distance was more comfortable for you? Did the picture get overwhelming when you moved it in too close? Did you get disconnected from it when it was far away? Or maybe the closeness motivated you, made you want to accomplish something immediately. Or perhaps the farther distance made the image more pleasant, less confrontational, easier to take.

Remember, these are *your* images; this is *your* show. Changing different aspects of your mental image gives you a freedom of choice. How you perceive something changes the impact it has on you.

Try looking at the image through a different lens of your inner camera. Make the subject bigger, gigantic, or smaller, minute. Put the picture in focus; make it blurred. Change the perspective—see your image from above, below, from the side. Play with it and notice how your feelings change as the submodalities—the aspects and parameters of your pictures—are altered.

Now turn up the volume. Bring in the sounds or the words connected to this experience. (If you're not getting the words, the sounds, ask yourself: If I *could* hear the words or sounds connected with this memory, what would I be hearing?)

Make the tempo *very* fast and turn up the volume to *very* loud. How does this affect the memory of the experience?

Slow down the tempo. Bring down the volume. What kind of impact does this have?

Now try keeping the volume down (if the sounds are words spoken by yourself or somebody else, bring the voice down to a whisper), and adjust only the tempo, the fastness or slowness of words or sounds.

Reverse it. Keep the tempo constant (the *tick-tock, tick-tock* of a metronome if you like) and play with the volume.

The changes will affect the way you perceive your memory. Aunt Em's voice is soft and slow and reassuring—you feel pleased and comforted. But now her voice is shrill, too fast, too loud—and you're nervous, irritated.

What we're playing with, on the imaginary dials of our unconscious, are visual and auditory submodalities.

Visual submodalities include focus, size, distance (from viewer to image), levels of brightness, black and white or color, color intensity, stills or movies, framed or panoramic, opaque or translucent.

How do you frame the picture in your mind's eye? Is it projected on a wide screen? Does it fill the whole landscape of your mind or is it small, the size of a postcard? As tiny as a postage stamp? Is it three-dimensional or flat, in focus or not, close up or distant? Are you inside the action looking out, or are you in the audience, watching the movie of your own life?

Auditory submodalities include volume, pitch, tempo, frequency, location, duration, and pauses or silences. When an inner voice is talking to you, is the voice soft or loud, high-pitched or low, close by or far away, fast-paced or slow, varied or monotonous? Does it have an echo, does

the sound reverberate; is it piercing, like a scream, or faint
as a distant foghorn?

SUBMODALITY DISTINCTIONS

VISUAL	AUDITORY
Framed or panoramic image	Volume
Color or black and white	Tempo
See self in picture or see through own eyes	Pitch
	Location of sound
Brightness of light	Duration
Size of image as a whole	Stereo of mono
Relative size (proportion) of objects and figures	Frequency
	Rhythm
Contrast of light and dark	Words and/or sounds
Moving or still images	
Focus sharp or blurred	
Color intensity (primary, pastel, or muted)	
Opaque or translucent	
Angle of viewing—above, below, to the side	
Dimensionality: 3-D or flat	

*Note: This is only a partial listing. Not all submodality distinc-
tions will be applicable to all memories/images. You may also
discover unique submodalities of your own.*

*Kinesthetic submodalities are not listed simply because I've
chosen to concentrate on the submodalities of seeing (visual)*

and hearing (auditory). These are easier to change and can be applied more generally than kinesthetic. Gustatory (taste) and olfactory (smell) submodalities are also not included.

Kinesthetic submodalities refer to primary physical sensations: the senses of touch (tactile), heat and cold (temperature), pressure, movement, contraction and expansion. A buzzing in your head, a tingling in your extremities, a rush of heat, pins and needles, goose bumps—all these are kinesthetic responses. You can recognize objects in the dark by touch—smooth or rough, soft or hard, sharp, rounded, silky, metallic, and so forth. Within yourself, the physical sensations might be a sense of pressure. Where does it start in your body? How far does it extend? Is the pressure the same over the whole area?

Movement is also a physical sensation, whether external or internal, in the rate of breathing, heartbeat, in muscular activity, the tension and relaxation of facial muscles, neck muscles. Kinesthetic submodalities are measures of exactly how (where, to what degree) you are feeling.

Submodalities are the qualifiers of experience, the way we code our experiences and enter them into memory. They are the units by which our brain distinguishes pleasant from unpleasant, past and future, fantasy and memory.

When we become aware of the submodalities we use in speaking to ourselves or projecting our inner pictures, we're able to make changes. We have choices about how we experience something, how we frame that experience for ourselves. With choice comes control. We can decide to act instead of being acted upon.

You can make extraordinary changes in the quality of your thoughts, your emotions, and your behavior with simple, easy-to-do shifts in submodalities; your brain learned to code your experiences without consulting you. And if at first you're not getting the results you hope for in the following exercises, relax and be patient with yourself. Your brain is talking to you in its own language of submodalities, the hidden resources you are just discovering and learning to use, like a child who keeps trying out words until the meaning comes across.

Changing submodalities can be as simple and quick as flipping through a photo album. Don't strain for it; it's an ability you already have, a magic tool waiting to be used.

◆

VISUAL SUBMODALITY RESOURCE EXERCISE

1. Think of something pleasant.

2. Make a picture of it. Look at the image and rate it on a scale of 1 to 10, with 10 being the most pleasant.

3. Make the image larger. Rate it.

   Return to the original image and make it brighter. Rate it. (After each change, put back the submodality to the way it was originally.)
   Bring it closer. Rate it.
   Add color (if missing), or make the color more intense. Rate it.
   Bring it into sharper focus. Rate it.

4. Notice which submodality changes make the image more pleasant. If you like, replay the image with those changes several times, until the changes are locked into place and appear automatically.

5. Enjoy the increased pleasure your magic tools can give you.

◆

AUDITORY SUBMODALITY RESOURCE EXERCISE

1. Think of something pleasant you tell yourself (such as "I did that well, I'm in great shape, I'm able to understand all of this"). Rate this on a scale of 1 to 10.

2. Listen for the pitch, tempo, volume, and location (where the sound is coming from).

3. Change the volume. Rate it.
   Return to the original sound. Change the pitch. Rate it. (After each change, put back the submodality to the way it was originally.)
   Change the tempo. Rate it.
   Change the location. (For instance, if the main sound is coming from the left side of your head, change it to right; if from inside your head, change it to outside.) Rate this change in location.

4. Find the submodality that makes what you say to yourself even more pleasant. Replay it, practice it, and keep it.

◆

14

Labeling Resources

Resources are skills, attitudes, aptitudes, abilities, emotions, and knowledge that help us do and become what we want. They are the possibilities and potentials within all of us, whether or not we recognize them.

Most of us rarely (if ever) think about the combination of molecules that makes up the air we breathe or about the force of gravity that prevents us from hurtling out into the void. It's the same with personal resources. We place no value on whatever comes easily. People who naturally sing in tune think there's nothing to it, but people who can't carry a tune for even the distance of a measure regard it with awe.

Or think of waking up in the morning. Sure, everyone wakes up eventually, but if you habitually wake up on time, get yourself dressed, do your chores, water the plants, make breakfast, feed the pets, the kids, bring in the paper, reassure your wife or husband, warm up the car or whatever else needs to be done, and then get to work or to your appointments on time, you are making use of what are invaluable resources. And if you don't believe it, just try to imagine your life if you *couldn't* do those things.

Label it; label that resource that gets you up in the morning at the right time and then sets you in motion in such a way that you can accomplish all the things you need to do before leaving the house or getting the kids off or settling down to work. What's the first word that comes to mind?

Is it *responsible? Reliable? Dependable*, maybe, or *trustworthy? Efficient?* A descriptive phrase as in: You can count on me? Set your clock by me? Or would you describe yourself in terms of your resource along more sensory lines, as *solid* or *sound* or *bright-eyed and bushy-tailed?*

Think of other resources you have. What about your ability to throw a party on the spur of the moment? You let people know they can just drop by and be sure of a warm welcome. Other people would fret and fuss; you take it in stride.

Confident? Relaxed? Easygoing? Friendly?

Even if you don't yet consider the resource you have to be a valuable one, label it anyway. And if you don't think *easygoing* is an important resource, leave it alone for the moment, let yourself start getting used to it. Or if, instead of *responsible*, you thought of *intense*, and you don't think intensity is a positive quality, let that stand. The first task is simply to uncover the resource. And being intense can turn out to be the resource that keeps you on track, that allows you to persevere and accomplish your goals more than any other resource possibly could.

In the same way, being easygoing might be the resource that gives you the necessary patience and coolheadedness to triumph over obstacles and discouragement and help others who are on the verge of giving in.

To make our resources available to us, we have to name them. Otherwise they become invisible, like the air, or intangible, like gravity.

When we name something, we take possession of it. We

make it our own, we are aware that we have it, and we are able to make use of it. Children begin to take control of their environment when they learn to use words. They can ask for what they want or need; they are changing their surroundings, remaking their world. Words bring awareness and control, which result in power.

Naming a resource is rescuing it from nonexistence. It becomes yours. You are made aware that you have this resource and you can call it up whenever you want or need it. The label becomes a handle you can grasp and hold on to.

Often, other people label our resources for us—"You're very generous"; "Thanks for pointing that out, you're really perceptive"—and often we can recognize at least *some* of the resources we have, like health, financial security, a good education, or physical attractiveness, especially those we can contrast with *not* having them. But sometimes we're blind to our most obvious resources, or we disparage whatever comes easily (on the principle of "If *I* can do it, it isn't worth much").

A man I once knew, an engineer, thought he had no resources. When I asked him to tell me something he did that he thought was very easy, he thought for a long while and finally came up with, "I don't know—maybe putting the children to bed." As he said it, the wrinkles of a smile formed at the corners of his lips. "I read to them most every night."

When he described how he did that, using the blankets and furniture in the room to set the scene for each story he acted out with his children, I remarked on how creative he was. "I don't know," he responded, shaking his head.

He made something come to life that hadn't existed before, I reminded him. That's what creativity is all about. "Creative?" he repeated, testing the word. "Creative?

Well, maybe, I guess you could call it that."

Once he accepted creativity as a resource he had, this man realized that he could be, and was, creative in other ways as well. He was playful, spontaneous, affectionate, imaginative—the resources tumbled out like toys from Santa's bag.

◆

RESOURCE EXERCISE I

1. Think of something you do that is easy for you.

2. Pretend to be someone else, someone you respect.
   Change your physical position: move to another chair or another spot in the room and look back at yourself.

3. From the perspective of this other person, look at what you do easily and listen to how you describe it.

4. Allow this other person to find and label the resource in the thing you do so easily.

5. Go back to your original position and be yourself again.
   Consider the named resource. Is it a resource you realized you had? When would it be useful to you?

◆

RESOURCE EXERCISE II

1. Do Exercise I several times until you have three or four resources. Start making a written list.

2. Ask other people what resources they see in you. Decide which one(s) of these you appreciate. Add them
   to your list.

3. Look at this list at least once a day for a week. Keep
   adding to it.

◆

15

Anchoring

Once you know what resources are stored inside your own treasure chest, how are you going to make use of them? Naming the resource brings it to light, yes, but that alone won't make it useful to you. A resource is like a tool: its value is created through use.

And, like a tool, it tends to get lost if you don't keep it someplace where you have easy access to it when you need it. Think of all the penknives and screwdrivers, thumbtacks, picture hooks, tape, and those ingenious gadgets that have managed to disappear just when you needed them most. All the wasted hours of searching, all the missing keys that had to be remade, all the forgotten items in your toiletry case that had to be replaced.

Like a tool, a resource must be available at the particular time and place when you need and want it. Possessing the resource of patience isn't going to help you unless you can call it up during the frustrations of trying to convince a hotel porter that you have a reservation when he insists your name isn't on the books. Being creative isn't necessarily going to do much good when you're filling out your tax returns, but if you can't call up your creativity when you're stuck in traffic with two cranky kids in the backseat, you'll have to contend with a lot of unhappiness. A first-aid kit needs to be taken along on the voyage for it to be of any use. The same goes for your mental toolbox, the magic of possibilities in the guise of resources.

You already have all the resources you need. Once you identify them, you have to be able to access them. This means immediate availability, the life jacket when you're drowning, not when you're trying it on in the store. You must be able to call up your resources instantaneously for them to make a positive difference in your life, and you have to be able to depend on your ability to summon the resources you need at any given time. This means that the access has to be under your conscious control.

Much faster than any computer yet devised, the human brain finds what we need. Hundreds of times a day, your brain is making thousands and millions of connections far beneath or beyond the level of your consciousness. When you pick up a fork, cross your legs, or turn your head, all these movements are the result of hundreds of automatic reactions, a chain of automatic stimulus-response events. You don't have to think about most of your actions and processes; they just seem to happen. When you climb stairs, ride a bike, or drive your car, you're not thinking about 90 to 99 percent of what you're doing. Your mind has already made the necessary connections.

The brain's incredible ability to utilize the stimulus-response phenomenon and make most behavior automatic frees our limited *conscious* mind for learning new things, adding on to the accumulation of memories and experience we already have, while in the *unconscious* mind stimulus-response reactions keep us moving, breathing, walking, talking, cooking, driving, washing, catching buses, humming, chewing—all the countless activities we rely on to keep things going on a regular basis.

Because we can depend on the automatic pilot of our unconscious, we can direct the units of our conscious attention toward learning, which is the creation of new connections, and we can make choices about what they are to be. Using the mind's natural ability to generate stimulus-response pairings, we form conscious connections in order to access and secure resources.

We do this through *anchoring*, a technique for consciously and deliberately pairing a chosen stimulus (anchor) with a desired response (resource).

Anchoring is a term we use in NLP. To understand it, simply think of the traditional anchor on a boat. When you lower the anchor from the side of the boat, it lodges on the bottom and holds the boat securely in place. When you anchor something to the floor or wall, it means you have secured it there.

With human behavior, an anchor is a chosen stimulus that secures a specific response. Anchoring is based on the work we know as Pavlovian conditioning. In the experiment that made him famous, Pavlov rang a bell whenever he brought his dogs their dinner. The dogs naturally salivated at the approach of food. After several repetitions, when the dogs had been conditioned to hearing the bell in connection with receiving their dinner, Pavlov rang the bell *without* bringing food. The dogs salivated—to the sound alone.

This is psychology's famous conditioned response: a learned but automatic form of behavior. Food was the stimulus that generated the response of salivating. When the ringing of the bell was paired to food often enough it began to replace the food as the original stimulus, so that the dogs would salivate to the sound of the bell alone. To the dogs, bell and food represented the same thing. (Of course, they still salivated when presented with food!) Pavlov had *conditioned* the dogs to respond in a new way to the stimulus (the ringing of the bell).

The experiment was designed to show that it was possible to teach automatic behavior (a seeming contradiction in terms), and therefore the results are rather more spectacular than useful. (As a rule, dogs don't get much benefit from salivating at the sound of a bell.) However, Pavlov demonstrated that the ability to utilize the stimulus-response phenomenon is based on a natural learning capability in humans and other animals. Pavlov used dogs to illuminate this natural ability in humans to make connections or associations through stimulus-response pairing.

Anchoring is the pairing of a chosen stimulus with a specific response. After several repetitions, the stimulus will automatically produce the response because stimulus and response have become associated in the person's unconscious. They have bonded, in a sense. The elements have come together. The stimulus cannot exist without the response.

Many of us believe we have free will. However, all of us are automatically anchored to a multitude of stimuli that we don't acknowledge—don't even recognize.

Unnoticed, like the air we breathe, these stimuli are the catalysts that produce inescapable responses of mood and feelings, action and thought. A fragment of a song brings to mind a person's face; the smell of baking bread propels you back to a room when you were eight years old; a tone of voice makes you irritated without any known cause. When someone holds out a hand for a handshake you don't have to "think" about responding, you just do. A sneeze might automatically bring out a "Gesundheit!" or "God bless you!"

These are all examples of anchors, a particular stimulus paired or associated with a specific response. Anchors are extremely important tools for getting to and maintaining a resource when we want and need it.

Most of the time we become anchored without being aware of it. We associate certain responses to certain stimuli as a matter of course, or conditioning, and we assume this is the way things have to be. Most of us learn certain "rulcs" as children—saying *please*, using knives and forks, controlling body functions in public—and they become automatic, so that we're surprised or offended if someone doesn't follow them.

These are anchors we don't think about. We can, however, consciously create anchors by purposefully selecting a gesture (stimulus) and an experience (memory) of a resource (response) and pairing them together several times until the gesture alone (held to the count of ten) will bring back all the feelings and sensations of the resource—automatically. The memory becomes the response. The resource (confidence, for instance) is contained in the memory, and by pairing the gesture (stimulus) with the memory (response), you elicit the resource. You make an "o" with your thumb and forefinger, or you make a small fist, and suddenly you feel confident.

You can anchor someone else, leading him or her through the steps, or you can anchor yourself. The ability to self-anchor lets you make fullest use of your resources, by giving immediate access and putting it, at times even literally, at the command of your fingertips.

Because it may be a new and unfamiliar technique for you, let's go through self-anchoring together, step by step. Then you can try it on your own.

To anchor yourself, first choose a gesture, something simple like making a small fist, pressing thumb and forefinger together in an "o," or gently holding your earlobe. This becomes your anchor for this resource. Make sure that the gesture you select is repeatable, so that you can do it in exactly the same way each time.

Think of a resource you want more access to. Remember an experience of feeling or having this resource in the past and allow yourself to relive the memory as fully as possible. Imagine you're back inside the experience: seeing what you saw then, hearing what you heard, feeling what you felt. While you do this, hold your chosen gesture. Continue to hold for a count of ten. Release.

Repeat this several times, calling up a memory of yourself feeling the resource you want more access to, while holding your gesture (anchor). Take your time and enjoy the process. You can use the same memory each time, or you can call up different memories in which you experience the same resource. In other words, if your resource is *confidence*, you might choose a memory of being confident while writing a proposal or planning a party or choosing a gift or standing up for something you believe in. Each time you hold your anchor, you relive one of these memories.

After you've done this four or five times—reliving your experience while holding your anchor—let go of the gesture and the memory, look around you, relax, and take note of your surroundings. (This is what we call "break state.") Then hold your anchor for a count of ten. You will feel your resource (confidence) come flooding back.

You've paired the stimulus of your gesture with the memory or memories of your resource, and now, by repeating your self-anchor, you bring back the experience of your desired resource. You have immediate automatic access to the resource whenever you need or want it. You don't have to think about it. Hold the gesture and it's there.

◆

SELF-ANCHORING EXERCISE

1. Think of one of your favorite resources, such as confidence, creativity, strength—any one you like.

2. Think of an experience, a time of your life when you had this resource strongly.

3. Remember that experience as though you were living it now. See what you saw then, hear what you heard then, feel what you felt then, until it becomes as though it's happening now. As you relive this experience, make a soft fist and hold for 10 seconds.

4. Release your anchor (the soft fist). Look around, take a deep breath.

5. Repeat step 3. Do this three or four times.

6. Take a deep breath, look around, think of something else.
   Remain like this for several seconds.
   Now use your anchor. Make that soft fist and hold it for 10 seconds.
   Notice what happens.
   The feelings associated with that resource will come flooding back.

You have now anchored this resource. Whenever you feel you could benefit from having this resource, all you have to do is hold your anchor.

Note: Please treat your resources intelligently and respectfully. Do not expect your resources to solve all your most difficult situations. Use the anchor/resource for situations that match the intensity of your anchor. An anchor may not hold a boat in the midst of a hurricane in the open sea. If you anchor a resource of confidence and use it when asking your boss for a raise, it will work wonders. If, however, you use that anchor when the boss fires you unexpectedly, anchor and resource may become overwhelmed by external circumstances.

◆

16

Future Conditioning

Future conditioning is the term we use in NLP for creating an anchor in the future. It means attaching a resource (assertiveness, for instance) that you might need in a future situation to a stimulus (the anchor) you've already established and then transferring it to the future situation—Thanksgiving with relatives, maybe, or asking for a bank loan. (It becomes much easier when you actually do it.)

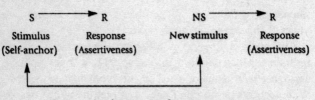

The new stimulus now gets the same response as your original self-anchor.

Let's say you've anchored your resource of assertiveness by pressing your thumb and pinky together. Whenever you press your thumb and forefinger together you feel assertive.

Think of the relatives you'll see at Thanksgiving and focus on that one uncle you can never stand up to. Picture his face in your mind's eye and press your thumb and pinky together for ten seconds. Do this three or four times, or as often as you need for the response to become automatic.

Now when you think of this uncle you'll feel assertive. His face has become the automatic stimulus for your response. You've transferred the stimulus (your self-anchor) for your resource of assertiveness to his face.

As you do your anchoring, you can select whatever gesture works best for you. But do *not* use the same anchor for different resources—it will muddy the anchor and weaken if not nullify the response. To anchor, you could gently pull an earlobe, press your thumb and forefinger together, or touch your elbow, knee, eyelid, back of your neck, or hand, for example. Just make sure that whatever you use as an anchor is very specific, so that when you repeat it you can do it in exactly the same way.

If you're using a word as an internal anchor (something you say to yourself), practice saying it out loud first to make sure you get it the same way each time, with the same intonation, volume, and pitch—and then you can say it to yourself (internally) as an anchor.

Anchoring is a magic tool that lets you instantly call up resources. Much faster than dialing 911, it gives you the assistance you want or need in the moment you need it. With anchoring, you don't have to regret the words unspoken, the things you could have done, or would have or should have, but didn't do because you were missing your resource of assertiveness or confidence or creativity, or whichever of your resources was needed at the time. The could haves, should haves, would haves, or *l'esprit d'escalier* ("the spirit of the stairway," meaning words that come to you *after* the opportunity for saying them is past) that plague many of us can be erased by this simple tool of anchoring, which is, in the literal as well as in the deep sense, a way of getting in touch with yourself.

The advice in *Hamlet* given by Polonius to his son—

> *This above all: to thine own self be true,*
> *And it must follow, as the night the day,*
> *Thou canst not then be false to any man*—

has become a cliché mainly because it's as true now as it was when Shakespeare wrote it. In order to communicate clearly to others, you must first communicate clearly with yourself. To do that, you have to be able to access your resources. Like plugging into an old-fashioned switchboard, anchors let you connect with the resource you need whenever the call for it comes in.

◆

FUTURE CONDITIONING EXERCISE

1. Self-anchor the resource of confidence. (See Self-Anchoring Exercise in chapter 15.) Test it.

2. Choose a person with whom you want to feel more confident, or think of a place in which you want more confidence than you have now.

   (Please don't overwhelm your resource. Make sure it's a person or place with whom or where it's possible and realistic for you to have increased confidence. Do not pick a person or place that reminds you of a traumatic event in your life.)

3. Picture and hear that person or place inside your mind. As you do this, use your self-anchor for confidence. Hold it 10 seconds. Release, take a deep breath, look around. Do this three times.

4. Now, just think of the person or place. You will automatically feel more confident. And the next time you see this person or are in this place, your resource of confidence will be triggered automatically.

You have transferred the stimulus for confidence from your self-anchor to the image of the person or place. Now the sight of that person or place (in actuality or on the screen of your mind) will automatically bring up the resource of confidence. Once you've established this connection, you will never have to "think" about having more confidence in that situation. It will simply happen.

◆

17

Physiology

Look at you. Yes, you, the one who's reading this book. Put it down a moment and go to a mirror. Look at yourself. What do you see?

How do you come across? Do you look like a person who's essentially resourceful? Someone other people look up to (no matter what your height)? Or do you give off the message that things aren't much good and there's nothing you can do about it?

The way you carry yourself, the way you hold your body—this is what we mean by *physiology*. It's the message you send out about how you feel about yourself.

Physiology is a resource too, so obvious that no one pays much attention to it, like the resource of memory. And yet, physiology may be the first thing someone notices about you. It's your walking advertisement (or apology) for yourself.

In working with submodalities, we've seen that each of us has the power and ability to change the meaning and impact of thoughts and memories. You can affect the outcome of an event by the way you approach it, by the take you have on it through the pictures and sounds in your brain. If something appears dark and small and out of focus to you, it's a pretty sure bet that the outcome will not be positive, unless or until you change your perception of that event or person or concept.

What is true on the micro scale of submodalities is also true on the large or macro scale of your whole body. If your posture is hunched over like a question mark, you are not going to make a dynamic impression, to put it mildly. Equally important (and at times even more so), your physiology will affect the way you think and feel. Chin tucked under, eyes cast downward, shoulders hunched over, chest caved in: Is this a recipe for or a description of depression?

Billy Crystal has a hilarious routine in which he elaborates on the importance of looking good. "You look *mah*-velous," he says, and keeps repeating the word. "*Mah*-velous. It's not important how you feel, it's how you look—and you look *mah*-velous."

Of course, the truth in that humor is that once you look marvelous, or at any rate believe you do, you will feel marvelous. And when you feel marvelous, why then you'll . . . (you can fill in the rest).

NLP offers an instant way to look marvelous. It's called *resourceful physiology*. In an instant, as if by the waving of a wand that transforms a pumpkin into a glass coach or a ragamuffin into a princess, you can go from down to up, from negative to positive, helpless to confident. An instant body-lift, it has you looking and feeling great in seconds. All you have to do is concentrate on two areas of your body: your pelvis and your rib cage.

A resourceful (read *confident, upbeat*) physiology happens when (1) you center your weight in the middle of the pelvic region of your body and (2) you lift your rib cage. If you throw your weight to one hip, as in the typical model's stance, you are not centered. When you lift your rib cage, you should not be hiking up your shoulders. We're not talking about a stiff, military bearing. The resourceful physiology is relaxed and natural. Lifting the rib cage lifts your chest, your entire upper body, including your head and chin, and allows your shoulders to remain rounded and re-laxed.

Try it.

Lift your rib cage, center your weight. Hold this posture.

Now slouch down, feel how your ribs seem to crunch together. Your chin drops toward your chest.

Lift the rib cage again. Your chest expands, there's more space to breathe, your neck and chin lift, you can take deeper breaths, and you're probably feeling taller, stronger, and more in charge.

Now shift your weight to one side. Notice how you feel, think, look. Center your weight.

In case you're still unsure about the power of positive physiology, try this experiment: Put your chin down, crunch up your rib cage, slump your shoulders, shift your weight to one hip, and try to think of a positive resource you have. Hard to do, isn't it?

Now center your weight and lift your rib cage. What happens? How many resources come instantly to mind?

Or try the opposite: Think of a problem and look down at the floor, your head down, rib cage caved in, your weight on one side or the other, and ask yourself how to solve the problem.

Now straighten up, center your weight, lift your rib cage, and look up. Think of the problem and possible solutions. Doesn't this alert new posture give you a brand-new per-spective on the problem?

The *way* we look at something influences what we're seeing. Remember the eye movements we talked about in chapter 7? One reason why looking up makes a difference is that when we move our gaze up above eye level we're putting ourselves in the visual mode. Looking down puts us into feelings, and if they're negative, we're likely to get stuck.

It's like the song about holding yourself tall when you're

in a storm: If you look as though you're brave, you're bound to convince others, and yourself as well, that you actually *are* brave. Holding your head up is the first step to feeling ''up,'' on top of things. The way you look and the way you feel are mirror reflections. When you're looking up, you'll soon be feeling up, and you'll notice that things around you are looking up as well.

Resourceful physiology is only one of the ways to access your resources. Remember that what we're doing here is finding ways to make the resources we already have available to us when and where we need them. It's the search for buried treasure, keeping in mind that the treasure exists, has always been there, and will always be there, ready to yield up more riches the more you look. Your treasures, your resources, are like the pages of a wonderful book: Each time you read them you find something new, something you may have overlooked the first time or, if you didn't overlook it, it didn't have the same meaning then because your life hadn't caught up with it yet. But later, and partly because of reading that wonderful book, you changed your life, you did new things, and now the pages— the resources, the treasures—come into their own.

As in communication with others, communication with self is an interactive loop. As you increase your ability to imagine in pictures and sounds, to project yourself into the past and future, your powers of imagination increase. What you uncover in yourself leads to new choices, which in turn lead to new directions and decisions, new ways of being and interacting. As you evolve, your resources grow with you, and you keep on discovering more of them, acknowledging them, naming them, finding ways to access them. These treasures, like love or understanding, have the capacity to increase the more you use them. You have everything you need to accomplish whatever you want. Believe it!

◆

RESOURCEFUL PHYSIOLOGY EXERCISE

1. Pick a spot on the floor and label it Resourceful Physiology.

2. Step onto the spot you've labeled Resourceful Physiology (RP). Center your weight in your pelvis and lift your rib cage.

3. Step off the spot; relax into your usual posture.

4. Step on again and go into your RP posture.

   Keep stepping on and off, practicing your RP whenever you step back on, until it becomes automatic and easy.

5. Think of a situation that happens often or repeatedly in which you don't like the way you handle yourself. Pick another spot on the floor and label it Difficult Situation.

6. Step onto that spot, immediately assume your RP posture, and live through the difficult situation, as though it's happening right now. Maintain your resourceful physiology. Notice how you feel and think.

The difficult situation has changed for you, hasn't it?

◆

RESOURCES RECAP

RESOURCES: The skills, attitudes, aptitudes, emotions, and knowledge we have that help us accomplish what we want. To make use of our resources, we first have to label them.

SUBMODALITIES: The language of the brain. Our most basic resources as represented by the finer distinctions of our sensory systems, V (visual), A (auditory), and K (kinesthetic).

ANCHORING: Deliberate creation of a stimulus-response connection; learning to condition your own response by establishing a specific stimulus that will elicit a desired resource. Being able to do this means you have your resource under control, to access where and when you want it or need it.

SELF-ANCHORING AND FUTURE CONDITIONING: Techniques that give you more access to your resources and increase your choices and control in a range of situations.

PHYSIOLOGY: A resource that can instantly transform your outlook. Learn to give yourself an instant body-lift and send out a cheerful message to yourself and others.

SOMELAND*

Long ago in the vast reaches of space a planet was born. She had one large land mass surrounded by oceans. Her name was Someland.

Someland was beset by terrible troubles, both internal and external. She was inhabited by fierce warring tribes; she suffered earthquakes, hurricanes, and erupting volcanoes that kept reshaping her geography. Someland's image as reflected in the heavenly mirror of her own atmosphere was constantly shifting; she'd get used to one image, and then it changed to another. This was very upsetting; she didn't know who she was.

Her external problems included meteorites, which kept crashing into each other and falling onto the planet, ruining still more of Someland's features. Not to mention the problems she had with the three moons that orbited her and the two suns around which she orbited. The three moons kept influencing her tides, pushing and pulling in various directions and causing great floods, tidal waves, and giant whirlpools. Her orbit around the two suns was in the shape of a figure eight, so that at night she was frozen by the cold and by day she was burned by the heat.

Her experience was of chaos and unpredictability. Only one thing was certain: Survival was an endless struggle. Someland felt despair; she felt as though she could not endure, since she didn't have the strength to withstand the terrible stress, the pushing and pulling.

Now remember, planets are lonely bodies—they cannot meet each other and learn from each other, nor can they

---

*ADAPTED FROM A STORY BY CHANNAH CUNE.

just lie down and die. What was Someland to do? In her desperation she turned inward. Instead of studying herself in the mirror of her atmosphere she looked at herself in a way she had never done before. She saw familiar parts, such as layers of earth and stone, underground wells, streams and rivers, caves, the roots of vegetables; and unfamiliar parts, such as layers of black coal, reservoirs of slow-flowing oil, streaks of gold and silver, gemstones shining. And beneath all this a heavy, stable area that could not be moved, pushed, or pulled even by the fiercest storm. It was a powerful magnet and source of energy.

Someland had never known this part of herself. "Who are you?" she asked.

"I am your core."

"And what are you for?" asked Someland.

"I am for you," said her core. "I am your center and I keep you stable in your solar system. External troubles only add to my power and energy. Now that you've finally found me, we can work together to influence our environment and reach our destiny."

"Why did you never speak to me before?" Someland asked.

"I had no voice," answered her core, "until you found me. You were just paying attention to your external world; now you are beginning to notice your internal treasures and resources. Think of the treasures you noticed today for the first time. You are much richer than you ever realized. Your hidden parts have been working for you all along."

Someland took her place in the universe. Knowing her inner core and her resources enabled her to complete her journey toward her destiny.

❖ ❖ ❖

PART THREE

*Success Is the Ability to Achieve
Intended Results*

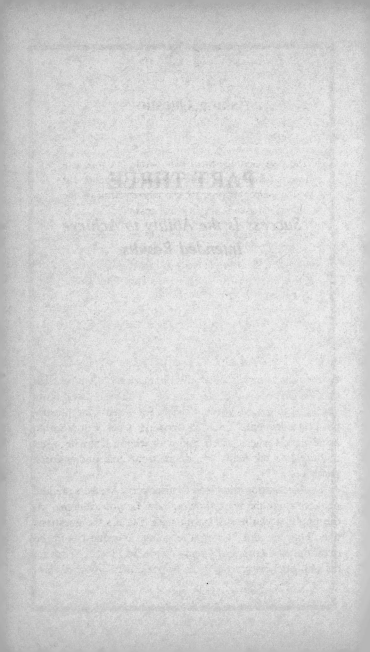

18

Asking Questions

The poet Gertrude Stein (who wrote "A rose is a
rose is a rose") was on her deathbed. Gathering her
last resources of strength, she raised herself on the
pillow and asked, "What is the answer?"

She fell back into a deep sleep. In the room people
waited as the minutes dragged slowly by. And then
Gertrude Stein opened her eyes again and her clear
voice commanded, "Never mind that. What is the
question?"

These were her final words. So the story goes.

Getting what you want isn't difficult, as long as you're clear
about what it is you're looking for. You have everything
you need to get whatever you aim for—that's the presupposition. The only catch is knowing what you want to
achieve, and where, when, and with whom. Knowing what
questions to ask helps you define your goal and make it
realistic.

It's the questions that lead to discovery. Answers are like
markers along the way, showing how far you've come, indicating that you're still on the path. But it's the questions
that define the direction you're going. The quest is in the
*quest*ion, as the ancient Greeks knew. In Plato's *Republic*,
the philosophers practiced the Socratic method for discov-

ering truth and knowledge, which, incidentally, were considered to reside within a person, not without.

The Socratic method, the way to get to truth, was by asking questions, in order to draw out the knowledge that the person already possessed but had no access to. (Education means, literally, "to lead out." The verb *ducere* means "to lead" and the prefix *e*-[which is the same as *ex*-] means "out of.") The job of a Socrates, or teacher, was to make a person *aware* of what he already knew. The questions were intended to make the disciple turn inward, to discover himself.

All of us have done this to some extent. We've questioned ourselves, we've relied on inner resources, on our abilities and experience to pull us through, whether or not we were conscious of doing it. After all, we're still here.

That in itself is proof we've survived, we've overcome the obstacles, we've managed to find a way. We did it by muddling through, by instinct, brilliance, by sheer luck—however.

And here we are, having come a long way. But now what you want is something more than survival; you want success. The accomplishment of your goals. And now the questioning begins. What do I want? Where should I look for it? How will I know when I have it?

Unless you ask the questions, you'll never know if you've found the answers.

How can you start a journey if you don't know where you're headed? How can you recognize what you've found if you haven't defined it? How will you know you've arrived unless you have a clear picture of where you meant to go?

Part III is about defining what you're after and then making use of your resources to achieve it. You define your outcome in the same way as you describe something you've lost. If it's a piece of jewelry, or if your pet has disappeared, how could you make sure someone else would recognize it? How would you describe it in the Lost and Found pages of your newspaper or if you were filing a police report?

You'd be very specific:

ANTIQUE GOLD RING, NARROW BAND, WITH FIVE SMALL DIAMONDS SET IN A CIRCLE AROUND A BLOOD-RED RUBY.

Or:

THREE-YEAR-OLD CALICO CAT WITH A BUSHY TAIL, WEARING A LEATHER COLLAR, ANSWERS TO THE NAME OF ALLSPICE, LEFT EAR SLIGHTLY RAGGED. LAST SEEN TUESDAY MORNING NEAR ALBERT'S GROCERY STORE ON WEST BEECH.

You can characterize your lost property or lost cat with such fine exactitude that anyone who came across it would recognize it. You're able to do that because you can see it with precision in your mind's eye—a picture, photograph, maybe an ongoing film—while you describe it.

You need the same clarity in defining your goal or outcome. If you can imagine it, if you can focus it on the inner screen of your thoughts as precisely as a picture of the gold ring or the calico cat, you're already on your way. Once you've formed an achievable outcome in your mind, you're 90 percent of the way there. Even a distant goal becomes reachable if you break it down into well-formed outcomes, clearly marked stretches along the winding road to rainbow's end. Getting down the road isn't the hard part, it's knowing where and when, with whom and how, you want to go.

Let's go back to the first question: What do I want? It's

the essential one. This short string of four monosyllables is at the core of who you are and what you're doing. It's the question that shapes the choices you make, the career you pursue, the mate you select, your decision to have children or not, to travel, to become a collector, to invest your energies into material concerns or spiritual ones, and it's also the question to ask when you're planning a dinner party, drawing up a contract, buying a car, or redecorating a room.

It's the standard question you can ask anyone, any time, about more or less anything. What do I want? focuses the mind toward an outcome, defines the thing or action that you're moving toward.

The shoe salesman asks the question to find out what kind of selection he should bring out from the storeroom.

"I want a pair of shoes to wear to my nephew's wedding," the woman replies.

Now the salesman will ask about the outfit she plans to wear, how formal it is, what color and pattern, of what material. The questions become specific, each one helping to define the outcome, which is the pair of shoes to wear at the wedding. Each question leads to the elimination of a number or even class of possibilities, narrowing the field until it's pretty clear to both salesman and customer what the pair of shoes should look like. At this point he brings out the selection, and the woman will try them on, choosing a pair or not, depending on how well the shoes match her expectations and whether or not they have a comfortable fit.

Seek and ye shall find. Ask and it shall be given. Questions are at the basis of knowledge, of information, and are what give humans in general and each of us specifically the capacity for changing and controlling our own environment.

19

Defining an Outcome

Basically, questions serve one of two purposes: to get a specific piece of information ("Where's Main Street?"; "How many eggs go into the recipe?") or to point the mind toward a goal or outcome ("Where am I going?"; "What do you want to be when you grow up?"). Implicit in the question is a sense of movement, a direction you've taken. The purpose of these questions is to drive you forward.

What comes after the question, What do I want?

If you've answered with *I want to be happy* or *I want to be successful*, this won't help you very much unless you have a specific idea of what you mean by those words. What *is* happiness, by your definition? What is success? How can you pursue a goal or outcome unless you've defined it? If your destination is simply "the city," you'll never get there, not until you describe *which* city, *where*, and then get on the train, plane, or road that leads you there.

If you can dream it, you can do it, but to transform a dream into reality you first have to translate it from an abstraction to specifics.

You need to take its dimensions and measurements. Like building a dream house, first you have to ask yourself where you're going to build it, in what country or part of the country, what particular kind of space, land, environment. Then you design it or have an architect design it for you, asking questions about rooms, bathrooms, kitchen; where the windows and doors go; laying it all out in plans and blueprints. After that, by degrees, will come the hundreds of details and decisions about the specific materials that will be used: floors and cabinets, door handles, latches and paint.

Questions are part of the process of building your house. They are intrinsic to it, part of the interactive loop we talked about in describing communication with others and with self. The questions make it take shape; each answer leads to a new question, which is based on what came before ("What color is the bedroom?" leads to "What color are the cabinets?") and which defines the question that follows ("What kind of handles should we put on the drawers?"). The questions are almost organic, forking and branching like a tree as it grows, reaching into every space in your dream house, until all the pieces are there and the house is ready for you to enter and live in.

Think of the house as your goal, whatever it is. You reach it by increments, or steps: the plans, the decisions, the specifics of construction. These steps are your outcomes, and you move from one to the next as each is accomplished by asking the right questions.

The following plan could be called a blueprint for success. It shows how to reach what we'll call a smart outcome by asking the questions that lead to specific answers, to ever sharper and finer definitions. These questions have a natural progression and must be posed in the order they're listed. Creating your smart outcome follows the same sequence as building your dream house: Until you know where, specifically, the house will be built, and then where each of the rooms will go and what the view(s) from these rooms will be, there's no point asking about the bedroom windows. Step by step: You build a dream the same way you build a house, starting with the foundation.

We'll refer to this blueprint throughout Part III, as we discuss each aspect of creating an achievable outcome.

◆

BLUEPRINT FOR SUCCESS
How to Reach Your Smart Outcome

Definition

1. *What do I want?*
   Answers must be stated in positives.
   Answers must be under your control.

2. *How? What or who? Where? When? With whom? How much? How long?*
   Answers must be specific.

3. *How will I know when I achieve my outcome? What will I be doing, thinking, feeling?*
   Answers must give evidence of success.

Check

4. *How will my outcome affect my entire life? Family and my intimate relationships? Social life? Work? Health? Spiritual concerns? What are the advantages and disadvantages of achieving my outcome?*
   Answers must be ecological for the entire fabric of your life.

Implementation

5. *What resources do I have or could get to that would help me achieve my outcome?*
   Answers must *label* resources that you already have or could get that would be specifically helpful.

6. *Where am I now along the path to achieving my outcome?*

   Answers must define how close or how far you are in relation to success and give the specific next steps you must take to reach it.

Summary

A smart outcome is: stated in positives, under your control, specific

A smart outcome has: evidence of success, ecological consequences, use of resources

◆

20

Goal or Outcome?

An outcome is not a goal, but you can't achieve your goal unless you have well-formed outcomes.

A goal is something you want to get, have, do, achieve, or become in the future.

An outcome is a specific aspect of that goal.

An outcome is achievable because it is under your control. If you want someone to love or admire you, this is not an outcome. It is not under your control.

A goal is often *not* under your control; it's a dream you hold out in the future. So if your goal is to be loved or admired, you might create specific outcomes that can help you achieve it.

A goal can be your secret ambition, your motivation, your passion. It's the fantasy that keeps you going, your own private Cinderella story that you believe in against all odds and despite your better judgment: it brings you pleasure and hope. It makes the workaday world a lot more bearable.

- I want to be a movie star
- I'm going to become boss of the company
- I'll publish a best-seller
- I'm going to be a doctor one day (even though I haven't gone to college)

- I'll compete in the Olympics
- I'll play shortstop for the Yankees

All these are goals. Goals can be vague and generalized or they can be as clear and bright and big in your imagination as seeing your name on a billboard, but they are not under your control, and you cannot make them happen unless you break them down into attainable outcomes.

Let's take the first one: You want to be a movie star. You can imagine it perfectly, in all your sensory modalities. You picture yourself on a big screen, your face in close-up; you hear the clamor of fans and autograph seekers as you step out of your limo on Oscar night, wearing a shimmering dress, your skin caught in the glare and heat of the klieg lights and camera flash.

It's vivid, sensory-specific; it's all there in sight, sound, and feeling. If you can dream it, you can do it. True, but first you have to dream or think it in a way that makes it achievable.

Look at your blueprint for success, Question No. 1: What do I want? The answers must be stated in positives and must be under your control. Your answer is certainly stated in positives—I want to be a movie star—but is it under your control?

Absolutely not.

Let's stop here a moment to make sure that what we're looking at actually *is* an outcome. Is this a dream that's achievable? Or is it a bright bauble held out in the future, the gold at the end of the rainbow, the pumpkin transformed into a glass coach, the ugly duckling become a swan? Is this the fairy tale you use to motivate yourself?

If so, fine. It's valuable; it can serve the purpose of giving you an escape hatch when reality threatens to crowd you in. Impossible dreams are wonderful, and enormous goals can give you a sense of grandeur, or of mission.

Sometimes we need the great far-off dream to give meaning to the routine and monotony of our lives. But don't mistake the goal for the outcome.

To be a movie star—that's the Cinderella part, to turn into something or someone else, a sudden metamorphosis from caterpillar to butterfly. Dreams of glory. Great for the fantasy, but it doesn't really give you much to work on.

Becoming an actor, however, or working in some aspect of the movies might be possible outcomes for you, still held out in the future like a goal but attainable through very specific work and training—and probably by giving up other things you might have done, financial rewards, social pleasures. The dream of becoming a movie star may or may not be realized—it's out of your control—but the outcome of acting, even of acting in movies, *can* be achieved.

Without a dream, you have nothing to work on. Unless you have one, how can you make it come true?

A goal is a dream for the future that doesn't have to be well-defined (according to the requirements for a smart outcome) or under your control. An outcome is something you want to achieve that is specific and within your control.

Forming an outcome is all in the questions. They show you what to focus on; they direct your attention along certain tracks and not others.

Your Goal Is Your Dream. Your Outcome Moves You Toward It.

21

The Well-Formed Outcome

A well-formed outcome is an essential part of success. To create one, you must define what you specifically want and under what conditions you want it. This is also an essential part of your communication with other people.

The employer who hopes to motivate employees must first understand what each of them expects to achieve or accomplish in the organization. Equally important, someone who works in a company or who's applying for a job should be aware of the company's expectations and how well he or she would adapt to them. Where is the organization headed? What are the long-term goals, the short-term objectives?

As an employer myself, I use the blueprint for success in chapter 19 to help me assess what a person expects from the job that's being offered. I also use it to help my employees direct their attention and energies in the direction of a smart outcome.

Teachers and students, lawyers and clients, lovers, clergymen, contractors—everyone who is in a relationship, whether professional or personal, needs to know what the other person wants and expects from it.

In sales, "What do you want for this?" (implied: *How much do you expect to get?*) is the first question asked by any buyer; "What do you offer?" (*How much are you will-*

ing or expecting to pay?) is what the seller needs to know. The success of the deal depends on an agreement about outcome. Even the bargaining itself is dependent on each side's having a reasonable idea about how far to go in raising or lowering the price without risking the possibility of spoiling the sale. A real estate agent has to evaluate both sides of the equation—What can the seller reasonably expect to get? What can the buyer reasonably afford to pay?—before beginning to broker a deal.

What do you want out of this relationship? is the implied question in every dating situation, in every listing in the personals column, in every X-meets-Y. Is my outcome the same as yours? If one of us wants a fling and the other wants a family, the result will be frustrating at best, possibly disastrous.

What do you want for the future? If I'm looking for love and you want diversion, we'd better get our cards on the table right from the beginning to avoid pain later on.

And when we're ready to marry or commit ourselves to a long-term relationship, it's very important to make clear (to oneself as well as to the other) what we want in terms of where to live, having children, dealing with money and with each other's families, pets, hobbies, habits—whatever is relevant to the particular situation. If my outcome isn't the same as yours, is there a way we can negotiate? Can we adjust or adapt our outcomes? How much is under my control? How much under yours?

Well-formed outcomes belong to every aspect of human endeavor—business and love, politics and education, in the physical sphere as well as the spiritual—and are as important in communicating with others as with oneself.

22

The Outcome Stated in Positives

In answer to the question What do you want?—the first rule on the blueprint for success is that the desired outcome must be stated in positives. This may seem self-evident. Since an outcome is something you want to achieve, have, or accomplish, you must state it in terms of what you actually *want*, not what you *don't* want: "I want to go home for the holidays"; "I want to learn to speak Japanese."

Examples of *not* stating in positives would be: "I don't want to be alone," or "I don't want to miss out on signing the contract."

Think about it. How could you go about trying to achieve something you *don't* want? But many people have a habit of thinking or speaking in negatives. Whether this is something they learned as children (some families stress negative over positive, giving their children more "Don'ts" than "Dos") or it's a way of reducing the risk of failure, these people focus on what they want to avoid.

There's nothing wrong with this. All of us move between attraction and avoidance, pleasure–pain, the tendency to go *toward* what we want or what gives us pleasure and *away from* what we don't want or what causes pain.

This is called *directionality*, and it derives from the instinctual behavior of the newborn, who moves toward warmth and shrinks back from cold. Later it translates into a cognitive pattern. Some people habitually move toward what they seek; others move away from what they hope to avoid. Neither pattern is better or worse, and most of us, even those who are definitely positive, will at some point or other assert what we *don't* want in order to eliminate some unproductive choices.

But this won't put you on the path to where you're going. If your outcome is that you don't want to go to Cleveland or you don't want to travel alone, that's not of much help when you plan your next vacation. In terms of formulating an outcome, you need to go *toward*. If you can't think it, you won't be able to get it. How could you begin to imagine something that *isn't*? And how can you achieve it? How do you not bake a cake?

Some years ago, when I was giving a training workshop in Belgium, I was told about an experiment being conducted by a driving school there. One group of student drivers was shown a large hole in the middle of the road. The drivers were told to focus on it and to concentrate on *not* driving into the hole. Most drivers headed straight for the hole and drove right into it.

In another group, the student drivers were told to focus on the pavement beyond the hole and to concentrate on driving *toward the pavement*. Guess what happened? You're right, of course. Most of the second group of drivers got safely around the hole.

Don't think of elephants. Especially, don't think of a pink elephant with large ears!

Don't think of chocolate cake, and above all don't think of having a slice of it!

Not doing something you've been told not to do requires superhuman effort. It's virtually impossible. I've tried this in workshops, asking people to think of a cat *not* chasing a mouse. They can't do it. Some of them might think of a cat sleeping—but that's not what I asked them to do.

Think of:

A CAT
NOT
CHASING A MOUSE

The only way you'll be able to do this is by thinking of the cat *chasing* the mouse and then putting a slash through the image you have.

It's like the sign that tells you where not to park by showing a picture of a parked car with a thick line running through it. Or NO SMOKING signs, or NO MORE NUKES: They all show a canceled image—as if something that's still on the retina of your eye gets turned off.

Our minds can't represent negatives. Whatever I tell you *not* to think of, you first have to think of and then erase or paint over.

A successful outcome depends on having a positive input. Thinking about what we want directs our minds toward the outcome. We picture it (visual), tell ourselves we can do it (auditory), feel what it's like to have already accomplished it (kinesthetic). Only then are we motivated. *If you can't think it (imagine it), you won't achieve it.*

However, sometimes we have to go through the negative to get to the positive. Young people, adolescents in particular, can become overwhelmed by the unfolding choices in their lives and will insist on the negative as a way of eliminating the abundance of possibilities: "I don't want this; I don't want that either." And all of us, at any age, sometimes focus on what we don't want, don't like, what we want to be rid of. (In politics, as elsewhere, being opposed to something you think is wrong can be as important as standing up for something you believe is right.)

That's OK as a starting point, just as long as you're

aware that you *are* being negative. (Or, if you're helping someone else define an outcome, keep in mind that you're hearing what the person *doesn't* want.) Then your next step is finding out what you or they *do* want instead. You might start by asking questions that are *away from* (referring to what's *not* wanted) and then go *toward*.

When you're doing Smart Outcomes with someone else, you start by backtracking them to make sure you've understood what they intended to communicate. You try to get a clear understanding of what *isn't* wanted in order to redirect the focus toward what *is*. Then you begin asking what they *do* want, pacing and leading them toward a positive outcome.

Here's a dialogue I had recently with Laura (not her real name), a biology teacher in her early fifties who lives by herself in Manhattan and runs into the same problem every year.

Laura: I have spring break coming up, and I don't know what I'm going to do with it. I don't want to be in my apartment again; I never end up doing anything. I don't want to stay in the city; it's cold, it's miserable. I don't want to spend a lot of money. I don't want to go somewhere alone.

Anné: OK, so you don't want to spend your vacation in the city in your apartment, you don't want to be cold, you don't want to spend too much money, and you don't want to go somewhere alone.

Laura: No.

Anné: All of these are what you don't want.

Laura: It's like this every year. It's why I end up at home.

At this point we've pretty well established what Laura *doesn't* want. Now I try to direct her toward finding an outcome she *does* want, something she can state in positives.

Anné: This time, what would you want instead? Instead of being cold, being in your apartment, being alone, spending a lot of money, what would you rather do?

Laura: Well . . . (laughing self-consciously) *I guess I'd like just the opposite. I'd love to be in a nice, warm place with people around that I know—or maybe I could meet them—you know, people I have some connection to, maybe people like me, who are interested in biology? Or frogs, in particular. I love frogs, you know.*

Now we've arrived at Laura's first attempt to frame a positive outcome. It's still vague, and eventually it will have to be something that's under her control, but at this point we're just trying to focus it clearly. To make sure I understand, I backtrack her answer:

Anné: So you want to be in a nice place that's warm, warmer than the city. Where there are people around who share some of the same interests that you have. Teachers of biology, people interested in frogs.

Laura: Now that you say that, it occurs to me—if I'm not stuck in the city, I don't mind being alone. In the woods, with animals, I wouldn't mind being alone. It's in the city that it bothers me.

Anné: *You might consider going somewhere not too far away that you don't have to fly to. Maybe you could drive there or take a bus: some place that's warmer than New York. Maybe you can find a place that's having some kind of conference to do with biology or—why not?—maybe even frogs. Sometimes the zoological societies advertise meetings or expeditions you could join. Or, as you just said, maybe if you're not in the city you wouldn't mind so much being alone. Does this give you any thoughts about what you'd like to do with your vacation?*

Laura: *Yes.* (Brightening) *I think I'd like to . . . Yes. I've been thinking about frogs. I'd like to observe them. Maybe in the Everglades? . . .*

Anné: *I'm sure they have some programs there, lectures or movies in the evening. It could give you a structure.*

Laura: (continues musing, following her own train of thought) *It wouldn't be so bad being alone in the Everglades, would it? Because there'd be people around everywhere, park rangers.*

What's happened is that Laura has moved from thinking about what she doesn't want to what she does like. This is a shift in directionality. She's no longer thinking of the negative aspect, what she wants to avoid or get rid of; she's now thinking of what she wants to achieve for herself. She's thinking about reaching her outcome, not about the obstacles or problems in her way.

The kind of questions you ask yourself (or another person) produce a specific mind-set, or directionality of thinking, that's either problem-oriented or outcome-oriented. This doesn't mean that this type of questioning generates success; it simply establishes the direction in which your (or the other person's) thoughts are headed; it puts you on a certain track, with success as your destination.

Here is a list of some common words that indicate directionality. Use them in pacing and leading another person, or to recognize your own directionality of thinking and help you switch your thoughts in the direction of outcome and success.

TOWARD	AWAY FROM
Want	Avoid
Get	Get rid of
Achieve	Can't
Go for	Don't
Include	Shouldn't
Accomplish	Won't

Instead of moving away from what she doesn't want, Laura is now going toward what she does want. This is the first step toward defining her smart outcome.

◆

SMART OUTCOME EXERCISES
A. Stated in Positives

1. Think of something you don't want, something about yourself you don't like, or a situation you want to avoid.

2. Try to imagine it by giving yourself all the reasons you can think of for why you don't want or like it. Use these questions to guide you.

   - What's wrong?
   - What's my problem?
   - Why do I have this problem?
   - How is it limiting to me?
   - Who or what is to blame?

Write down your answers. How do they make you feel?

3. Think about this problem or situation in the future. What do you see? Feel?

4. Change your posture. Walk around, take a deep breath. Ask yourself, "If I don't want [the problem or situation], what do I want instead?" Use these questions to guide you.

   - How do I want to be different?
   - What could I do or feel instead?
   - What are some other possibilities?

Write down your answers.

5. Tell yourself what you *do* want. Make pictures in your mind. How do you feel about this? Picture this outcome in the future. What does it sound like? Feel like?

❖

23

The Outcome Under Your Control

The second rule on the blueprint for success in achieving a smart outcome states that the desired outcome must be under your control. We talked about this rule when we were defining the difference between outcome and goal. Attaining peace on earth is not under your control. Attaining peace in your household or relationship *may* be, just so long as it doesn't depend on what someone else does or on getting someone else to change. You control your relationship to the degree that you take responsibility for it. The only person you can change is yourself.

If you want somebody to become interested in you, or you want your children to call you on a certain day every week, or you want your boss to be impressed by your work and give you a promotion, you might as well stroke your rabbit's foot. Because the only person who can get you what you want is you. You can't change somebody else.

That doesn't mean you give up on the somebody you're interested in. It just means that you take responsibility for what you want to happen. You go after it. You transform your goal into a workable outcome.

Let's say there's someone you want to get involved with. Fine. Let that be your goal. Now ask yourself about the outcome: What can I do, *that is under my control,* that will bring me closer to my goal of being with this person?

There will be a lot of concrete answers. Going to the places where he or she is likely to go; taking up an interest in whatever your special him or her is interested in. Asking this person out—to join you or be your guest at an event you're sure he or she would especially like (movies, bird walks, dancing, concerts). Up to a point you have control over the outcome. But nothing you do is going to make the other person fall in love with you. Leave that to chemistry and concentrate on getting right as many elements as you possibly can.

That means you'll have an outcome of spending an evening with this person, having lunch with him or her, taking a walk. That's as far as you can go in making your outcome specific and under your control. You cannot include in your outcome statement: "I want so-and-so to like me, care about me, pay attention to me." Your outcome is only about *you* and what *you* can do, with the resources you have, to achieve or accomplish whatever it is you want.

That means, instead of saying "I want my husband to act differently," you switch the focus and think about what that would do for *you*. If your husband did change in the way you want him to, what then? How would it make you feel?

Let's say he's always late when you're going out together. You want him to be different, to be on time, so that you don't have to squeeze into the last row of the movie theater, or run for the train, or apologize to your host or hostess yet again, and so on.

Now imagine that you wave your invisible wand and he starts being on time. How is this affecting you? How does this change the way you feel about your evening out together? What are you thinking, feeling, doing?

Chances are you're probably more relaxed, smiling more, and your voice is softer. What the change in his behavior has done for you is to change your mood, your attitude.

You're feeling the way you want to be feeling. So now you revise your desired outcome. Instead of: "I want him to change his behavior (and be on time)" your outcome has become: "I want to feel relaxed and calm when I go out with my husband in the evening."

Now you think of ways you can achieve this, ways to bring about your own sense of tranquillity: by taking a long bath, listening to music, drinking a glass of wine, using a self-anchor for the resource of calm.

"I want to impress my boss with this work," says the man I'll call Doug, who works for a real estate firm that rents studios and offices in foreign countries to traveling professionals, "Because I want her to give me more responsibility."

"So you want your boss to give you more responsibility. Great," I tell him. "What would that do for you?"

> *Doug: I wouldn't be so bored. That's what it would mean. I wouldn't be so bored with my work.*

> *Anné: OK. If you had more responsibility, you wouldn't be so bored with your work. What would you be feeling instead?*

> *Doug: I guess . . . that time would go faster. I'd have more to do; I'd be thinking about things, getting ideas.*

> *Anné: You want more to do, so you'd have more ideas. And what would that do for you?*

> *Doug: I think I'd be feeling a whole lot better about myself.*

The first step toward change is creating an achievable outcome, under your control. "I want my boss to give me more responsibility" is obviously not under Doug's control.

When I asked what having more responsibility would do for him, he said he wouldn't be so bored. That's in the negative (how can you do "not bored"?), so we had to turn it around to positive.

Doug wants to feel better about himself, which means being more creative ("getting ideas") and having more responsibility. How he will actually set about doing this is still down the road; what he's doing here is laying down the plans.

Remember, outcomes give you a structure, just as a blueprint does. Before you start building, you have to have your outcome clearly in mind and under your control. That means you are responsible for it. You can't have control without responsibility.

People have said to me, "I'll do something about my life when the fighting stops in [wherever]" or "when my lawsuit is resolved," "when my daughter marries," "after my teeth are fixed," "when I sell my house. . . ."

There's always time *not* to achieve. Blame it on the world, on the weather, on other people. "If my boss appreciated me." "If my husband were kinder/made more money/stayed home more often." "When my kids graduate." "When my parents move." All these are ways of telling yourself you're not responsible. You're telling yourself that your failure to achieve your goal has nothing to do with you. It's someone else's fault. Or it's the fault of outside forces over which you have no control: the snowstorm, politics, the economic situation.

"Who, me?" is what you're saying. "It really isn't up to me at all." Your excuses pile up. Other people are "lucky"; other people get the "breaks." Other people "have it better" than you.

Those "other people" have created achievable outcomes, under their control. They take responsibility for what they do and what happens to them.

Once you take responsibility for the outcome you're constructing, it's yours. And that means, even if for some reason your outcome can't be achieved immediately, you can try again. You've got the blueprint.

◆

SMART OUTCOME EXERCISES
B. Under Your Control

1. Think of a person you have frequent interactions with and whom you'd like to change in some particular way.

2. Make it specific: "I want so-and-so to do/feel/be _____" [put in the change].

3. Imagine the person has actually changed in this particular way. How does that make you feel? What does it do for you? What positive impact does this change in the other person have on you?

4. Ask yourself what you could do to make yourself feel better in this same way.

5. Restate your outcome, with "I" as the one who changes. (I want to do/feel/be _____"). Write it down. Think about it. How does it make you feel?

◆

24

The Specific Outcome

> I know where I'm going,
> And I know who's going with me . . .
> —Old Irish ballad

Now that you've stated what you want in positives and it's under your control, you have the basic foundation of your outcome. The next rule deals with the specifics.

Actually, we've been talking specifics all along. It's impossible to imagine your outcome otherwise. Try building a dream house without specifics—it vanishes in thin air.

You need to nail down the house or the dream with concrete details. Where is this taking place? What is the size, what are the dimensions? When will you have it? With whom? The life of the imagination is very exact—it deals in pictures, sounds, words, touch, temperature, taste, smells—and each of the representational systems of the imagination (of our thoughts) reaches into a multitude of submodalities. We think in very specific particles or bits of information, represented through our senses. There's no way we can think of something we want, now or in the future, without making it specific, filtering it through a modality and modifying it through submodalities.

That doesn't mean we're conscious of doing this. The process of thinking, of representing ideas to ourselves, is largely automatic. In shaping an outcome, we access the information we need from our unconscious and bring it into the conscious mind. Only then can we control it, fine-tune it, and adapt it to our life and lifestyles.

Making the outcome specific is bringing it into being. Asking yourself "What, where, when, and how *specifically* do I want it" clarifies your objectives.

To say "I want to be happy/rich/successful" gives you no direction, no definition. But when you start asking "With whom do I want to be happy? How, specifically, do I want to become rich? When, specifically, do I want to achieve this success?" you can begin making headway.

Generalities get you nowhere (which is where this generality gets you). Certainly, they bring you nowhere closer to your outcome. When you get down to the specific wording of your outcome, the first thing to check for are words that have no precise meaning, words like *satisfaction, fulfillment, happiness*. These are generalities.

I call these words *fat*. They're excess—not helpful, not well-defined, and certainly not part of a well-formed outcome. Shake them out.

Remember the Rolling Stones' song, "I Can't Get No Satisfaction"? No wonder. Big fat word *satisfaction* is way out of control. What does it look like? How does it feel? How would you know if *satisfaction* came along? By what would you recognize it? ARE WE HAVING FUN YET? blare the bumper stickers. Who knows? What do we mean by "fun"?

Getting to the specifics and testing for the fat words or generalities are part of the same process. It relies on asking questions that help you define the measurements, dimensions, and proportions of what you want and then gives the test for whether or not you've achieved it.

Come meet Sherri (not her real name). She's a high-fashion model, very successful by most standards. She gets a lot of work, makes extremely good money, and has as many friends and dates as her schedule will permit. Yet she came to see me a few months ago, saying, "I'm not really getting enough satisfaction out of my work."

Now the first thing I need to know is what she specifically means by "satisfaction." Without that information I can't help her to form an achievable outcome.

> *Anné: What do you want out of your job that you're not getting?*

> *Sherri: Well, I like modeling; I like the money, the travel, the clothes. But, well, sometimes I don't really feel it's me, you see what I'm saying? There I am, in somebody else's concept of who I'm supposed to be, showing off somebody else's clothes. I guess what I want is more say about what goes on, I want it to have more to do with* me.

> *Anné: What would that do for you?*

> *Sherri: I feel everyone's looking at me as though I was a dodo. I'd like more satisfaction.*

> *Anné: OK, you want more satisfaction. How do you do that? What do you do to be satisfied? Where, specifically, can you think of doing it? When could you be satisfied?*

> *Sherri: That's really interesting. I never thought of it that way, so specifically like that, but when you ask me these questions, I realize that I want to see things through my own eyes instead of through the eyes of other people. It's as though I were seeing things directly, without the veil, without those others. I want to see things on my own. I want to be in control of my being, my life.*

Anné: OK, is that what satisfaction means to you? You want to see things directly, on your own?

Sherri: Yes. That's it. Seeing on my own, creating the pictures myself—that's what would bring me more satisfaction.

Anné: You said you want more satisfaction from your work. If I understand you, what that means to you is having more control, so you are seeing things through your eyes. Instead of being the object in the picture, you want to create the picture. So your outcome is to create: for you yourself to create the picture.

Sherri: That's it.

This is what satisfaction means to Sherri. And we got to it by being more and more specific. I asked Sherri to be sensory-specific, and with each image (Sherri is primarily visual), she had a clearer insight (literally, in-sight, a picture within) about what would give her satisfaction as she focused in on her specific outcome.

◆

SMART OUTCOME EXERCISES
C. Getting to Specifics

1. Write down an outcome (something you want) from Smart Outcome Exercises A and B in chapters 22 and 23.

2. Look at this statement and see if there are any fat words—words that don't produce specific images for

you. Ask yourself about the fat words in your outcome statement:

- "How specifically do I experience _____ [your word]?"
- "What specifically do I see, hear, and feel/sense in my body when I experience _____ [your word]?"
- "Who or what specifically do I mean?"

Write down your answers and then restate your outcome with greater specificity.

3. Ask yourself about your outcome. "With whom/when/where/for how long do I want _____?" [Which specific question you ask will depend on the type of outcome you are describing.] Write down your answer and restate your outcome with this information.

4. Compare your first outcome statement (step 1) with your last statement (step 3). Which one increases your feelings of being able to get what you want?

◆

25

Evidence of the Outcome's Success

The next rule involves evidence of success, so you will know when you're achieving your outcome. Sherri was able to formulate her outcome by being sensory-specific. She defined what she meant by satisfaction—"having more control," "creating the picture," "seeing things through my own eyes"—and in doing this she was able to specifically describe her outcome.

I then asked her for evidence: "How would you know if you *were* more satisfied in your work? What would you be doing? What would you be seeing? What would you be hearing?"

Evidence is a word we use in NLP to test the validity of an outcome, to make sure it's achievable. But testing the evidence is something most of us do all the time naturally, as a matter of course. We test-drive cars before buying; we try on clothes, sample the wine; we test ourselves all the time in all kinds of ways, and whenever we're in danger of falling in love, we ask, "Could this be it?" or "How do I love thee? Let me count the ways."

How do you know you're in love—or having fun yet, or satisfied?

Specificity and evidence are two sides of the same process, both referring to the same kind of information. When we're going for the *specifics* ("How/what/who, *specifi-*

cally?''), we're trying to get a clear picture of what the outcome is. When we go for *evidence* (''How will I know''—*specifically* is implied—''when I've achieved it?''), we're testing that outcome to see how we can ascertain or convince ourselves that we're successful.

Basically, we're asking, ''What do I want and how will I know when I'm getting it?'' We measure the answer in terms of the second question: ''What will I be seeing, hearing, feeling?''

I asked Sherri that question.

Sherri: I don't know about hearing or saying, but I know I'll be feeling as though this were mine. This life, I mean. I'll be seeing the pictures, pictures with me in them, or just the landscape, the animals. I'll be feeling free, like starting out new. See what I'm saying? I'll be feeling really, really good.

Anné: Where would you be doing that? Can you picture it?

Sherri: I would be walking on the . . . [She pauses, as if lost in thought.] *The landscape I'm thinking of is in the desert, where we just did a shoot and I was sort of placed into it. I had on this satiny thing, ''deep sunset,'' they called it, a really dark coral, a fiery color, like a flare going up from the sands.*

What I'm feeling now is, I'm sort of positioning myself. Me, I'm putting myself where I'm supposed to go. I'm the one doing it. Paying attention to what my own body is telling me instead of whatever they're shouting about, about where to put my legs, arms, whatever.

Anné: And what could you be doing? Just imagine— if you were in the midst of this work, out in the desert, having a full, satisfying experience—what could you be doing?

Sherri: *This is interesting. You know what? I see the sand, and there's a bright blue sky, and I'd like to be the one who's looking at it and framing it in the way I want. I would love to be out there taking pictures of this incredible landscape. That's what—that's what I really love about this job. I love seeing these incredible places.*

Anné: *You want to stay in the same industry. But what I'm hearing you say is, in order to have more satisfaction, instead of being the object of the picture you want to be in control of the picture. You want to be—*

Sherri: *Exactly.*

Anné: *—taking the picture, setting up the scene, instead of being set.*

Sherri: *This is incredible.*

Anné: *So instead of somebody else telling you how to move, you would be creating the movement in the scene.*

Sherri: *It would be through my eyes.*

Anné: *It would be through your eyes, you would be framing the picture yourself, and you'd probably be saying things, telling other people how to stand, what the picture includes.*

Sherri: *Yes, I would be* taking *and* creating *the pictures! That would be great, Anné. That would just change my whole life.*

This is what we call the evidence procedure: what's the sensory evidence that you're achieving your outcome?

◆

SMART OUTCOME EXERCISES
D. Evidence of Success

1. Continue to use the same desired outcome as in exercise C.

2. Ask yourself: "How will I know when I am getting what I want? What will I be doing, feeling, thinking? Write down your answer. Add this to your outcome.

3. Look at your smart outcome. It's stated in positives, under your control, specific.

   See this outcome. Hear it. Feel it.

   Now add the evidence information. See it, hear it, feel it.

   How does this increase your pleasure or sense of accomplishment?

◆

26

The Ecological Outcome

How will your outcome affect your entire life? The rule here is that the outcome must be ecological within the fabric of that life.

By *ecological* I mean our personal ecology, the interrelating systems that we are composed of. Any change we make in our lives, even something very simple—a short trip, a new car—will have an impact on the systems we are and the systems we're part of.

There's been a lot written and said about such changes, as part of the current interest in chaos theory, in meteorology, and in many developing branches of the physical and social sciences.

What I want to concentrate on here are the changes you can foresee or predict in your own life as a result of achieving your outcome.

I picture this (the outcome) as a pebble dropped into a lake (your life), causing ripples to spread in concentric circles out from the center from the point of impact—which is the point or moment of change.

The pebble is the core of the change, the new outcome. Each spreading circle represents another layer or dimension of self, alone and in relationships: from the physical self out to the mental, emotional, and spiritual selves, out to relationships: the most intimate first (family, lovers, closest

160

friends); then colleagues and relationships at work; social relationships; on to community, country, global involvements; and for some people even farther into cosmic alliances. Each of us is different, and for each of us the layers may have slightly different names. It doesn't matter; we are all layered, like the Russian dolls you open up to find another doll within, and another, and another.

In estimating the future impact of your outcome, you have to consider, in addition to the advantages you expect, the possible disadvantages that even the most desired and well-formed outcome may bring. Achieving everything you hoped for professionally may have consequences you didn't intend, in your love life, in your family life, perhaps in your physical life as well, if it means less time for the gym or giving up those skiing trips you love.

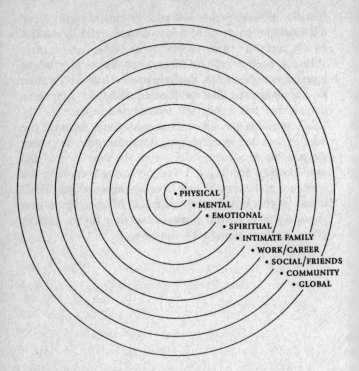

The widening circle of questions.

Marianne, the mother of five, who had been trained as a speech clinician, returned to the workforce after the last of her children was grown and discovered that her marriage was undergoing new and unexpected stress as a result. Also, she found that the financial advantages turned out to be much less than she'd counted on, since she now had to hire other people to care for her aging parents and take over chores around the house while she was at work.

She resigned from the job and tried to pick up where she'd left off at home. But the ''damage,'' if that's what it was, had already been done. She was thinking of herself as a person entitled to her own life, not always in the service of other people's needs or desires.

It took another year for Marianne to discover a way of juggling her obligations at home (which she didn't want to give up) with her outside interests. Eventually she found a compromise that suited her, entailing fewer hours away, and doing some of the work at home, but much of the disappointment and struggles of that year could have been avoided if she'd worked out the ecology of her decision ahead of time.

To check out ecology, let's go back to Sherri for a moment. Sherri has already formed her outcome: to remain within the industry she knows but to switch from working in front of the camera to working behind it—not the model but the photographer.

The ecology check rounds out a smart outcome. Let's look at the implications and consequences of this outcome on the rest of her life.

Anné: I want you to imagine that it's two years from now. You've achieved your outcome. You're now the photographer. You're the one to look through the camera and see the world through your eyes. You're in charge; you're doing it. You're creating the images. Look at your life now. How has it changed?

Sherri: Actually, I'm much less sure of things. I'm in charge, and that means it won't be so easy to get work.

Anné: Not won't. Pretend this is happening now.

Sherri: OK, isn't. It isn't as easy to get work. Some days I get up and know I have to hustle.

Anné: So you have less financial security?

Sherri: Yes. I didn't realize . . . it's a lot harder.

Anné: What else? Is this impacting your relationships with men?

Sherri: Yeah, well . . . (She laughs, shrugs.) *Competition. Guys don't go for that so much. The old ego stuff. They like me where they can keep an eye on me. So it's not the same, not as easy.*

Anné: What are the advantages of your new life?

Sherri: I'm on my own!

Anné: You like that.

Sherri: Love it!

Anné: What's the impact on your physical well-being?

Sherri: Gained a little weight, six or seven pounds. I don't have to worry about it.

Anné: Does that mean you're enjoying your food more?

Sherri: I never cared about food that much, but I can have a drink now and then—no problem.

Anné: Anything else?

Sherri: Yes. I feel freer in my body, bigger—as though I've grown, literally. I'm planning the shots.

Anné: Now that you've achieved your outcome, do you think it's worth it? Even though you have less financial security, you have to hustle more for work, and, being independent, you scare off a lot of guys? Have you lost any friends? Made any?

Sherri: Not really. I don't think I got particularly close to anyone through my work.

Anné: So, on balance, was it worth it?

Sherri: The one thing that really bothers me is my brother. I take care of him, you see; he relies on me.

Anné: So the biggest disadvantage has been the financial insecurity?

Sherri: Yes, but you know, if I make it I'll earn more than I did modeling, because I can go on for years.

For Sherri, the ecology is clear-cut and the disadvantages easy to see. The knowledge she has gained—that financial security is *not* going to be there for her the way it is now—could be very important, not as a reason for her to give up her outcome but as an essential piece of information she can use to reduce future risks.

Sherri recognizes the major disadvantages of leaving a high-salaried job and striking out on her own. Yet she feels it's worth doing. To paraphrase the old ad: "If I have only one life to lead, let me lead it as a photographer"; that's what Sherri has decided. Sure, there are risks. There are risks in everything, even crossing the street. Risk is part of growth, and growth is life.

Once you frame your outcome, you run it through the

ecology check, the widening circle of questions. This is a reality check as well. Here you come up against the risks and disadvantages of your outcome as well as the pleasures and satisfactions.

◆

SMART OUTCOME EXERCISES
E. Personal Ecology

1. Think of something really outrageous that you might have fantasized about having or achieving.

2. Pretend you have it. Now consider what effect this "success" has on your family life, work, health, friends, sense of self-esteem. Do you think your "success" is worth it?

3. Go back to your outcome exercise. Ask yourself, "How would getting this outcome affect my life? My family? My friends? My work? My health? My evolution?" Write down the answers.

4. Make a list of the advantages of getting this outcome. Make a list of the possible disadvantages of getting this outcome. (If this question draws a blank, ask yourself, "What are the advantages of *not* getting this outcome?")

5. Look at your answers to steps 3 and 4. Consider the impact of your success. Ask yourself if the outcome is worth it. If it is, consider any negative effects of

success and make allowances for them or modify your outcome so that you minimize these effects. If your outcome is not worth the negative effects on your life, go on to another outcome.

◆

27

The As If Frame

When I was doing the ecology check with Sherri, I asked her to pretend that she'd already accomplished her outcome. We call this the As If frame in NLP, and it's exactly what it sounds like: everybody's oldest game of make-believe. It allows you to do a reality check on your outcome by projecting it into the future and seeing what effect it has.

The As If frame is simply pretending you already have the outcome or change you want. This enables you to gather information that might ordinarily be unavailable to your conscious mind, since the As If frame suspends judgment and capitalizes on our ability to make believe. This is not an idle exercise in directionless daydreaming. Once you have a well-formed outcome and use this technique, you will be surprised at how many ideas you get, how much new information, pleasure, and excitement about your future possibilities. It is extremely helpful in checking out whether the consequences of success are personally ecological for you.

As If lets us make a kind of reality check on our outcome by projecting it into the future, living it, and taking careful notes about what happens.

As If means moving into fantasy in order to gather practical information that helps reduce the element of risk in our undertaking. Through fantasy to reality. We make believe in order to make what we believe in have the strongest possible chance of coming true.

Here is As If, a guided fantasy tour.

Find a comfortable chair where you can be quiet and undisturbed for ten minutes. Sit down. Place your feet on the floor, your arms on the arms of the chair. Relax. Close your eyes if you feel like it. Follow your breath—in and out, in and out. Allow yourself to notice how your back feels against the chair; feel the temperature of the air on your face, feel the weight of your hands. As you breathe, let the air you take in go to any area of tension you might have in your body—neck, shoulders, back, stomach.

As you relax, bring to your mind your outcome—whatever it is you want to have or achieve. Got that? Good.

Now you are walking down the street. Up ahead you see someone who looks familiar. The closer you come, the more familiar the figure seems to be . . . and then you realize this is your future self.

It is six months into the future and you have achieved your outcome. You have succeeded in getting what you wanted.

You are going to daydream now. Please notice everything you see and feel and hear in this future world. Look at and listen to your successful future self. Notice the weather—it's different from six months ago when you were reading this book and developing your smart outcome, creating your blueprint for success. Remember? Of course you do—and now you have achieved what it was you wanted then.

Watch and listen to yourself go through a typical day in your (new and future) life. See what kind of room or space you're in, what clothes you're wearing, how the furniture is arranged, the walls and windows. Are the windows open or closed?

Now step inside yourself, become the future You. Notice how you're feeling, how you see other people, hear them. What is your life like now that you've achieved your outcome?

Look at the colors and shapes around you, the rooms of your home. Listen to the sounds, feel the temperature, the breezes or stillness. Smell the cooking if you like. Pay attention to your interactions with your family. Are they different now? How are the members of your family responding to you? How are you responding?

Now go to your place of work, see and hear your colleagues. Pay attention to how you are feeling and thinking about them, about yourself, about your job. What specific task or project are you working on today? How is it going?

Now move on to other interactions, your friends, your social life. What are your friends doing, saying? See them, hear them. How are they responding to you? How are you responding to them? How does this make you feel?

Move on to your health. Take note of your body, how you're feeling physically, your energy level. Are you tired? Alert? How do you look? How do you feel emotionally? Pay attention to the inner you, the spiritual self. Notice how you feel and think, how you relate to yourself. Allow yourself the time to daydream about all aspects of your life now that you have accomplished what you wanted. . . .

Now start to come back to the present, to the here and now, sitting in your comfortable chair, creating your outcome. Come back through time. Take a moment to relish your experience and reflect on what you've learned. Has this experience given you new information? Using this information, you can now further adjust or refine your outcome.

As If Exercise

1. Simply enact As If right now—as if you had already made a change. How would you be feeling, thinking, acting?

2. Go into the future—pretend you have achieved your outcome. Project yourself into a specific time: next week, next month, a year from now.

   Once in the future, be sure to use verbs in the present tense: I am; How is this change affecting me? How are others in my life responding to me? Use descriptions of weather and holidays to enhance the reality of your experience.

3. Helpful lead-in phrases:

   · Act as if . . .
   · Let's suppose that . . .
   · Pretend/make believe that . . .
   · If I/you were to . . .

   You can do this by yourself and with others.

28

Implementing the Plan:
Resources

Each outcome demands specific resources. Which of your resources would be most helpful in achieving your outcome? Sherri can call up several essential ones: creativity, perseverance, physical stamina (she evidenced all these in her work in the fashion industry over a number of years), a deep knowledge of the field she's working in, a network of connections, and the solid support of her family. On balance, even if the possible disadvantages are considerable, she can well afford to take the chance of starting out on a new career.

For each desired outcome we look into the future, not with a crystal ball but by realistic prediction based on everything we know about ourselves and surroundings, and make an estimate of how the change will affect us. It's like creating a profile: assets and liabilities, now and possibly in the future. What resources do we already have that we can count on? Which do we need to develop? How can we use these resources in achieving our outcome and in protecting us against possible disadvantages or risks?

We each have the "hidden treasures" of chapter 12, resources that are specifically ours: the talents, abilities, strengths, and knowledge that we can count on in the future. Each of us has the resources we need for a particular outcome. To help you discover which of your resources to call up for a specific outcome, try the exercise that follows.

◆

SMART OUTCOME EXERCISE
F. Resources

1. Look at the smart outcome you've been developing through the exercises. Read over what you've written down.

2. Consider it as if this were someone else's outcome. What resources would you say were needed to successfully accomplish the outcome? Write these down.

3. Pretend to be someone else, someone who knows and likes you. From the point of view of this person, write down some of *your* most important resources. (Write down your own name and under it, a list of your resources as someone else might see them.)

4. Come back to being yourself. Look at your outcome. What resources do you think you need to accomplish this outcome?

5. Look over your answers to steps 2, 3, and 4. Which resources do you already have? Write them down. Which of the resources don't you have—yet? Write

these down. What resources do you now have that can help you learn, develop, create the other resources you need to get your outcome? Write down the answers.

◆

29

Implementing the Plan:
Strategy

The blueprint for success is divided into three sections: the *definition* of the outcome (questions 1–3), the *check* (question 4), and finally *implementation* (questions 5 and 6).

This last question—How far are you along the path to achieving your outcome?—completes the plan. You might be surprised to discover that you're closer to achieving your outcome than you'd imagined. But in any case, whether it's only a few more yards or still a longer stretch to the fulfillment of what you set out to accomplish, your blueprint is finished. It needs nothing more but implementation.

Implementation shows how to actually make it happen, how to get your dream off the ground (or put your dream house in place). You have the plan and the materials (resources), you've checked everything out, you have the permits and license, and all you still need is a time frame to let you know how far you've come, how much farther there is to go.

Using the blueprint for success, the very last thing to check for is where you are in terms of the overall outcome. Are we having fun yet? If not, when? Have you already attained the success you were after? Or is it still far beyond you, like a mirage that vanishes whenever you approach?

How can you tell?

Make a movie of your outcome. It's your story; you've created it, put it together. You know all the elements in it: the characters, location, setting, maybe even the script. It's time to watch it now, from beginning to end.

As you watch and listen to this movie, try freezing the frame that represents your outcome. See yourself in it. (If you have trouble visualizing this, ask yourself "If I could see myself achieving this outcome, what would I/the image look like?" and then describe it.) As you do this, hold a self-anchor for confidence.

Adjust the image until it's exactly right for you. This means playing with the knobs of submodalities: going larger or smaller, closer or farther away, adding color (to black and white) or making the color more intense, increasing brightness or subduing the light, sharpening the focus or blurring it. Play with the auditory submodalities too. Listen to the words that are describing your outcome and adjust tempo, speed, volume, and pitch until it comes out perfect. Click your image into place. Now imagine a path leading out into your future and place this image wherever you want your outcome to be. Release your confidence anchor.

Look at your outcome on the path ahead of you—it's the Emerald City at the end of the yellow brick road, or throwing a successful party, moving to a new home, creating your own company, changing the way you talk to yourself, being patient with your children—and calculate the distance from where you are now. How many more steps along the way? What do the steps represent?

Each step is a resource you need to overcome a particular obstacle. You may not be able to see them all from your starting point—the fears you have to conquer, the knots to untangle, problems to resolve—but as you advance on your outcome, the steps will become evident. Maybe you have an inner voice saying, "You'll never get this; you can't do it; you're not good enough." If that's what's holding you back, you'll have to play with submodalities, changing the position of the voice, taking it out of your head, placing it behind you, to the side; or adding music, speeding it up; maybe combining several submodalities (see chart in chapter 13) until you can leave that message behind.

Write down whichever obstacles ("steps") you can identify—three or four, even if they're not completely clear. Now make an image of each of them, as you did of the outcome as a whole. Imagine it. See your outcome on the path ahead of you and place the obstacles like stepping stones along the way. Tell yourself: "As I take each step, using these resources and removing these obstacles, I am getting closer and closer to achieving my outcome."

When you can imagine all parts of your strategy, when you have defined and checked your outcome, and have designed a plan for accomplishing it step by step, you'll find that the road to your dreams is paved not only with good intentions but with solid information, clear thinking, and the imaginative use of resources and possibilities. The road is long or short, depending on your distance to the outcome, but you have no doubt that you'll make it. Every step along the way is clear to you. You can see yourself reaching the mountaintop or the pot of gold, and you find that way up over the rainbow becomes the place where dreams become actuality.

◆

OUTCOME STRATEGY

1. Make sure your outcome is well formed and achievable.

2. Create a still photograph or slide that represents this outcome for you. See yourself within this image. Play with submodalities until you get it exactly the way you want it. Now put it out in front of you on your path into the future.

3. Identify the steps that will bring you to the successful accomplishment of your outcome. Create an image of each of these steps. Put them on your path like stepping stones between now and the future, when you will have accomplished your outcome.

4. Think of the resources that will help you with each step along the way. Imagine implementing them.

5. Look at the path to your outcome and at the steps leading to it. Describe this process to yourself. Make an image of it and say to yourself, "I'm on my way. I'm already beginning to achieve _____. [whatever your outcome is]."

❖ ❖ ❖

THE CHINESE MERCHANT

Once upon a time there was a very old, very rich merchant in China who wished to retire and spend the remaining days of his life studying, meditating, and tending his garden. But first he had to find someone who could successfully run his empire, since he did not want to see his life's work wasted.

He decided upon the perfect test and sent out notices of the search for his successor. On the appointed day, many people came to apply for the position.

The test the old merchant had devised was deceptively

simple. At one end of a large room stood massive carved-oak double doors. These doors had a golden chain going from one to the other, secured by a great golden lock. The applicants were told that behind these doors lay the merchant's incredible treasure, and that whoever could open these doors and look upon the treasure would become the merchant's successor. In front of the doors stood a single chest with many drawers, which contained the clues for success.

After an entire day, none of the applicants had succeeded in solving the puzzle. The old merchant was very disappointed. He noticed that the applicants fell into one of two categories. There were those who turned all the drawers upside down and rummaged through the contents, rushing back and forth to try each item they came upon as a way to open the massive doors. These, the old man thought, would be good salespeople but could never run his empire. The other group was composed of those who would carefully and meticulously open one drawer at a time, examine its contents, and select something from each to try on the doors—always to no avail. These, he thought, would be good accountants.

But the day ended and no one had succeeded. Just as the merchant was about to go to bed a young man appeared at his door and asked for an opportunity to apply for the position. The old merchant was tired and disappointed but nonetheless decided to give this young man a chance.

After listening to the instructions, the young man went quietly to the oak doors and the golden chain and looked very carefully at them. Then he touched them lightly and discovered that when he pushed on one of the doors it slid open easily—for it was not attached to the golden chain.

Behind the doors it was very, very dark. In the middle of the darkness he could see two gleaming red eyes, and he heard a dangerous-sounding hiss coming from the cen-

ter of the room. The young man went to the chest and opened the drawers one by one until he found a candle and matches. He lit the candle and held it in front of him as he stepped in behind the double doors. There he saw a large poisonous snake in a cage with the door open. The young man retreated back to the chest and in one of the drawers found a long ruler. He took the ruler into the room with him and used it to shut the door to the snake's cage.

Behind the snake was the treasure. With the candle lighting his way, the young man looked upon the magnificent treasure of the old Chinese merchant, and in this manner he became the merchant's successor.

◆ ◆ ◆

PART FOUR

You Can Turn Failure into Feedback

30

What Is Failure?
What Is Feedback?

A person without a problem
is like a warrior with a broken sword.

Sit back. Relax. Take a deep breath.

Allow yourself to daydream.

Think of some mistakes you've made. Now look at your whole life up to this point and try to imagine what it would have been like if you *hadn't* made those mistakes.

Think of the positive things that would not have happened if you hadn't made those mistakes.

Take a few minutes to recognize the opportunities these mistakes provided and all that you learned and gained because of them.

Failure includes mistakes. Failure means not achieving the outcome you intended, because of some miscalculation on your part, because something you couldn't foresee or control made it backfire, because the timing was off, or because of any number of reasonable or unreasonable causes that make things go wrong. You didn't get what you wanted.

Or you got what you wanted—the job, marriage, a long-awaited trip—but it turned out not to be what you'd expected. Things happen; people are not trees (they can move despite having roots), and what was or used to be will change as the person grows and develops.

Life happens. Failure happens. People make mistakes. They say the wrong thing, fall in love with the wrong people, fight battles they later wish they'd never heard of.

But each mistake is a possibility. Jeannette marries Bob and moves to Australia. Five years later she sees it was a mistake, Bob isn't the person for her, they can barely speak to each other without getting into an argument, *but* Jeannette has found a wonderful job there, which has led to a new career she loves. If she hadn't made her "mistake" (Bob), she might never have discovered her talents and satisfactions down under.

Someone else makes a career choice that turns into a dead end—he's a specialized technician with a large corporation that seemed to specialize in nothing so much as downsizing—but he meets the person who becomes the love of his life.

How often has this happened to you or to people you know? Missing a train, walking into the wrong room, saying something you didn't mean to say: These are the trivial mistakes of everyday life that open up new opportunities. You take the wrong road—and find undiscovered country, a beautiful setting for something you have in mind, a picnic, a wedding, a scene in a play you're writing.

You go to one of those multiplex theaters and buy a ticket to the wrong movie—which turns out to be the best thing you've seen in years, and helpful too.

Mistakes are like tiny time warps, a little hiatus in the usual routine, an interruption of the automatic cycle of A ∅ B. A mistake is a new response, and it can provide a new outlook. It can give you a new approach, open up new possibilities, show you a hidden territory you've stumbled on by accident.

Bill Gates, the fabulously wealthy founder of Microsoft,

got his start by being fired. The discovery of penicillin came about by mistake.

Even the discovery of America was an accident. Christopher Columbus set out intending to find a sea route to India—and by mistake ran into the New World. (Also by mistake, he discovered that the world was round.) Did Columbus fail? Well, sure he did. If failure means not achieving your outcome, Columbus failed in a big way.

Romeo and Juliet failed—and theirs was a failure that ended in death. Though ultimately their love for each other resulted in the coming together of their families, the Montagues and Capulets, and the bringing of peace to Verona, the young lovers themselves were unable to turn their failure around. They were too young, too lacking in experience, not able to learn from the enmity and bitterness around them how to prevent their own demise. They themselves became the mistake: The deaths of Romeo and Juliet (both of them the results of mistakes) became the accident that permitted the two warring factions to come together, the deep wound that leads to eventual healing.

Failure happens when you want something—to get, be, or do something—and don't achieve or attain it. Failure also happens when you think you *should* do or achieve or acquire something because someone else—or convention, or society (religion/morality)—wants or expects you to.

Expectation leads to failure, especially if the expectations are unrealistic or have little to do with the individual involved. If a man feels he *should* support his wife and family, or a woman feels she *should* be a wonderful mother, failure is getting ripe to happen.

Failure is a sense that you haven't done the right thing or you haven't done enough. Failure is when you're not keeping up with the Joneses or—depending on what you see as the expectations of your family, class, upbringing— not getting *ahead* of the Joneses.

In other words, failure happens when you don't have a smart outcome. It's not getting what you want if what you want isn't a reasonable or possible thing for you to get or accomplish at this point in your life.

Failure leads to disappointment. That's natural. You want something; you don't get it; you're disappointed. Or you make a mistake, an error of judgment or timing. You say the wrong thing and offend someone without meaning to. You drift off into a daydream in the midst of a lecture and don't know the answer when you're asked about this part on your exam.

Small mistakes like these, or large failures on the scale of a career, relationship, or major project, are devastating, frustrating, disappointing, annoying, all of that. But they can also provide a gateway into new fields, new learning, and new opportunity.

Mistake or failure—something happens that's not what you intended, not what you wanted. "That is not what I meant at all," J. Alfred Prufrock says in T. S. Eliot's poem. OK, these things happen all the time. Now the question is, What next?

Failure is often part of a cycle: You try, you fail, you give up. The road you set out on turns into a dead end— and that's it, end of story. You wish you'd never started, wish you'd never tried, but in any case it's over now. Best thing to do is forget about it.

Is that how you think? Forget about it? Lose all that information and experience? Throw out the feedback?

Babies and bathwater! The feedback you can get from failure lets you start on a new path that can lead you to destinations you haven't yet dreamed of.

Feedback is the information we gain from experience. More than "gain," it's like a *harvesting* of experience, gathering up the fruits so we can begin again—either by planting the same crop, the same type of seeds, but in new soil, or by doing something different this time. Feedback is new information, a new way of looking at things, profiting by what went wrong before to make sure it won't happen this time.

Feedback lets you start again, gives you a new lease, lets you reassess your former goal or outcome. "What did I do wrong?" and "Why didn't this work?" lead naturally to "Do I still want this outcome? Am I still the same person I was when I set out on this career/project/relationship? What has changed? What can I do about it?" And, most important of all, "What have I learned?"

The ability to learn from your mistakes is one of the most valuable resources you can have. It lets you move on to the next step, prevents you from being caught in a rut, and lifts you out of boredom, mediocrity, even a sense of helplessness. "What can I do about it?" If you're asking that seriously, the answer is *a lot*!

In fact, failure is a necessary part of growth. How can I know what I'm doing right unless I see what I do wrong? How can I improve my backhand, my cooking, my public speaking unless I'm sensitive to my weaknesses or mistakes and then do what I can to correct them?

Failure is a dead end only when people are unable to learn from it. Paradoxically, it's often success, and particularly early success, that is limiting.

Success can limit you because you stop learning. If you get everything you want at the beginning, you miss the opportunity to learn about things that can help you grow and develop. Without the experience of failure, you don't develop resilience or flexibility. If you're not tried and found wanting, how are you going to develop the resource of strength?

Think of sports stars who are washed up at thirty; child prodigies in science or the arts whose success prevents them from maturing at a normal rate. Or beautiful women and men, those who were always stunning and relied on their beauty to get anything they wanted.

What happens when these women and men grow older? What happens to their self-esteem, their self-image? Very often, they have a hard time living with the reality of aging and the loss of their youthful charms. These are the people who become obsessed with plastic surgery, whose standards become impossible to match. They *have* to be beautiful; beauty is the only way they know how to live. It's the way they interact with other people; it's how they're used to accomplishing whatever they're after. Not to be beautiful becomes a failure. Not to be young is a failure. Aging itself is failure.

People who are used to success often find they don't have many resources when the attribute or talent that has brought them success fails. To view aging as failure—as, unfortunately, too many people in our society do—is to be unable to deal with the real world. It means you can't learn from experience. You're locked into a cycle that says: Failure is bad; you have yourself to blame. If you fail, it says: You're no good.

This is like the old stimulus-response behavior we talked about in Part II. Here, Failure leads to Bad, and Bad leads to Self-Blame.

When we turn failure into feedback, we interrupt this response and replace it with a new one. Now it becomes Failure $\varnothing$ Information. And Information leads to Opportunity. Instead of driving us to a dead end, failure can put us on a new road.

31

Back from the Future:
Learning from Failure

There's no such thing as failure—
only not enough time.

"Growing old isn't so bad—when you consider the alternative," said Maurice Chevalier, coupling wit to his wisdom. He certainly didn't regard aging as failure, any more than did George Burns, who used it to great advantage until he died at the age of 100.

The future is the greatest way we can learn from failure, but the "future" I'm talking about here is a *sense* of future. In order to have a sense of the future you must be able to perceive it as being *other* than the present and the past; that's why it offers you countless possibilities. Because the future is *unknown*, things are possible that otherwise wouldn't be. When the time that comes after now is experienced as the same as the present or the past, you do not really have a sense of the future. And to transform failure into feedback, to make something new happen, you must have a sense of the future as a time that has never yet existed.

The future gives comfort when something bad happens: "Five years from now, you won't even remember this . . . you'll look back and laugh." There's an implicit recognition in these words that we'll be different in the future. Our pain won't hurt as much; things will have happened; it's a new life out there.

Time is in the past, present, and future. The past holds our memories, experience, knowledge. The present is the here and now, this unique moment. The future is our potential, dynamic and moving.

Thinking of the future as different from the past and present gives time its magical quality of change. Tomorrow anything is possible! Things change, grow, die, and are born. As long as you have a sense of the future as different from what came before, changing, moving, transforming, you know that you can learn, change, evolve, and succeed where once you failed. All you need is time, which belongs to the future.

Let's look at a practical example. You're taking the kids to the zoo, your nieces and nephew, all three of them. It's a beautiful day, but nobody seems to notice the weather. They've been fighting since the moment you arrived, each of them wanting to go somewhere else. Glenn wants to see the gorillas, Dina wants reptiles, Beth wants birds.

Then there's lunch: It's a nightmare. They can't decide what they want; when they do, they change their minds; when they get their trays to the table, each wants what another's having. Dina spills her drink; Beth leaves most of her lunch untouched; Glenn eats too much and gets sick.

By the time it's over, you're exhausted, the kids are crying, and you wonder whatever made you think of doing this in the first place.

How do you turn this to feedback?

You go into the future. After you've had your shower, drink, workout, or whatever it takes to make you feel human again, you ask yourself, Do I still want to take the kids on an outing?

Yes.

Would I ever take them to the zoo again, or to some place like it, where there's lots of choice?

Yes, again.

OK. This means my outcome remains the same (taking the kids to the zoo), but to avoid going through the same torture in the future, I have to look at the whole experience and see what I can do that's different.

We could decide which animals to visit by drawing lots. I could let them pick slips of paper with numbers on them—first, second, third, and then we go to see the animals in order. To solve the food disaster, we can take a picnic. Have each child name a favorite food, and I pack it all up ahead of time, letting them choose one treat or maybe a beverage from the zoo cafeteria when we get there.

To be able to learn, to get the feedback, you need a sense of future. What would it be like in a month's time? It will be warmer at the zoo then; the trees will be in bloom; the kids won't have so many clothes to put on and take off; it'll be prettier, balmier, a better time to go. Or a year from now, when the kids are older?

Future means the possibility of change. Things will be different, the earth goes through revolutions, seasons change, people aren't always the same.

When you're stuck in failure, it's as though you were caught in a net, captured inside a bubble in time. This is how it will always be, you feel; I don't have the power to change it.

"It will always be the same." If this is how you feel in the situation, in the failure, you won't be able to do anything about it because you don't *want* to do anything about it. You're stuck inside the bubble.

But prick that bubble of time, and you can get outside of it; you can look around, move, act—you can do something about it.

You're turning a static event into a process. Instead of

AT THE ZOO
WITH THE KIDS

like a slide or a still photograph that you bring out each time, you make it into a film. It's not just one awful event, one picture framed in memory, it's a series of pictures, movements, changes of scene that you watch in your mind. You can slow it down (to see exactly what happened at a certain point) or speed it up, and it becomes something ongoing, something that can change.

ARRIVING ►	SEEING ►	SEEING ►	PICNIC ►	ANIMAL
AT THE	THE	THE		RIDES
ZOO	MONKEYS	SNAKES		

Feedback is active. You're doing something about the failure; you're learning; you're changing what you do and how you do it through the new information you've gathered.

You do that by looking into the future. The future is not simply *then* instead of *now*, as if you were choosing between different types of muffins. It's a sense of time as something different from what you've known before: the future as you *haven't* experienced it, in which things have changed, you have changed, and life isn't exactly predictable based on what you're doing and feeling now. The time ahead of you offers the possibility of new approaches, new choices.

Though you can't know the future (meaning tomorrow or next week or decades from now), you know it will come and that it will be different from whatever you've experienced in the past.

For some people this thought is disquieting or even scary, because it implies uncertainty. But there's little you can do about it. You can try to picture the future the way you did with outcomes, using the As If frame, in order to broaden your scope, to foresee possible implications and consequences you might otherwise have overlooked. But As If is make-believe. It works as a test for the ecology of your outcome, but there's no way you can step into your actual future, the future as it is taking place, even if you're talking about something as close as tomorrow.

But think about it: If the future were *not* different from the present, we'd have nothing to look forward to. No expectations, no outcomes, no development.

"Nothing remains the same" is the definition of life as a process.

Of course there are some constants, some predictability—otherwise we'd go too far into chaos and destroy ourselves. The sun rises and sets each day, our house stays where it is, the sidewalk outside my office is always there, the furniture remains where I left it. However, in terrible disasters and catastrophes these constants do change—though fortunately this is unusual—and when they do the effects are overwhelming and extremely disruptive.

Kimberley gives a dinner party, inviting her future in-laws to meet some friends of hers from the Career Counseling Center where she works. She likes her boyfriend's parents very much—almost, she jokes, better than her own. At least she feels freer with them.

The dinner party is going to be an unusual event, not the setting-out-to-impress-his-folks kind of thing but a much more informal get-together, treating his parents as if they were friends, contemporaries of hers.

No lace or linens, just a red-and-white checkered tablecloth, a stew, some wine, salad, bread, and cheese. Simple, classic, and fun—that's how Kimberley plans it, but then everything goes wrong.

It turns out that George, her boyfriend's father, is a vegetarian and won't touch the stew. His wife doesn't eat cheese. The French bread burns to cinders before Kimberley remembers she put it in the oven to crisp it up.

Later, cleaning up after her guests have gone home, Kimberley tells herself she was a fool to try, she's a lousy cook, it was a terrible idea, and everyone probably had a miserable time.

But then she remembers the way her boyfriend's parents hugged her when they left—with genuine warmth—and she realizes that some parts of the evening were in fact OK, especially the company. Her guests all seemed to get along very well, they were relaxed, they found a lot to talk about, and she saw them exchanging addresses before they left.

She recognizes that food was not the primary focus of the evening. It was congeniality, making new friends, getting people together who had a lot in common and enjoyed spending a few hours in one another's company. Next time, she thinks, and already she's on the track of turning failure to feedback. *Next time* means the future.

She puts the dishes in the rack and looks back on the evening from beginning to end. She sees it like a film—the people arriving, introductions, small talk, then sitting down for the meal, the disaster with the stew, the burned bread, the cheese, the good-byes, the cleanup, dishes in the sink—right up to this very moment of the present.

She runs it through a second time, picking out what was good about the evening, what worked. Next time, why not suggest that everybody meet for dinner at a restaurant? It wouldn't have to be fancy; the new corner bistro might be perfect, and people could order what they wanted. Nobody would mind paying for themselves, Kimberley was sure. Or she could try again at her house, but this time she'd ask her guests ahead of time if they had a food intolerance or preference. Or, with a slightly larger group, she could ask each person to bring a dish—that way, people who were particular about food would be able to prepare it the way they wanted.

Kimberley uses her failure to come up with new ideas.

First she moves out into the future—next time—and asks herself if she still wants the same outcome. The answer is yes, for the most part anyway. (She wants these people to come together again, though not necessarily in the same place or with the same menu.)

She then asks, What did I do wrong? What can I change in the future—next time? She looks at a rerun of the evening, sees what there was that she wants to keep and what she wants to change, and forms a new outcome based on the feedback.

Here's another example.

Dave is giving a speech to a group of real estate agents, talking about the importance of having good communication skills and establishing good rapport. As he talks, he notices that people are fidgeting, some people are leaving, and others are looking bored, doodling on their pads, not paying attention.

Painfully, he gets to the end and receives sparse applause. He feels terrible. He knows the speech was a complete dud. He feels stuck in his failure, downcast, sure no one will ever ask him to speak again.

Then he steps into the future. He bursts the bubble of the present and looks ahead, forward, and realizes that he wants to give speeches again and wants to learn to do them better. He loves talking to people about communication skills and improving rapport.

"Yes!" he tells himself. "Despite everything, that's what I want to do. It's important, I can *feel* how important it is, it's exciting to me—and I want to convey that excitement to other people."

How to do it?

When Dave looks at the movie of himself giving his speech, he sees that he really *was* boring. He gave out the information, yes, but there wasn't any life in his words and sentences. He was technical, the room was hot, it was after lunch—Hell, he thinks, even *I* would have fallen asleep.

What I've got to do, he decides, is liven it up. I want to convey my own excitement. I'll tell stories; I'll talk about actual experiences, mine and other people's. I'll give the audience exercises for them to do right there in the auditorium. They've all got pads, and it's better than doodling. We'll take some true-to-life sales situations and work on them, the audience interacting with me, too busy to be bored.

He'll be able to get everybody involved, and the audience will love it. Dave is learning from his mistakes—his "failure." And if he keeps learning like this he'll be in demand; he may even get on the circuit of popular speakers and in time become a drawing card at the annual National Convention of Realtors.

Failure to feedback.

◆

FUTURE EXERCISE

1. Where you are right now is your present; what you had for lunch today and last summer's outing are your past; what you're going to do this weekend is part of your future. Imagine for a moment your coming year: work, family, trips, holidays, visits with relatives.

2. What would it be like to be able to predict everything that is going to happen to you—down to the last detail? Imagine this.

3. Take one of the most pleasant days of the last few years. Imagine what your life would be like if *every single day* in your future were exactly the same: no difference, no surprises.

◆

32

Dissociation

To turn failure into feedback, you need

A sense of the future

An outcome

The ability to dissociate

The three are interdependent. It's a cybernetic loop: each component feeds into the next and changes it. You need a sense of the future to be able to dissociate, step back from yourself, and form an achievable outcome. If you don't have the ability to dissociate, you can't think of a future different from the present, and you won't be able to create an outcome. And by definition, having a well-formed outcome means you can project yourself into a time you haven't yet experienced (the future) and see yourself in a new perspective.

The steps are linked like beads on a chain. Dissociation, Future, Outcome, Future, Dissociation: In any order it comes up to the same. You turn a failure around by looking at it from a new angle, as an observer, and then using the information this gives you for the future. (Without a future, a time to come that's different from the present or past, there would be no way to change anything.)

Dissociation is the ability to watch yourself as if you were an actor in the movie of your mistake or failure. You look at and listen to yourself without censorship or shame, without any sort of judgment. You just see yourself doing what you did, saying what you said, and then you use this information, returning to your outcome, placing it into the future, and doing it differently because of what you learned from observing yourself in or with the failure.

Or else the information you get from dissociating can make you decide *not* to go for the same outcome in the future.

If you're traveling with a friend, for instance, and she wants excitement while you want rest, this could lead to an unpleasant experience for both of you. Your friend is up at dawn, anxious to start sightseeing, and you want to take it easy, have breakfast in bed, read the paper, and eventually stroll down to the beach or along the streets of the town, window-shopping, sitting in cafés, taking it easy. What next happens is that either you're both so eager to avoid confrontation you end up doing nothing at all, or else one of you ''sacrifices'' for the other, and nobody gets to do what she likes. You feel pushed; your friend feels held back.

When you come home, you decide it was a terrible mistake, your friendship is on the line; how could you ever have imagined that the two of you could get along?

Here's where you dissociate. You look at your mental film or slides of the vacation: There you are, there she is; here's the beach, the sights of the town. What went wrong? What can you learn?

You're watching the film of the two of you trying to have a good time together, and at the end you ask yourself: Do I still want this? Do I want to travel with her again next year?

No.

But this doesn't mean you've lost a friendship. You can

see that you two are temperamentally different (which may be why you became such good friends in the first place), and when you're on vacation, taking time out of your usual life, each of you wants something different.

Fair enough. Don't travel together. You tell your friend how much you enjoy her company—in your regular life, coming from your separate ways to meet for a meal or the movies, for hours of conversation—but you think it would be best if each of you goes on her own vacation.

The outcome has changed; the feedback from failure provides new information: I really like this person, but I don't want to travel with her.

The feedback frees up your life, gives you more options, allows you to break the cycle of doing what you feel is expected (traveling with your friend), failing at it (you get annoyed at each other; you interfere with the other's idea of a vacation), and then blaming yourself or her. That cycle could jeopardize your friendship, whereas the feedback you get from stepping back, watching yourself (being dissociated), lets you keep the rewarding parts of your relationship and discard the rest. No more throwing out the baby with the bathwater.

Crucial to changing your behavior in the future is the ability to watch yourself in the past, becoming your own audience as you go through the experience, gathering the information that allows you to adjust, alter, or reject your former outcome.

Dissociation changes your perspective. Instead of being inside the experience, seeing through your eyes and hearing through your ears, you are now outside, the audience instead of the actor. You step back to watch the experience from a certain distance and gain a degree of objectivity.

Being dissociated is nothing more or less than being your own observer. It's not to be confused with what psychologists refer to as "disassociation," meaning a person split off from experience. That is a clinical pathological condition and definitely not what we're talking about here.

Dissociating is the skill of seeing and hearing yourself from the outside, as if you were someone else. It is the ability to be disinterested, to simply notice and record the behavior without exercising any judgment. This is an extremely important position to take in problem-solving. And it's easy, too. You probably do it naturally a lot of the time: stepping back, seeing yourself from a distance, observing yourself with a certain objectivity.

But in order for this ability to become really useful, a tool you can use to learn from failure and overcome it, you have to become aware that you have it, and then you have to practice until it becomes automatic. Then, when you decide you want to dissociate, it's easy and immediately available. Dissociating becomes a resource that you can call up instantly when you want to create a buffer of distance between you and a problem or failure. You have the choice, in any given situation, of becoming your own observer and either using the information to help you achieve what you set out to do or rejecting it in favor of a more realistic and achievable outcome.

Joanna has a new house in the country with more than an acre of land. Finally, her own garden: a dream come true. She pictures the trees and flowers, plans how she'll landscape her new property. She thinks of it as a kind of Eden.

In early spring she prepares the ground and plants all of her favorites, the flowers from seeds, the trees from saplings. When the dry season comes, she realizes that to water the entire acre is fabulously expensive. She will have to choose which plants to keep, which to let die. It's hard, selecting among the plants she loves.

In Joanna's garden the flowers are planted close together to make beautiful arrangements, the colors like something out of a Monet painting. After two years the flowers are all in bloom, but some have crowded out the others. The following year she has only three different species; they've taken over the flower beds. And soon it's the same with the trees; some of the fast-growing trees have expanded beyond the area she planned for them. Close to the house, her favorites have sent down roots that have started growing into the basement, undermining the foundations of the house. She has to cut them down, have them removed.

Is this the end? Is she a failure?

She looks at the trees being carted off. She asks herself, Do I still want a garden?

You bet! More than anything.

She imagines her garden in springtime—next spring, the spring after that—and as she does the possibilities begin to excite her; she feels good about herself again and about her garden; she has all her original enthusiasm and more.

Joanna realizes she made mistakes. She recognizes the miscalculations and discouragements of the past years. She dissociates, observing herself through time, reviewing the decisions she made, the plantings she selected. And then she forgets failure and disappointment, forgets about self-blame, and asks herself, What can I do differently in the future?

Step by step come the answers. She will plant a smaller area, not the full acre but within a parameter that she knows she can water effectively. In the flower garden, she can arrange the spreading plants to the left of the wall, where they have lots of room; the others to the right. Her favorite tree will be moved farther from the house.

When she does all this, she discovers that her new landscaping is actually better than the old plan. It's not a garden of Eden, it's a real place where kids have room to run without stepping on flowers; she puts up a badminton net and croquet wickets for when the grandchildren come to visit. She discovers that moving the tree farther from the house allows sunlight to pour into her bedroom in the morning, and she feels happy as a bird, at peace with her world.

◆

DISSOCIATION EXERCISE

1. PAST
   Remember a pleasant visit with a friend. Pretend you have a snapshot of this visit and that you're looking at a picture of the two of you.

2. Turn this snapshot into a home video of your visit, and watch and listen to yourself and the other person.

3. PRESENT
   Imagine that there's a video camera somewhere in the room with you now and that a part of you is behind it, looking at yourself through the lens. Say something out loud and listen to your own voice—notice the tone and tempo.

4. FUTURE
   Think of how you would like to spend a special weekend. See yourself in the place you want to be, with the people you'd like to be with, doing whatever activity you want to be doing. Listen to yourself. Watch this movie as if it were a trailer, a preview of coming attractions.

This is dissociation—watching and listening to yourself in a past memory, future activity, or even now, in the present.

For some of you, seeing yourself will be easier than hearing yourself, and for some it will be the reverse. It doesn't really matter. As long as you can begin to imagine seeing yourself or hearing yourself, you are dissociating.

◆

FEEDBACK EXERCISE

1. Think of a "failure."

2. Ask yourself, Do I still want _____ [whatever it was you didn't get or do]?

   If no, go on to another outcome; if yes, continue.

3. See yourself in the "failure" experience. As you're watching, ask yourself, "What can I learn from this experience? How can I be different in the future?"

   Rerun this movie several times, until you've gathered some new information, new ideas for the future.

4. Based on this feedback, do you now want to change your outcome in some way or to keep it as it is? Make an image of the outcome. Imagine a path running ahead of you through time and space that represents your future. Decide where in the future it would be realistic to place this outcome, when you could realistically accomplish it. Place the image of your outcome there in your future path.

5. See yourself being different, doing things differently—using the information you gathered in step 3 as feed-

back in order to achieve your outcome this time. Tell yourself, "I have the time I need to succeed."

Remember: You can always use the blueprint for success (see chapter 19) to further define your outcome and increase your chances of success.

◆

33

Chunking

- *What do I want?*
- *Do I still want it?*
- *What do I want now?*
- *What can I learn from this failure?*
- *How can I be different, or do things differently, next time?*

Questions provide direction and perspective. With each suc-
ceeding question, you define your outcome a little more
clearly. Never mind the answers; it's the questions that
show you where you are and where to go next.

This is the process of transforming failure into feedback.
The questions help us break down experience and information into smaller, more workable pieces. Instead of trying to change *everything* about a situation or about our
behavior, we can focus in on specific details.

Questions also open up a broader view and help us understand the larger picture that shows us the purpose behind
our behavior and concerns. At one end of the questioning
is the microscopic "What, *specifically*, do I want to change
in this recipe?" At the telescopic end we have "What is
my purpose in doing this? What will this do for my life?"

The way we break down information into smaller details
or expand it out to the generalities and larger assumptions
of life is what NLP calls *chunking*. This is a power tool

that you've probably been using for most of your life to help you make decisions. It's as natural a human activity as calibration, and we can't help doing it. But we *can* improve our efficiency. Learning to make use of our mental toolbox means we go on doing what we've always done, except that we're aware of what we do, how to do it more efficiently, and how to get to it when and where we want. That means we have conscious control over the natural processes that we would ordinarily not think about. The difference is incalculable.

Chunking is a way of organizing our thinking by creating *categories* of information. Categories are frames we use to identify pieces of information that we experience as being similar in some way. Hardness, for instance, is a category or frame that might include rocks, metals, wood, and plastics but not feathers or foam.

Each "chunk" is a piece of information that can be put into a larger category (chunking *up*), subdivided into smaller categories (chunking *down*), or replaced by another chunk within the larger category (chunking *laterally*). So, for instance, "rose" can be put in the larger category of flower or it can be subdivided into specific kinds of rose: tea rose, red rose, sweetheart rose, silk rose, and so on. Or, within the larger category of flower, it can be replaced by "lily" or "daisy" or "orchid."

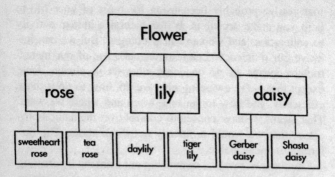

Chunking up means expanding the information into a more general concept. Chunking down particularizes the information, making it more specific. Lateral chunking means going across a category and finding a parallel idea or synonym within the large chunk that defines them both. If the larger heading (big chunk) is attractiveness, the specific instances of the concept might be: beautiful, pretty, handsome, lovely, charming. These five adjectives are all types of attractiveness. Parallel ideas or words linked by a common thread are lateral chunks.

Chunking arranges and streamlines information by organizing it into frames or categories. Is X like Y? In what ways? How are they different? (Are apples like oranges? Both are types of *fruit*. Apples grow in cold climates, oranges in warm. Apples are smooth-skinned, oranges are pockmarked. Apples are red, oranges orange.) After we chunk up to *fruit*, showing how the two are similar (lateral chunks), we ask how they are different. Now we create new categories (cold climate, smooth-skinned, red), and we can chunk down, finding many parallel instances, or lateral chunks, within each. The category (large chunk) of *red fruit* would give us cherries, plums and strawberries, while *pockmarked fruit* gives us grapefruits, lemons, tangerines.

Chunking is a screening process that goes on all the time in our minds. It allows us to discriminate and differentiate ever more finely between what we want or mean and what we don't. It lets us define and redefine relationships between ideas as well as between people, situations, experiences, or memories, finding new possibilities, new ways of looking at or thinking about things, new solutions to problems approached in a new way.

We depend on this built-in classification system to organize our thoughts, sensations, and behavior. If each experience were separate and not related to other experiences, we'd have no memory, no consistency, no knowledge. Knowledge is built from the relationship between ideas, between experiences. Chunking is a filing system for these ideas and experiences.

To make clear how chunking works, let's take a simple word: *train*. What larger category is *train* a part of?

There are a number of possible answers. One might be *transportation*. That's the larger chunk, the more general category of which *train* is a part. Many other pieces of information can also fit into this category, other chunks besides train: car, plane, subway, horse and buggy, Rollerblades, Metro, taxi, ship, bicycle, camel. Chunking up is moving to the more general category. *Transportation* broadens or generalizes the concept of *train*.

Chunking down means making it more specific, breaking it down into smaller categories, specific instances of *train*, as in express train, local, electric train, commuter train, Orient Express, the 6:22, Amtrak, and so on.

Moving within a category is lateral chunking. This means grouping words or concepts together that are similar, synonyms or substitutes within the larger category. Train, car, horse, bicycle are all lateral examples, meaning they are similar in size and all of them fit in the category of transportation. But if we change the large chunk, or main heading, from *transportation* to *vehicles*, our sideways chunking changes. Horse is not a vehicle. It doesn't belong here. We've defined what we're *not* talking about as a way of clarifying what, specifically, we mean.

Chunking is natural: we do it all the time. However, problems set in when we assume that other people chunk the same way—that they think in the same categories as we do.

Take the topic of abortion. One side debates from the large chunk of *personal freedom*: Does a woman have the right to decide on her own, without government interference, whether or not she wants to go through with her pregnancy? The other side debates from the large chunk of *murder*: Does anyone have the right to take a life?

There's no way these sides can meet, unless they begin to talk from the same large chunk. Either they agree to talk about murder—whether or not the unborn child is an individual, a citizen in the eyes of the state, and therefore entitled to the same rights and protection as all other citizens—or about personal freedom. But unless they agree on the basic issue (large chunk) that they will debate, there's no point even calling it a discussion. The two sides are talking to themselves.

Becoming aware that we organize information and experience into categories and recognizing how we do it allows us to question the particular categories we create, the way we frame things to ourselves and others. This gives us the choice to expand our frame, make it more specific, or move laterally to find an alternative.

Having control over the categories we make enables us to solve problems (for ourselves or others) by changing the frame. For instance, if someone says, "My family is difficult," you might respond by asking, "Who, specifically?" This is chunking down.

Or you could start by chunking up to get an overview:

"Families overall are complex and multidimensional."

Lateral chunking would be: "Friendships are difficult, relations with other people are difficult, relations between generations are difficult."

Each type of chunking changes the frame of reference, the particular category that's being considered. Moving from one to the other is like looking at a sculpture from many different angles. What you see, whatever particular configuration of space and form, depends on how you look at it. From far away you see the broad outlines; from close up, the texture of the sculptured material, small curves and embosses. Or you can look at where the sculpture has been set down and ask yourself, What else could I place there?

In terms of your life's goals, outcomes, and decisions, it's usually important to get the larger frame, the overall picture. Chunking up will help define the mission or purpose behind whatever you're doing or planning to do, placing it in the larger context of your life. This helps motivate you.

Let's say you've been job hunting for months without success. Or you've been trying to sell somebody on a project. You're getting fed up. You don't even feel like making that extra phone call or filling out the application form they hand you at the interview anymore. It all seems nothing but a waste of effort.

You're frustrated, mired in rejections, feeling "what's the use?"

This is the time to stop and take stock of what is happening. You chunk up, asking yourself the larger questions: "What am I doing this for?" "What will this project do for me?"

Here you're clarifying the purpose behind your actions. Chunking up helps you redefine your goal and expand your possibilities. You ask yourself, "What am I doing this for?'' and your answer might come back: ''To make money.''

The overall objective is defined. Now you ask yourself: ''Is there anything else I can do to make money?''

You chunk sideways, looking over the options. You could take care of children at home; do telemarketing by phone or on the Internet. Maybe open up a shop (get a loan), offer your skills as a consultant, take special training courses as an investment toward a better job in the future, join the armed forces. Each of these options is part of the larger category *make money*.

Or you chunk down, becoming more specific in how you will go about getting this job, selling this project. Chunking down lets you get out of the trap of Overwhelm.

Instead of being overcome by the sense of having failed, reaching a dead end, being ''no good,'' you ask yourself very specific questions: ''What did I do here that didn't work? How could I do this differently?''

Chunking is the means by which we transform failure into feedback. When we fail at something, we have an opportunity to get more information about our own abilities and resources by asking, ''How can this (how can I) be different in the future?'' Everybody fails, at least some of the time. Without failure, we'd never risk ourselves, never aim higher than our reach.

Reassessing goals and outcomes—looking back at the man who got away and realizing we no longer want him, or letting go of an old dream of buying a sports car (because it's not practical), and freeing that money for something else instead—this is the freedom that feedback provides.

If you haven't done or achieved it yet, whatever it is you've been dreaming of or hoping for, maybe it isn't the right or practical outcome for you. Or maybe it just needs a sharpening of focus and a dose of the future. Moving across space and time, changing categories, gaining specificity—you're able to go from outcome to failure to new outcome. Chunking is an amazing tool: like a computer in some ways and also like a zoom lens, going from wide angle to close-up. Using it, you can move from close scrutiny to panorama, from minute concerns to a worldview.

Turning failure into feedback means knowing there is a future that is different from the present or the past and you can break through the bubble of time that keeps you stuck inside failure. You learn from failure and advance into the future, armed with the resources, questions, and organized thinking that lead to new possibilities and new adventures along the exciting path that is always changing and where nothing remains impossible forever.

FAILURE-TO-FEEDBACK RECAP

FUTURE: A time that is qualitatively different from the past and the present, in which you ask yourself, "What can I learn? How can I do things differently?"

OUTCOME: Ask yourself, "What do I want in this situation?" If you still want the same outcome, move it into the future.

DISSOCIATION: Seeing and hearing yourself in a memory, in the present, or in a future possibility. Then ask yourself, "What can I learn? How can I do things differently in the future?"

CHUNKING: Organizing information and thinking into large categories (generalizations) or smaller specifics (details).

TRANSFORMING FAILURE INTO FEEDBACK: Chunk up to your outcome and chunk down from there into smaller specific pieces of information. You can learn from your failure what to change the next time and how to fine-tune and overhaul your outcome.

◆

CHUNKING EXERCISE I

1. Pick a word, something concrete, an object in your environment: chair, car, book, television, plant. Write it down in the center of a piece of paper.

2. Chunk up from the original word, find the larger category it belongs to. Write this above your first word.
   Ask yourself: What large category is (chair) a part of?

3. Chunk laterally. Think of other words that belong in the same larger category as the word you first thought of. Write these on the same line as that word.
   Ask yourself: What else is similar to this (chair)?
   Keep in mind that your examples here must also fit into the larger category of which chair is a part—e.g., "furniture."

4. Chunk down. Below the word you first thought of, write down the finer distinctions or subdivisions (details, specifics) of that word.

Ask yourself: Which specific (chair); what type of (chair)?

Make diagrams. It's fun, it shows you the kind of categories you're in the habit of making, and it limbers up the mind!

◆

CHUNKING EXERCISE II

1. Think of something you want to accomplish or change.

2. Chunk up. Ask yourself: What will this do for me? What will accomplishing/changing this mean in my life? (This puts your outcome within a larger frame, adding perspective and broader meaning.)

3. Chunk laterally. Ask yourself: What else in my life is like this? What else have I accomplished that was similar to this?

4. Chunk down. Ask yourself: What can I do first? What resource can I use? (Most steps of the blueprint for success are examples of chunking down.)

◆ ◆ ◆

THE LITTLE KITTEN

There was once a little kitten named Squirt who lost her entire family when she was only a couple of weeks old. She grew up by herself in a large barn where there were several big old tough tomcats. They treated little Squirt as a nui-

sance and beat her up whenever she approached them. Squirt became terrified of these cats and avoided them as much as she could. Eventually she got older and stronger and moved on to other barns and other places. She caught enough food for herself to eat and her life was all right except that she was very lonely. She couldn't find anyone to play with or talk to. There weren't many little kittens around, and whenever she saw one it was protected by big cats, and Squirt was terrified whenever she saw a big cat. That meant she couldn't play or talk to any cats at all, and the other animals were different from her and she couldn't speak their language or feel close to them.

One day she was exploring a barn that had lots of furniture in it and she came upon a big sheet of something shiny that stood propped upright against the side of the barn. As she approached this shiny thing she saw a very large cat coming toward her—and, as always, she got very frightened and ran away. This time seemed different, however—she couldn't hear or smell another cat—so she again approached this interesting object, and again she saw this large cat and ran away. This maneuver was repeated several times until Squirt's curiosity led her to practically touch noses with this strange, very large cat. She began to hiss and so did the stranger; when she stopped, so did the other. Squirt sat there, extremely puzzled, until a little black-and-white kitten came by and ran up to the shiny object—and Squirt saw there was another kitten who looked just like the first one. Whatever the kitten did the other kitten did also, and whatever Squirt did the big stranger did.

Suddenly Squirt knew: That was herself! That big cat was Squirt! She looked at herself and saw how big she was and suddenly the thought came to her that if she was a big cat herself, maybe there were other big cats some-

where who would play with her and talk to her—and if they were mean she was big enough to take care of herself now. Squirt went off and found lots of friends and was never lonely again.

❖ ❖ ❖

PART FIVE

The Map Is Not the Territory

34

Patterns of Language

Language is not experience,
but language can create experience.

Language is the code by which we enter thoughts, memories, and imagination, enabling us to leap through time and space, move backward and forward, go to places we've never been and times that never were. It's part of our vision, how we shape experience so we can both keep it and share it. Language is an essential part of what makes us human.

Whatever language we use, whether Tutsi or Sanskrit, whether by tongue and larynx or fingers and facial muscles, as readers or writers, speakers or signers, we depend on language for thought and communication with ourselves and others.

Language is a communication code for all humans, no matter what language an individual speaks. Languages are the specific instances: Chinese and Swahili and Finnish and any of the thousands of other systems of putting together words and syntax.

And then we have *Words*, the carriers of language, the specific units of expression. Words represent experience, but they are not themselves experience.

Language as a whole is a representation of experience, but it is not the experience itself. In this way, language is like a map. A map represents territory: the state or region, the city, county, borough, neighborhood, even a single street (a map can be a large chunk or small chunk). A map tells you where to turn or how far one place is from another. It can be detailed enough to show every stream, every alley, every house in the area. But basically the map is one thing, the part of the world it represents is another. A map is the lines and sometimes colors drawn or printed on a piece of paper. The place itself is vast (by comparison) and filled with sounds and sights, with movement, houses, hills, rivers, garbage dumps, seagulls, restaurants, parking lots, schools, fire hydrants—whatever. The map is not the territory, and yet we need the map to know where we're going.

"The map is not the territory" is an NLP presupposition that's taken from Noam Chomsky, whose transformational grammar revolutionized our view of language as a representation of how the brain works.

A similar statement would be "The menu is not the meal." As any dieter can tell you, you don't get fat eating the words on the menu, even if the descriptions of the food are luscious, even if you have a picture accompanying each menu selection. You can taste it in your mind, maybe, and your mouth is watering, but it's not the same. It's not the real thing. Food has smells and flavors and colors and textures; a menu has designations, labels, or descriptions of the dishes offered.

Language is a representation of experience, as the menu is a representation of the meal, the map is a representation of a place, and a portrait (photograph) is a representation of a person.

Language is not experience.

What's important about this in terms of learning to communicate better with ourselves and others is recognizing that people assign different meanings to words because of their different experiences. An experience may be universal—love, motherhood, anger, war—but each of us has private memories and meanings. Referring to *love* or *mother* can bring on very different associations in different people. Each of these words could have hundreds of meanings, in all the shades of individual definitions. How can I communicate *my* experience to *you*?

"I hate milk" and "I hate foreigners" might look like similar utterances, but below the surface they are leagues apart. The only way we can understand the difference is by knowing the specific experience of hate.

"We are the world" and "We think the world of you"—the way we can understand the difference between those two sentences is in recognizing what each speaker means by "world."

A person cannot *literally* convey experience to another. We use language, with all its possibilities and constraints, to convey an impression of what we mean. The map is not Texas but it is a representation of Texas, containing certain details and omitting others, according to how the particular map is devised (a road map, a topographical map, a map of air routes).

Language is not experience; however, language can create experience.

A map can show where something is hidden or reveal how things are connected, what lies near what, how to get from here to there. This chapter is about "reading" linguistic patterns (the map) and discovering what kind of questions we need to ask to uncover more about the individual experience or meaning (the territory).

These questions take us beneath the words or patterns of words to get at the actual experience of another person or to better convey our own, so that we can communicate more clearly, have a better understanding of what the other person means, and make sure that our own message carries the meaning we intend.

In Part I, The Meaning of Your Communication Is the Response You Get, we discussed the interaction between the sender and the receiver of a message: how to get your message across by paying close attention to the response and then using it as information to vary the way you're sending your message. It's about communication as a cybernetic loop.

Here we're talking specifically about patterns of words. This is not about the type of sensory language a person is using; it's about the word patterns of everyday speech that often send out misinformation or incomplete information, though the speaker (and sometimes the listener too) may not be aware of it. For instance, if I'm having an ice cream cone on a warm June day and I tell you, "I like it," I might be sure of what I mean by "it," and I'm assuming you know what I mean, that you're thinking of the same "it" I'm thinking of.

But in fact, I may have been thinking of the flavor of the ice cream, and my "it" referred to pistachio. You answer "So do I," but what you're thinking of is the warm weather. "It," an unspecified pronoun, is part of a common word pattern that can lead to confused communication.

The word patterns we'll be talking about in this chapter are easily identified aspects of common speech that carry with them an assumption that you know what I'm saying—though in fact I can't know what you're saying without knowing what you're thinking, what's on your mind. To do that, I have to ask you specific questions.

When I say, "I like it," and you answer, "So do I," no real communication has taken place. Instead, it's a kind of fairy communication: the words are there, the dialogue switches from one to the other, but nothing of any substance or meaning has been said.

However, if when I say, "I like it," you challenge me with a question—"What (specifically) do you like?"—and I tell you it's the flavor of the ice cream, you can now give me actual information back ("I like it too"; "I prefer chocolate"; or "I was thinking of the weather, how much I like the heat.") Now we can have a dialogue, exchange views and information, reassure each other of our similarities or simply that we're friends, interested in everything about each other. Bonding, or rapport, depends on clear communication, understanding what the other one means, what each is referring to. And clear communication depends on rapport, which is a sense of mutual understanding.

In order to get from words to meaning, we need to ask questions. Knowing which questions to ask for which kind of word pattern is like knowing how to ask directions for where you're going.

Usually, when we know we're lost, we can ask specifically, "Which is the way to X?" or "How do I get back on the highway?" or "How many miles to the nearest gas station?" The questions are determined by the need for precise answers.

When we're lost in a conversation or a communication, we're often not aware of how we wandered off, and we don't know how, specifically, to set about finding the way back to meaning. This can happen when we're talking or reading; we need to translate from the words and word patterns in front of us back to the meaning that was intended by the speaker or writer.

In order to map the territory, learn to read between the lines or simply to recognize that we sometimes don't understand what's being said, we need special tools in the form of questions.

Do *you* know what you're saying? Do *I* know what you're saying? Do you know that I know? And how do we find out?

By asking questions.

35

Linguistic Patterns

"When *I* use a word," Humpty Dumpty said in a
rather scornful tone, "it means just what I choose it
to mean—neither more nor less."

—Lewis Carroll
Through the Looking Glass

What's the connection between language and meaning?

Let's take a look at how language—all language, any
language—is basically structured. There are three levels.

First we have what is called the surface structure. This
simply refers to the words people use, the actual words that
are spoken or written. What I'm saying here, the words
you're reading, is the surface structure: "The train was
late."

The next level is deep structure. Deep structure provides
the details of what happened—to whom, when, where,
how: "The train pulled out of the station at 4:42 and remained on schedule for 11 minutes, when somebody pulled
the emergency cord, which brought the train to an almost
instantaneous stop just 500 yards outside Bellrose station,
where it remained for the better part of half an hour while
the cars and tracks were being checked, until we finally
started moving again, arriving in Redbrook, which is my
station, too late for me to get to the movie."

Beneath that is what we call the reference structure,

which is the actual experience itself, the sensory experience of the train ride.

If reference structure is the *actual* experience (through the senses), deep structure might be called the *virtual* experience (through language).

The surface structure simply informs us that something happened. This is the level of everyday conversation, the world of habitual phrases, ordinary sentences: the words people use to do their jobs, buy their food, get their bus passes and subway tokens, ask directions, and talk about themselves.

This is the level on which we communicate, almost all of us, almost all of the time. That's because we would never communicate anything if we had to fully describe everything about our experience every time we opened our mouths.

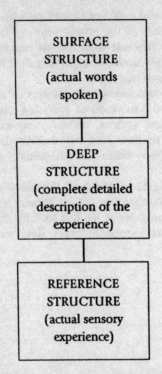

As an example, let's take a simple three-word sentence: "Joan hurt me." That's the surface structure. The deep structure might be: "When Joan, my oldest sister, was cooking a turkey on Thanksgiving morning she took a pan of boiling water off the stove, and as she was carrying it over to the counter, she slipped and some of the hot water splashed on me, over the back of my hand and halfway up my arm, and it burned terribly and left a red, scalding mark."

Or it could be: "Joan is like my best friend, and she was at this party on Valentine's Day, and when she saw me come in, she just sort of smiled lukewarmly and didn't introduce me to any of the people she was with. And then she sort of walked away from me, and she really hurt my feelings a lot. She made me feel really rejected, that she'd sort of given up on me."

Can you imagine communicating regularly on the level of deep structure? If we didn't fall asleep listening, we'd probably wear out our jaws talking.

Now look back on the full descriptions of "Joan hurt me." In the first instance, it was by burning the speaker's arm, in the second by snubbing her at a party. When the examples came up in a workshop I was giving, one of the students challenged the first statement. "That isn't accurate," she said. "Joan didn't hurt her, it was the boiling water. It's obvious Joan didn't mean to."

Others disagreed. "Joan hurt me" made absolute sense, they said. You can hurt someone even if you don't intend to. The statement didn't refer to intention, it referred to the burn.

"The burn," argued the first student, "was caused by boiling water, not by Joan."

What happened was that each person had a different experience and understanding of the word "hurt." Think about it a moment. What's *your* definition of "hurt"?

Most people would agree that it means "to cause pain." After all, words do have a generalized meaning we can usually agree on. Otherwise there would be no dictionaries and we'd all turn into Humpty-Dumptys, speaking our own language that nobody else could understand.

Understanding: How would you define it?

To one of us *understanding* means compassion, the ability to empathize with another person. To the other it means clarity of vision, being able to see things clearly and notice their interrelatedness.

Under ordinary circumstances, you and I can use the

word "understanding" back and forth, and our personal definitions (one kinesthetic, the other visual) are close enough so that it's not going to cause a problem.

However, under stressful circumstances, whether professionally (where it might be crucial to the success of an undertaking to figure out *exactly* what's meant) or emotionally (where people are having trouble with their relationship anyway), if we both use the same word but are talking about very different experiences, it can mean the end of communication. Like ships passing in the night or, even worse, ships colliding in darkness.

Or take *love*. That word can also touch off an explosion. What do *you* mean by it? What do I? Your private definition of love is going to be based on your personal experience, and the same goes for me.

The meaning of words is connected to experience, which is different for each person. Sometimes it seems a miracle that we can communicate at all. We use words all the time, and eight times out of ten our personal experiences are similar enough that we know or can identify with what the other is saying. If you tell me you love Corduroy, your cat, and I don't like cats of any kind, I'm even allergic to them, I still know what you're talking about.

Words have no meaning by themselves. The map is not the territory. Language is not experience. Words are just words. Words acquire meaning because they are associated with and descriptive of experiences you've had or I've had and they connect our individual meanings in a definition common to us both.

◆

WORD GAME I

1. Write down your definitions of: hurt, smart, beauty.

2. Ask at least three different people to define these words—ask them to describe their understanding of these words.

◆

WORD GAME II

1. Write down your understanding of: respect.

2. Ask three or more other people what their understanding of the word is. Write down the definitions. Just write them down, don't judge.

3. Look at the definitions. Compare them. How are they different? How are they similar? Can you predict where there might be conflict between these definitions in a stressful situation?

◆

36

Language Patterns:
The Metamodel

Language enables us to make distinctions. We do this by labeling, calling things by a certain name (animal, success, food, beautiful). The labels help us to create categories and to keep order in our thoughts and memory.

Because our conscious minds are limited in the amount of information we can be aware of at any one time, we create habitual patterns, sequences of behavior that are repeated predictably. This lets us do most of what we have to do without "thinking." With language, it's the words we use habitually that form the patterns. We can't think through everything consciously each time we speak, so we condense concepts into the shorthand of word patterns.

By recognizing linguistic patterns, we can discover what questions to ask to get to the experience underlying the words. We go *through* the language to reveal the meaning.

We're going to look at five basic language patterns, part of what NLP calls the metamodel. Each pattern has specific questions attached to it, questions that challenge the underlying assumptions and clarify your communication. This means you get a clearer understanding of what the other person is saying; it also helps you define more precisely what you yourself are trying to say.

When I talk about *love* or *understanding* or *relationship*, I'm so used to these words that they've become disconnected from my experience. By asking myself very specific questions, I can begin to reconnect with my actual experience of a word.

Think of language as a code. It's up to you to break through the code and get to the important message or secret cache. *Metamodel* refers to a set of linguistic tools that help you crack the code (*language*) and get to the importance or richness of the experience (*meaning*) that the words represent.

The five patterns of the metamodel that we'll be discussing refer specifically to certain kinds of word groupings, patterns derived from Chomsky and modern linguistics.

1. The first pattern is *unspecified nouns and pronouns*. This simply means that the noun or pronoun isn't specific. You don't know who, what, or which is meant. Unspecified words are "fat" in the sense we talked about in chapter 24, meaning words that are not well-defined, not specific enough.

   "My relatives are driving me crazy." The noun here is "relatives." It's not very specific—unless the speaker has only two relatives. Do we know *who* is driving this person crazy? Does she mean *all* her relatives? Probably not.

   "Where does this go, honey?" What "this"? Honey's in her study, hubby's in the kitchen. Does he think she can see through walls? *This* is an unspecified pronoun.

   "I don't like them." This statement is perfectly clear if somebody's pointing to a bowl of Brussels sprouts while saying it. But if your child comes home from school complaining, "I don't like them, Ma,"

you'll have to find out who "them" are. *Them* is another unspecified pronoun.

"I don't like my teachers," he elaborates. But
which teachers? Who, specifically?

The trap we all fall into is assuming we *know* who
(which one) the person is talking about. Often it's not
critical to communication; however, when it is, we
need to be aware that we *don't* know and we have to
bring out our tools, the specific questions, that will
crack the code, go beneath the pattern, and discover
the intended meaning.

The pattern of unspecified nouns and pronouns
takes the question: "Who, what, which, specifically?"

A gentle warning: When you use the word "specifically" in a question, ask it with a pleasant tonality
and expression. Otherwise, people may feel you're
giving them the third degree and will get annoyed at
you instead of giving you the information.

2. The second pattern is *unspecified verbs.*

We distinguish between nouns and verbs because
they refer to different patterns of language and thinking. A noun describes a static event; a verb describes
a dynamic process.

In order to make them specific—to find out what
the speaker means, coming from his or her outlook or
preconceptions about the world—we ask definitive
questions. With nouns or pronouns the question is
who, what, or which, specifically? With verbs, it's:
"How, specifically?"

Remember the simple statement we used in chapter
35, "Joan hurt me"? It took a long time unraveling.
Hurt is the verb, the process. It looks small but, as
we discovered, it can be "fat" inside. What I mean

by *hurt* and what you mean can be very different. Does hurting have to be intentional? Can it be emotional as well as physical? What we have to ask is "How, specifically, did she hurt you?" to get the information we need.

When it becomes crucial in a situation (professional or emotional) to define a word precisely, you better make sure you know what the other person means. With verbs, which refer to a process and are ongoing, you have to keep checking to make sure you're both talking about the same thing. Even the word *stop* is a process, as in: "I've got to *stop* having this kind of relationship." But how, specifically, do you "stop"? How do you experience "stop"? How do you *do* "stop"?

Remember: *What?* leads to information about nouns and pronouns. *How?* tends to directionalize the person's thinking toward the process, which is ongoing, dynamic, and changing.

3. The third pattern is *nominalizations*.

These are probably the most fascinating of all the linguistic patterns—a bit complex, but worth it.

In the English language we have words that we treat as nouns—like *relationship*.

"My relationship is deteriorating": "relationship" is the *subject* of this sentence.

"I want to get out of this relationship": "relationship is the *object* of this sentence.

Traditional grammar says that the subject or object of a sentence is always a noun or a pronoun. So here, relationship is treated like a noun.

Trouble is, it *isn't* a noun, not behaviorally, at any rate. Relationship is a process. It comes from the word *relate*, and *relate* is a verb. It moves, it's ongoing. It's

not a noun like "lamp" or "bedroom" ("my lamp
is deteriorating"? "I want to get out of this bedroom"?).

Or take: "I have trouble making decisions." "I"
is the subject, "making" is the verb, and "decisions"
is the object of that sentence, which makes it, grammatically, a noun. But it isn't one, not like "popovers" in the sentence, "I have trouble making
popovers."

The problem is that these types of words—*relationship, decision*—are grammatically treated as
nouns. But behaviorally they are verbs. They represent a process. Each of them comes from a root verb,
an ongoing process, not a finished event.

In the sentence "My relationship is deteriorating,"
relationship is treated like a thing, a noun, something
that's complete, finished. As such I have no control
over it. It exists independently of me; I don't have
any responsibility there. I can put *relationship* up on
a wall, where I can admire it or throw darts at it.

What I have to do to get out of this nominalization
is to change the word back from a noun to a verb,
transform it into a process, something I can *do* something about. The question here is, "How, specifically,
do you (do I) relate?"

Transforming something that's fixed into an ongoing process means becoming involved in it. "I can't
get no satisfaction"—until I figure out how, specifically, I get to be satisfied. What do I do? I have to
take an active role; only at that point do I become
part of the process, which means I can change it. How
do I (could I) experience "satisfy"? I take responsibility and gain control.

Certain word endings often are clues to a nominalization. These include:

-ance (grievance)	-ness (happiness)
-ing (loving)	-iency (leniency)
-itude (ineptitude)	-ful (hurtful)
-ment (fulfillment)	-ship (friendship)
-ity (capability)	-ence (indulgence)
-able (achievable)	-ion (decision)

And then there's "-tion" (attention), as in "I want more attention from you." Now, anyone who speaks English knows what that means, right?

Maybe.

Let's say someone you care a lot about says that to you, and you resolve to do something about it. All week long you do everything you can to show you care. You ask questions about how the day went, you work up an interest in anything and everything he or she is doing, you share news and gossip, you watch TV together, you even buy flowers—and at the end of the week, the person says to you, "How come you never pay attention to me? I thought we'd agreed."

"Never pay attention? What are you talking about? I've been paying attention to you all this time." And knocking yourself out, you feel; it's just not fair.

But then you hear: "How many times in the past week did you touch me? Did you hug me even once when I came home from the office? When was the last time we held hands?"

So that's what it was about! "Why couldn't you say so?" you ask.

"I *did!*"

Or this: The student asks the teacher, "Why did you give me such a low grade?"

"Because you don't pay attention."

"What do you mean? I take notes, I write down everything you say."

"But you never look at me when I'm speaking."
Or it could go this way:

Student: Why did you give me such a low grade?

Teacher: Because you don't pay attention.

Student: But I'm always looking at you.

Teacher: But you don't respond. You don't ask questions.

This is nominalization: sounds like a noun, behaves like a process. You want attention? Tell me *how* you want me to attend to you.

Besides word endings, two tests can tell you if a word is a nominalization or a true noun, the "wheelbarrow" test and the "ongoing" test.

First, does this word fit in a wheelbarrow? It doesn't matter how big the wheelbarrow would have to be, if the thing being described could fit into one, it's a true noun, not a nominalization. "House" fits in a wheelbarrow; "mountain" fits in a wheelbarrow—albeit a very large one. "Relationship" doesn't fit in a wheelbarrow. "Decision" doesn't fit. If it doesn't fit in a wheelbarrow, it's a nominalization.

Second, if you can put the word "ongoing" in front of the word and it makes sense, the word is probably a nominalization. (You have an ongoing relationship but not an ongoing lamp.)

4. The fourth pattern is *polarity words*.

Polarity words represent one extreme or another, the polarities: all, none; everybody, nobody; always, never.

When people think in absolutes—right/wrong, good/bad—they're limiting the possibilities of choice. This is polar thinking, and we will be talking about it in Part VII. A strong signal that someone is doing polar thinking is the use of one of these words or phrases: "All or nothing." "I never understand what's going on in class." "Everything is up for grabs." "Nobody cares one way or the other."

There are two ways to respond to the patterns of polarity words. The first is by exaggeration:

"My friends never invite me to their parties." The polarity word is "never." If you extract this word from the sentence and exaggerate it—simply repeat the word as a question and put a lot of emphasis on it—you'll probably surprise the speaker. Chances are, the person using "never" didn't realize it and, as you soon discover, didn't actually mean it.

You repeat: *"Never?"*

"Well . . ."

"Never, *ever?*"

(Silence, thinking.)

"They've never, ever, asked you to *any* party?"

"Well, a couple of times . . ."

You've broken that pattern. You've brought the person down from the extreme position and provided an opportunity for choice.

"I always screw up when the big boss asks me to do something."

"Always? You screw up *every single time?*" You can add even more polarity words and exaggerate through your tonality. You *must* exaggerate; it doesn't work otherwise. If you repeat in a normal tone of voice, "So you always screw up?" the response will be "Yes." These speakers probably don't even hear their polarity words.

"I can't go to that party, I have nothing to wear—everyone's in Armani."

Sure thing. "*Everybody's* in designer clothes? *Every single body? Every last person?*"

"Well, a lot of people—"

"And you have *nothing* to wear. *Not one thing, nothing.*"

"Not a thing—unless I just throw together some kind of outfit . . ." The "unless" means you've bumped her from the absolutes, the polarity words.

The second response to the pattern of polarity words is by counter example: finding the exception to what seems an absolute rule. Instead of exaggerating, you ask, "Has anyone, ever, come to one of these parties who wasn't wearing designer clothes?"

Or, to the person who says, "I always screw up when the big boss asks me to do something," you respond, "Has there *ever* been a time when you didn't?" You want to get the counter example so they can't hold on to the extreme.

"It *always* rains when I go to the hairdresser."

"Right," you say. "But think back: has there ever been a time when it didn't?"

5. The fifth pattern is *mind reading*.

The other four patterns have focused on particular types of words: nouns and verbs that aren't specified, nominalizations, and polarity words. Mind reading is different, in that it's not so much a particular type of word or phrase as it is a way of thinking, a certain assumption. Mind reading is when I assume that I know something about you, about what's going on with you, although I don't have any concrete external evidence. Or it's when I assume that somebody else should know what's going on with me, even though

I haven't given them any kind of solid information.

We do it every day. A wife gives her husband a fiftieth birthday present. He thanks her in a half-hearted way and finally admits he was expecting something else—the Rolex he'd always wanted.

She's startled. He was expecting a Rolex from her?

Of course, he says, she certainly knows him well enough by now, how long he's wanted one. She should have known.

He's assuming that his wife is reading his mind. He never actually told her he wanted a Rolex.

Or this: I'm talking to a class and there's a student sitting in the first row who's looking at me and frowning. His eyes are narrowing, the eyebrows are pinching together, vertical lines sprouting up between them, horizontal lines deepening across his forehead. I'm thinking, Oh, God, he doesn't understand a word I'm talking about. What am I doing wrong? How can I get him to understand the material?

I'm mind reading. I'm assuming the changes in his facial expression that I'm calibrating mean he doesn't understand. But then he says something brilliant, and I realize he's been concentrating very hard and following me precisely.

People do this all the time; they assume they know what someone else is thinking even though they don't have any specific evidence.

Someone hasn't called for a few days.

Oh, my God, you're thinking. What did I do? He must be angry with me. But I haven't *done* anything he could be angry about. What's the matter with him anyway? The hell with him!

And then it turns out the person's been ill, and you wish that instead of having been offended (through mind reading), you'd called to find out what was going on.

Or what about this scenario?

She: You turn down the light as soon as you come in the door because all you think about is bed.

He: Bed? What bed? I have an infection in my eye.

Or:

She: You didn't like my cooking. You didn't have more than one serving, and you didn't even finish that.

He: That's because my stomach hasn't felt right since I came down with the flu. Your cooking's wonderful. I love it.

Or play it this way:

She: You didn't like my cooking.

He: How can you say that! I had three helpings!

She: But you didn't say anything.

Mind reading and polarity words can go together. ''You never want to do anything on Sunday,'' because you wanted to stay home and work last weekend. People assume you're going to do things in the same way you've done them in the past.

Usually, mind reading interferes with communication. It can also be destructive. If someone tells herself, ''There's no point trying out for that job; they'll think I'm too stupid [or inexperienced or young],'' her mind reading is probably costing her a job.

"You wouldn't understand this, it's too technical."

"You wouldn't like this, it's not your sort of thing."

All these are mind reads. The question to ask when you hear this kind of assumption is, "How, specifically, do you know?"

How, specifically, do you know that the people interviewing you will think you're stupid?

How, specifically, do you know I wouldn't understand [like] this?

The question is the challenge; it breaks down the rigid categories and lets in other possibilities. And once you start challenging your assumptions, you free yourself from the prison of your own thought.

Just a little aside: Mind reading can also come in the form of intuition. And sometimes it's accurate. Intuitive thinking is one of the most creative processes of the mind. But it's important to know that you *are* mind reading and that you don't actually *know* this is true. As long as you remind yourself that this is your intuition, which may or may not be accurate, you can go on to make creative guesses.

A modern form of mind read is the messages people leave on telephone answering machines: *You're probably still asleep and that's why you're not answering the phone,* or, *Yesterday you said you were sick and now there's no answer, so I guess you're out on the town.*

Meanwhile, the machine's owner is sitting in the doctor's office, feeling absolutely rotten, or some emergency has forced her to rush out.

For that reason, you might want to curb your first impulse the next time you're leaving a message. Just think how infuriating it is when you have to listen to someone's assumptions about you—particularly if they're dead wrong!

Unspecified nouns, unspecified verbs, nominalizations, polarity words, and mind reading: These five linguistic patterns are a trap we fall into regularly. They're dead ends. The questions we use to challenge the patterns are ways to get out of the trap and gain a clearer view of what we or someone else is saying.

These are questions that simply directionalize our thinking, whether we're speaking the words or listening to them. The questions lead us beneath the surface structure of words to connect with the deep structure—the details, the specifics—and with the experience itself.

If you use polarity words or mind reads—"Nobody would hire me"; "You're going to be bored by what I tell you"—you may find that you begin to believe what you're telling yourself.

The map is not the territory, and language isn't experience. But language can *create* experience. What you say becomes what you mean, not the other way around. Your words become your message; the map becomes the territory; the menu is the meal.

When you metamodel yourself or the other person, you ask the specific questions that lead you to the deeper message, the meaning underneath the words. You see through the surface into the depths. Language, which is a representation of experience, becomes the looking glass through which you enter it.

Here are two examples of the use or misuse of language.

Libby is Marsha's boss in an advertising agency. Their department is responsible for the presentation of creative ideas to their clients.

Libby: *Boy, are they driving me crazy! Every time I see them, something else is wrong with that project.*

Marsha: I know what you mean. They really don't know what they want. All they know is it should have excitement and be innovative.

Libby: Well, we'll have to give it to them—even though I don't think we'll ever satisfy them. Get to work on that last draft, and please put some excitement into it.

Marsha: OK, I got it! Excitement, excitement! I know just what you want.

Libby and Marsha have used a lot of fat words—unspecified words and nominalizations—and they've assumed they know what the other is talking about. Maybe they do, maybe they don't. However, in the high-pressure world of advertising, can they afford to misunderstand, to "miscommunicate"? Missed communication can mean missed opportunities. They could be talking about two different clients or two different projects. They could be miscalculating what their clients mean by "innovative" or "excitement"—or what the other means by these words. They're also limiting their ability to communicate by the use of polarity words, like *ever, never, every time*. These create an extreme position without options.

Here, a father and son are talking about the son applying to college:

Father: How are the applications going? Let's see what you've done.

Son: Well, I'm confused by them. They're depressing.

Father: Yeah, well, you give up too easily. You've got to have perseverance.

Son: *That's what you always say. You never listen to me.*

Father: *How come you don't want me to help you? Other kids let parents help.*

Son: *You can't help me! Forget it!*

The father and son are getting into a very typical misunderstanding. The father really wants to help, and the son wants his help, but there's a breakdown of communication.

The father assumes the son is having trouble with his applications. But this assumption may not be true. The father misses an opportunity to learn what the son means by "confused" and "depressing." He mind reads that his son gives up easily; this upsets the son, who then responds with the extreme position that his father never listens to him. This leads to more mind reading on the father's part about the son not wanting to accept help from him. Both of them are using the word "help"—a verb, a process word—without knowing what the other exactly means by it. And so there arises another misunderstanding, which creates hurt feelings. It is a missed communication, a lost opportunity for mutually satisfying interaction.

METAMODEL RECAP

These are five of the linguistic patterns that make up the metamodel, along with the questions to be used in challenging them.

PATTERN	CHALLENGE
1. UNSPECIFIED NOUNS AND PRONOUNS	
People are strange. *They* are ripe.	Who, what, which specifically?
2. UNSPECIFIED VERBS	
He's *doing* it wrong.	How, specifically?
3. NOMINALIZATIONS	
I have trouble making *decisions*.	How, specifically, do you [decide]?
4. POLARITY WORDS	
Always, never, none, all.	Exaggerate: Always? Nobody? Ask for an exception: Was there a time when . . . ?
5. MIND READING	
You don't understand me.	How do you know [I don't understand . . .]?

These linguistic patterns are metamodel violations: words and patterns of words that obscure the meaning of the communication. To understand what the speaker is trying to say, the listener asks precise questions that guide the speaker toward exact meaning. You can do this with yourself as well as with another person.

◆ ◆ ◆

THE MONKS' DIALOGUE

*Provided he makes and wins an argument about Buddhism
with those who live there, any wandering monk can remain
in a Zen temple. If he is defeated, he has to move on.*

*In a temple in the northern part of Japan, two brother
monks were dwelling together. The elder one was learned,
but the younger one was stupid and had only a single eye.*

*A wandering monk came and asked for lodging, properly
challenging them to a debate about the sublime teaching.
The elder brother, tired that day from much studying, told
the younger one to take his place. "Go and request the
dialogue in silence," he cautioned.*

*So the young monk and the stranger went to the shrine
and sat down.*

*Shortly afterward the traveler rose and went in to the
elder brother and said, "Your young brother is a wonderful
fellow. He defeated me."*

The older monk asked what had happened.

*"Well," explained the traveler, "first I held up one fin-
ger, representing Buddha, the Enlightened One. So he held
up two fingers, signifying Buddha and his teaching. I held
up three fingers, representing Buddha, his teaching, and
his followers, living the harmonious life. Then he shook his
clenched fist in my face, indicating that all three come from
one realization. Thus he won, and so I have no right to
remain here."*

With this, the traveler left.

*"Where is that fellow?" asked the younger one, running
in to his elder brother.*

"I understand you won the debate."

"Won, nothing. I'm going to beat him up."

"Tell me the subject of the debate," said the elder one.

"Why, the moment he saw me he held up one finger, insulting me by insinuating that I have only one eye. Since he was a stranger I thought I would be polite to him, so I held up two fingers, congratulating him that he has two eyes. Then the impolite wretch held up three fingers, suggesting that between us we have only three eyes. So I got mad and started to punch him, but he ran out, and that ended it."

◆ ◆ ◆

PART SIX

*There Is a Positive Intention Behind
Every Behavior*

37

Behavior

> Complicated? Not really. [I'm] just a lot of simple
> selves.
>
> —F. Scott Fitzgerald
> *Tender Is the Night*

Everything we do, from building roads to making pictures
in our head, is a form of behavior. Every act, every gesture—speaking, listening, talking to ourselves or to others—
are all behaviors. Though we sometimes force the word
"behavior" into narrow straits of meaning—as in "being
on your best behavior," "well-behaved," "such behavior!"—the broader definition includes all our actions,
movements, and words, whether private or public, internal
or external. Behavior is the expression of who you are by
what you do.

Human behavior, like animal behavior, reveals the nature
of the species. It doesn't have to be conscious. Dreaming
is part of behavior. So is focusing one's attention on something.

When a cat sits absolutely still, completely focused on a
stirring somewhere on the ground or behind an armchair,
it's obvious to us that the cat is getting ready to pounce.
The cat is exhibiting its hunting behavior.

Does the cat know what it's doing? Probably not, at least
not in our terms. The cat isn't thinking, Here I am, getting

ready to catch that mouse hiding behind the chair. The cat is directing all its attention—hearing, seeing, smelling—on one specific area.

That's cat behavior. When we pay close attention to something—a drama we're watching on TV or on the stage, a difficult maneuver down a ski slope, changing diapers on a squirming infant—we direct all our senses toward a focal point without thinking about it.

As we've talked about earlier, the constraints on our limited conscious mind mean that most of what we do is automatic. That applies to behavior. Most of our behavior is not under our conscious control.

This is very important to remember, since our usual use of the word "behavior" is invariably about things we do consciously, or at least things we do that can be consciously adjusted. I'm referring in particular to the sort of behaviors that people advise you to change or give up in your life: the way you eat (diet), the habits you have, the dependencies or addictions you're advised to get rid of.

In fact, labeling certain behaviors as "bad" or "wrong" is counterproductive if what you want is to get rid of them. Drinking too much alcohol, smoking cigarettes, eating red meat, lying in the sun—all these behaviors or habits or dependencies are carried out unconsciously for the most part.

Your behavior is what you do and an expression of who you are. To change a behavior you first have to recognize it and then label it. As we discussed in chapter 14, first you identify and then you label whatever it is you're bringing up to consciousness in order to have control over it.

Behavior that's unconscious to you is often obvious to someone else. Most of us have had the experience of seeing ourselves through the eyes of another person or hearing ourselves, as when somebody pretends to be you by imitating your manner of speaking. You listen in amazement, wondering, Do I really sound like that?

Somebody makes a gesture that's typical of you, draws a caricature, walks like you, drinks coffee the way you would, and you're astonished to discover there's something about you so obvious that everyone seems to know it's there—except for you. It's not that you don't recognize this trait; you just never really thought about it before.

A teacher tells you to stop daydreaming. Your friend tells you to stop biting your nails. Your mother says she can't stand hearing you gnash your teeth. Your boyfriend asks if you always have to drive through city traffic as though you're in the Indy 500.

"Who, me?"

You. One of you, anyway. One of the dozens or hundreds of parts of you that work together to keep the unique, complicated individual that you are going. The part of you that gnashes your teeth isn't the same part that thinks up those funny one-liners for your clients at the agency, but it's just possible that the two parts have a lot in common. After all, they're both parts of the same enterprise, *you*, and to keep you going the gnasher might be defusing some of the pressure from the comedian, so the creative juices can continue to flow without interference.

Yo! You there, come out of the clouds!

"Who, me?"

What were you doing while I was talking to you/while the clients were waiting/while the radio announcer gave the phone number for the information you've been wanting to get? Where were you for that instant while we all waited to hear your answer about how the check should be divided/where our next meeting would be held/how the tickets to the rock concert should be distributed?

Maybe you were breaking a deadlock among the alternatives; instead of having to be limited to the choice of A or B, your creative self was playing with new possibilities. The part of you in the clouds was removing yourself from the controversy in the room, trying out other alternatives and now coming back with a brand-new prospect that everyone thinks is the perfect choice.

You weren't aware of it. You were not consciously trying out the different possibilities in your mind, though you were doing it nonetheless. The creative process that yields scientific discoveries and works of art depends on unconscious behavior of this kind. And all of us have a creative part that can come to our assistance whenever we need it.

We can summon it up without being aware of it. Sometimes if the right hand doesn't know what the left is doing, it's because each is doing its own particular job in order to get the work done. Different parts of ourselves may all be working on the same project, but the right hand/left hand division means that one part is busy keeping away the interference so the other part or parts can do the work. Parts will work together in the person's interest, even if they're unaware that the other parts exist.

And the person may not realize that each part is trying to contribute to the whole, that a part may be valuable either for its own sake or for the sake of the combined effort. But if you want to change behavior, to get rid of a part you don't like, you first have to understand why it's there and what it's doing for your benefit.

38

Parts

> Parts of people's psyche detach themselves from
> consciousness and lead an autonomous life of their
> own.
>
> —Carl Jung

The concept of "parts" has been around for a long time.
Dramatists have used it in the form of ghosts, former selves,
conscience, and other figures on the stage. Religion talks
about the parts of a person in the contest between good and
evil, innocence and experience. Psychology has been naming parts or divisions of personality certainly since Freud,
using a variety of terms.

Some psychologists have called parts "subpersonali-
ties." Freud spoke about the different "actors" in people.
Carl Jung talked about "archetypes"—the anima, the ego,
the self, the shadow—and he also encouraged people to
name their own parts, along the lines of "Little Red Riding
Hood," "Tarzan," "Little Boy," or "Little Girl."

Gestalt talks about Top Dog, Under Dog. Object Relations Theory refers to our introjects. Transactional Analysis
offers the divisions of Adult, Child, and Parent and then
subdivides these further into Natural Child and Adapted
Child, Nurturing Parent and Critical Parent, all of which
are parts of the same person.

You can talk of "selves" (as the heroine of F. Scott

Fitzgerald's *Tender Is the Night* says she is "a lot of simple selves"), or of "sides" or "aspects." You may be more comfortable talking about your rational and your creative *self*, or about your spiritual *side*, or your homebody *aspect*. It doesn't matter which term you use; you can continue with the one you're most comfortable with. NLP uses "parts," so that's what we'll be using here.

By "parts" I mean aspects or qualities of a person: the efficient part, the stay-at-home part, the nurturing part, the shopper part, the baby, the glamour girl, and all the other selves, parts, and facets that make up the whole individual whether or not the person is conscious of them.

Anyone who can be surprised at himself or herself, anyone who's said something that seemed to come out of nowhere, anyone who's done something "crazy" has had the experience of coming in contact with a part of the self he or she didn't know was there.

Jung believed that not only do we have parts we're not conscious of, we also don't necessarily have to know what the part is trying to do for us. And certainly, the fact that we have a part doesn't mean we communicate with it.

This is true of everyone. We're not talking here about any kind of psychological disorder, no multiple personalities or pathology of any kind. We're talking about everyday normal folks.

Everybody has parts, and I believe that parts continue to be formed throughout our life. The older we get, the more experiences we have, the more distinctions we create in our inner world, and the more parts we develop.

It's like the story of the wizard and the magic carpet. A young wizard wanted a magic carpet just like the old wizard's, so the old wizard taught the young one how to weave his own. But the young wizard ended up with a very plain carpet and complained to the master. The old wizard told him, "The older and wiser you are, the more experiences you have, the richer and fuller and more beautiful your carpet becomes.''

How are these parts formed, and how do they become elaborated throughout our lives? In three ways, basically: Parts are formed and developed around the roles that we play in life, around our attitudes, and around our emotions. These three can interweave, of course, and additional roles (becoming a mother, for instance; attaining a new position in society; taking over from a predecessor) can influence or forge new attitudes and emotions.

Roles can correspond to our intimate and family relationships—mother, wife, husband, brother—or they can be connected with our work. I have a part that's teacher, a part that's therapist, a part that's writer. There are major parts and minor parts or subparts, as there are major and minor roles. (I have a minor part that's actor.) And even though someone's main role in the family might be mother, she still has a part that's daughter or even granddaughter. (And she can have this part even if her parents or grandparents are dead.)

We also have roles we play at different times in life, at particular occasions, or with certain groups: family, co-workers; at reunions or during crises. Roles like peace-maker, or troublemaker, or stimulator. Or you play the negotiator or placator, the one who gets people together or calms things down.

Parts are also formed around attitudes and emotions. Most people have a loving part, a playful part, a creative part, an angry part, a detached part, a mean part, a nurturing part, a murderous part.

Having these parts doesn't mean we have to externalize them. Though everybody probably has a jealous part, that doesn't mean we're going to act like Othello. And though having a murderous part isn't uncommon (just listen to a group of children in a playground), most of us would be unwilling and morally unable actually to carry it out.

Parts interact; they are like an inner family. As we accumulate more experience and make finer distinctions, we generate more parts and our inner family grows. All of us have an inner family of parts and, like external families, they can be either functional or dysfunctional.

Whether a family is functional or not has little to do with being "happy" or having no problems. One family can be immersed in problems and still function well, while another family that seems to be happy can be very dysfunctional.

Basically, there are three parameters that determine whether a family is functional or not.

1. Does the family have good boundaries? Does each member of the family have his or her own space? Is this recognized, respected, and appreciated by the others? Each individual—each child, each old aunt or uncle—must be acknowledged as a separate entity, with the right to his or her own space.

2. Is each member playing an appropriate role within the hierarchy? Are the parents being parents and the children being children? Too often, because of extenuating circumstances (particularly when a woman is a single parent and has to go to work), an older child will be placed in charge of the younger ones. If this continues over time, the older child takes over more and more the role of the mother—or the father. At a certain point this becomes inappropriate. The hierarchy of appropriate roles must be respected, and even when children and parents are "good friends," the parents must be parents and allow the children to be children.

3. Do the members of the family know how to communicate with one another? Just because members of the family are all sitting in the same room and speaking the same language doesn't mean they're communicating. One of the hardest things for families to do is really communicate. They may be able to "open up," to talk about what they want, what they like or don't like, what their emotions are, but often they don't know how to listen. What usually happens is that when somebody starts to express what he or she is feeling, the others start to defend themselves. Once they're defending themselves, they're not listening, and listening is at least as essential as talking for true communication to take place.

Good boundaries, appropriate hierarchy, real communication—if you have these parameters in place, you have a functional family, whatever its problems. And the same holds true for the inner family of parts within each individual.

Whether or not your inner family of parts is functional, and just how functional—to what degree—will determine your ability to perform successfully in the world.

There are three parameters for a functional inner family.

First, parts are recognized as separate, each having an identity and function that is respected and appreciated by the others. That means acknowledging the hateful part, the bossy part, the mean, cranky, or stupid part just as much as the loving, generous, creative parts. Unless you acknowledge a part, you can't communicate with it. When that happens, the part or parts may remain hidden and sabotage whatever you're trying to do or change in your life.

Second, parts take their appropriate place within the inner hierarchy. Some parts are large and take up a lot of space; others are small and don't need much room. I'd say my teacher and mother parts are pretty large; my outrageous part is much smaller.

"Appropriate" also refers to when and how a part expresses itself. It's like in a family of separate individuals: Each member is involved with different activities and behavior. The six-month-old baby is very important; however, it isn't expected to participate in taking care of the house or making a living. So, too, each part within the inner family expresses itself in its own way, does its own work, and is appropriate to certain situations but not to others.

Our parts create a whole, each in its own space, perfectly balanced. Think of a beautiful Calder mobile: brightly colored, with parts of different sizes, different shapes, different weights, but all hanging from a central fulcrum, somehow or other in absolute balance. The system created by the parts achieves equilibrium. The same goes for a family and for the organization of parts within each of us.

Third, parts communicate freely. This means opening the channels of communication between all the parts and between the conscious and the unconscious mind. It also means being receptive to communication in whatever form it comes. In a real family, the baby doesn't make its needs known by words and sentences, but we learn to listen and watch for its signals. Unless we can do that, we can't tell when the baby's in danger.

Our inner parts communicate with us through images, sounds, feelings, or sensations. If we don't pay attention, "listen" to them, and recognize that they are "speaking" to us, we ignore parts of ourselves that may be trying to grow, change, and develop. If we don't communicate with our inner selves, with all aspects of who we are, we cut ourselves off from them and them from us, making it very difficult to function as an integrated individual.

The telephone company, in an unusual flight of synesthesia (the evocation of one of the senses by another), asked its users to "reach out and touch someone." We can do the same within ourselves, faster than phone, fax, or e-mail: We can call up any one of our inner family of parts, or as many of them as we like at a time, conference line or individual, letting everybody listen in or communicating privately, one part at a time.

❖

PARTS EXERCISE

1. Think of all the roles you play in your life—with your family, at work, in your social life. Write them down.

2. Think of some of your emotions—the comfortable and uncomfortable ones. Write them down.

3. Begin to make a list of your parts. Give them names. (Remember to include those you don't want or like.)

4. Look at your list. Notice which parts you like, which ones you don't like. Which ones are you mad at? Which ones scare you?

5. Look at these parts and ask yourself, "What is each one trying to do for me? What is each one's intention?"

❖

39

Positive Intention

Now that we know what our parts are and can identify many of them within ourselves, let's go back to the original presupposition: There's a positive intention behind behavior.

All behaviors are manifestations of one part or another; in fact, the only way we can know a part exists is through its behavior.

Behavior means actions, thoughts, symptoms, gestures; it is not the same as intention. Intention doesn't necessarily result in behavior, though all behavior is the result of intention.

If this sounds like something from *Alice in Wonderland*, that's fine. It's an appropriate setting for understanding this very simple but incredibly mysterious process. "You should say what you mean," says the March Hare. "I do," says Alice, "at least I mean what I say."

Your behavior is the expression of a part, a side, an aspect of you that is trying to communicate. But the *intention* of the part may be quite different from the expression. Let's say you're walking along with a friend and her baby and you see an old school chum across the street and shout over to him, waking the baby, who begins to cry.

Now, your *intention* was certainly not to wake the baby.

All you intended to do was get the attention of this person you hadn't seen since high school. (There was a positive intention behind your behavior, even if you ended up making little Jonathan cry. And the intention would have been positive even if it turned out that the person wasn't your high school pal after all, just someone who looked like him.)

We have to separate behavior and intention.

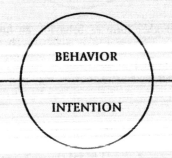

Here's an example.

It's Sunday morning. The phone rings, too early. You pick it up; a voice says, "Can I speak to Marsha?"

"This is Marsha. Who's calling?"

"My name is Gordon. I'm calling on behalf of the National Committee for the—"

Bang! Down goes the receiver. Rude, unprecedented— you shake your head, partly in annoyance at the caller, partly in bewilderment at your own behavior. You're not used to thinking of yourself as someone who's rude.

Hell-o! Suddenly there's a part of you expressing itself at 8:45 A.M. on a Sunday, a part you didn't know existed. It's Marsha the Meanie, the part that doesn't want Marsha to be disturbed this morning and is protecting her sleep.

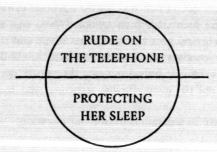

Or take another form of behavior, an inner voice that keeps telling you, ''I'm not smart enough.'' This is the manifestation of a part that could be trying to motivate you to study harder, take extra courses, read more. The intention is to get you to be the best you can be—to succeed.

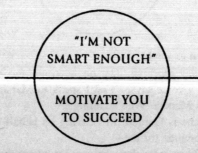

Whatever behavior we're talking about, whether it's external (actions) or internal (thoughts), remember that the behavior is separate from the intention. Both together form the whole part. The *intention* is always positive, even if you don't know about it. All you're aware of is *behavior*, which might not be positive at all—in fact, it could be totally the opposite. The *expression* of behavior (telling yourself you're not smart enough; banging down the phone, shouting across the street) represents the part that's communicating, which is how you know it exists. The *result* of the behavior is very different from the *intention*.

BEHAVIOR	Sharon, a fitness instructor in her late twenties, is unmarried, lives alone, and would like to have a significant relationship with someone. She tells herself she's not lovable. (What she tells herself prevents her from having relationships.)
INTENTION	The part that tells her she's not lovable is keeping her from being vulnerable— this keeps her from becoming intimate with someone and being abandoned. The intention of that part is to protect her from being abandoned.
BEHAVIOR	Jim loses his temper easily, over what seem to be trifles. (This makes people shy away from him, especially at work.)
INTENTION	The part that angers easily keeps Jim from feeling sad and scared about the work he does and the job he can't stand.
BEHAVIOR	MaryBeth has high blood pressure. (This prevents her from doing many ''exciting'' things.)
INTENTION	MaryBeth's condition keeps her connected to her mother, who had high blood pressure and couldn't put up with any ''excitement.''

These are examples of positive intentions within the individual (the *intrapersonal* system). Here the behavior serves a positive function toward oneself, either to protect or to motivate. We also separate behavior and intention in *interpersonal* relations or communication.

BEHAVIOR	A couple is getting ready to go out to a dinner party. The wife says to the husband, "That jacket looks awful with those pants—they don't match at all." (He gets annoyed; they argue.)
INTENTION	She wants him to look his best and make a wonderful impression on the people who will be there and who can help him get the job he's hoping for.
BEHAVIOR	A boss tells his employee she's not working hard enough, not doing enough for the company. (She feels unappreciated, resentful.)
INTENTION	He's trying to keep the company solvent and get her to be more motivated. He's sure that will help her enjoy her work and do better at it.

In interpersonal behavior (between people instead of parts), one person may have a positive intention toward another and be trying to send a positive message of encouragement or support. But the *way* this person does it prevents the message from getting through and may actually produce the opposite effect.

The same thing can happen within yourself. A part wants to motivate you to do something to increase your self-esteem and make you feel better. Or the part wants to protect you from something that might hurt you. (The positive intention is either to motivate or protect.) But you're not conscious of this. All you're aware of is something you don't like, maybe even hate, about yourself, the kind of thing that keeps you awake at night wondering, How could I have *done* that?

Think of the *worst* thing you know about yourself: something you feel ashamed of, that you feel you have no control over; something you do that you don't approve of, that you feel is wrong. Smoking, yelling at your kids, making a mess of your house, being unfaithful, drinking too much—any of these destructive behaviors has a positive function or intention, separate from the behavior itself.

I realize this sounds like a paradox: If you're doing something *bad* for you, how can that same something be *good* for you? (There's a Cole Porter song that goes, "It's so good for me, it's bad for me.") If someone's drinking too much and destroying himself, what could possibly be the positive intention underlying the behavior?

Many possibilities. The drinking could be calming this person down, giving a bit of relief from tremendous stress, or offering a bit of respite and even pleasure in the midst of grueling work or financial worries, illness, depression, or seemingly inescapable boredom. Maybe the overindulgence is nurturing someone through a particularly bad time. A woman I know was drinking way too much every evening during the period when her mother was dying of a particularly painful form of cancer. The drinking helped the daughter relax; she forgot about everything, fell into a deep sleep every night, and remained asleep until morning, when she returned to the hospital. Her drinking had the positive intention of "mothering" her during this very trying time.

Of course, drinking can be destructive and often is (particularly for other people), but it has a positive intention or function for the individual doing it. Acknowledging that there's a positive intention doesn't condone or support destructive behavior; recognizing what exists is not necessarily to excuse it. (We're not making judgments here, just trying to understand the roots of behavior.) It simply helps us acknowledge and understand what the part is trying to do and lets us begin to communicate with it. What the specific intention or function of the behavior (in this case, drinking) is for any particular person is determined by that individual's specific life and inner family of parts. There are as many answers, as many possible intentions, as there are individuals. It could even be that the intention of the part that drinks too much is to keep the person from going insane.

When you have a part of you that you don't like, what do you do about it? Some people try to get rid of it. They "hate" this part of themselves. Or they pretend it isn't there. People act as if they can't see, can't hear, don't know the part is there—like pretending not to see the nose on your face.

But ignoring what you don't like doesn't make it go away. Putting your head in the sand won't make the world around you disappear, it only makes you temporarily blind. Pretending your behavior doesn't exist makes you a victim of it. If you can't acknowledge a part of yourself, you have no choice about it; you can't make changes.

You have to start by acknowledging the part of you that does unpleasant, unnecessary, and even cruel things— wounding yourself or someone else by word or deed—because there is no other way to begin negotiating, coming to terms, and, finally, changing the behavior. You can't just *get rid of* behavior. If you could, no one would have ongoing problems like overeating, lack of self-esteem (telling yourself the same negative thing again and again), or any other habitual behavior. Most of us know from experience that when we try to change behavior *only* (going on a diet, for instance), it doesn't work. Or if it does work it's temporary; the behavior comes back or is replaced by something just as bad or worse.

We have to ask ourselves: What is this (undesired) behavior doing for me? What is the intention? Otherwise, the behavior goes on and on.

What does making a mess of my office do for me? What does yelling at my kids do for me? Each time you do it, you feel guilty about it, and you promise yourself you won't do it again. But it doesn't work, of course; the more you try to stop yelling, the more you seem to do it. And soon you begin to hate this behavior of yours; you hate this part of you, you want to get rid of it. Then it's an easy short step to hating yourself. But if you come to understand the intention—maybe it's to stop yourself from actually hitting them, maybe it's to motivate them to do better; whatever it is, there's a positive intention in back of the negative behavior—then you could begin to understand, to respect the part, and to communicate with it. Only at that point could you begin to change your behavior.

People will say, "I *hate* this thing I do—I *hate* this part that tells me I'm no good, that I can't accomplish or can't finish something—I want to get rid of it."

By the time they admit these feelings—to themselves, to a therapist, or just to someone else—they've probably been wanting to "get rid of" this part of themselves, to kill that behavior, for many years. Often, they've tried. They haven't succeeded, haven't made a dent. The undesired behavior continues and usually increases.

Only by recognizing that it's not possible to simply kill a part of yourself can a person begin to look at the problem in a constructive and communicative way. You change the focus from getting rid of the problem to understanding why it's there, separating behavior from intention.

◆

POSITIVE INTENTION EXERCISE

1. Think of a behavior, either internal (something you say to yourself or images you see on your inner screen) or external, that's not beneficial to you. (It could also be a symptom of some kind.)

2. Allow yourself to imagine that the behavior is separate from the intention. Imagine that the behavior doesn't reflect its own purpose.

3. Ask yourself, "What could this behavior (symptom) be trying to do for me? What could it be trying to tell me about myself and my life?"

4. Allow yourself to answer spontaneously, even if the answers make no sense to you. If the answer is negative, ask, "What is [negative answer] trying to do for me?" Keep asking this until you get something positive. Write the answers down and put them away for 24 hours. Then look at them again. Do they begin to make any sense? Do they give you any more ideas about other possible positive intentions behind the behavior (symptom)?

◆

40

Reframing

To understand why it's there, it helps to perceive a problem in a new way: get a different slant on it, see it in a new light, put another spin on it.

Before we get back to communicating with parts and specific ways of changing our behavior, let's take a look at a process we call reframing.

Make a little window of your hands, bring it up to eye level, and look through it at the "snapshot" you've captured. Look at it carefully, paying attention to details, to the composition of the picture. Got it? Good. Hold it a moment longer, imprint it on your mind—and let your hands fall to your sides. Look around you. Where has your scene gone?

Make a circle of your forefinger and thumb and look through it with one eye closed. Hold the scene long enough to imprint it on the screen of your mind. Let it go. Where is the picture now?

A picture is defined by its borders. The size and shape of the window determines what you can see through it. Reality takes on meaning by how we frame it. Looking at a cookie crumb through a microscope is a very different experience from looking at crumbs that have been left on the kitchen table.

What you see at any given time depends not only on

what's there but also on what you choose to see. The picture you capture through your hand frame is only a part of what's out there, of what it is possible to see. By "focusing" on this part of the scene or that, you change the "reality" in front of you.

What you capture in your snapshot represents what's "really" there, but you've interpreted it in a certain way, choosing what to include and what to leave out. Your picture is determined by your frame: what you see and how you interpret it.

We put frames on pictures; we also put frames on words. *How* you say something is often just as important as *what* you're saying. The "frame" can be your tone of voice, gestures, body language, or the particular words you use.

"Could you please speak a little more softly?" is certainly different from "Shut up!" though my intention remains the same. What I want is to have some quiet around me, but the way I ask for it—the way I "frame" my request (by my behavior)—will determine if I get it or not.

Reframing is a way of changing your perception of an experience—changing the meaning by changing the way it's presented. It's the *how*, not the *what*. We put things a different way; we change the behavior in order to accomplish the intention.

Reframes are like labels. What's the difference between a used car and a previously owned car? Nothing but the hype; it's probably the same lemon either way.

When something difficult happens, you can put a frame around the situation that says:

Because of the changed frame, the meaning of "This is terrible" changes to "This is exciting!"

It's all in the definition; the situation hasn't changed.

You can also do this by changing a word. Take a particular quality or attribute of a person and look at it from two perspectives. The same appearance can be "glamorous" or "trashy." The same behaviors that add up to "honesty" in one person's view turn into "simple" in another's.

This type of reframe often takes place with couples, to explain why they're no longer in love. "He's totally irre-

sponsible," Stephanie (not her real name) tells me, justi-
fying her reason for getting a divorce.

I ask her, "What was it about this man that made you
fall in love with him?"

"He was such fun," she says. "He was really spontaneous and a lot of fun when we got married."

Three years later and they're getting a divorce. What
happened?

"He's totally irresponsible," she says.

"Spontaneous" turned into "irresponsible." *He* hasn't
changed; his *behavior* hasn't changed. The word (and the
meaning behind the word) changed because the frame or
framework of the situation changed. The behavior was interpreted in a new way because the lifestyle and circumstances of the people had altered.

When you're dating someone, spontaneity—never knowing quite what to expect—is fun and exciting; it's thrilling.
But when you're married to someone, never knowing what
to expect isn't much fun; it can be upsetting or even fright-
ening. With Stephanie the initial frame was dating; then it
changed to marriage. Different frame, different meaning.

Somebody says, "He's really *cheap*." Somebody else
says, "He's just being *thrifty*."

A woman describes the man she lives with as "so *dependable*, I know I can count on him." A few months later,
"He's got no imagination, he's *dull* and *boring*." "Dependable" becomes "boring."

Simple one-word reframes are a kind of limbering-up
exercise, mainly to emphasize that the same behavior can
be seen differently according to the frame you put it in.
There has to be a line of continuity, of course; you can't
go from *thrifty* to *boring*. It's got to be *thrifty* Ø *cheap;*
dependable Ø *boring*. Here are a few more; try them on
your own or make it into a game with a friend.

ONE-WORD REFRAMES

Spontaneous	→	Unpredictable
Funny	→	Childish
Confident	→	Arrogant
Imaginative	→	Undisciplined
Generous	→	Spendthrift
Outgoing	→	Exhibitionist

This is verbal one-word reframing, a simple device you can use to find the silver lining in someone else's problem and help with a new approach. Ask your friend (or ask yourself), "How can this problem be framed in another way? How can it become an opportunity? How can this problem be taking care of you in a positive way?"

When you've found the reframe, feed it back. The "problem" becomes an "opportunity." For instance:

Other Person: I have to pay a lot of taxes this year.
You (reframe): *That means you must be earning more money than usual.*

Other Person: My parents never have time to baby-sit.
You: It must be a good feeling to know that they are busy and active and don't have to depend on you.

Other Person: My car's in the repair shop, and I won't be able to get down to the country on Saturday.
You: It's an opportunity to finally do all those things around the house that have been piling up.

Verbal reframing describes a problem from a different perspective and creates a sudden change. A simple reframe can work like a charm. Suddenly you see things differently: instead of thorns in your backyard, you've got a garden of roses.

Alison (not her real name), a woman in her early thirties, came to me because she was "chronically depressed," as she put it. She was happily married, a working journalist with a special interest in abused and battered women and children. But she'd been depressed since her teens, she told me, on and off medication, which "sometimes helped, sometimes didn't." She'd function normally for a while; then "it would get so bad I could barely do anything at all"; then she'd be all right again for a while. She was tired she repeated, of being "chronically depressed."

Alison told me about her work with abused women and children. She said she couldn't understand how anyone in the world who was at all sensitive didn't get depressed by the way human beings treated one another. How could "anybody with any sensitivity, seeing what goes on"—in particular, how women and children were treated throughout the world—"not get depressed?"

It soon became obvious to me that the part of Alison that became depressed was actually maintaining her sensitivity. I understood there was no way in the world she would give up her depression because that meant giving up her sensitivity, and being sensitive was extremely important to her. The part of her that became depressed had the positive intention of keeping her sensitive.

What I said to her was, "It's really important to you that you're sensitive. So how about if, instead of calling you 'chronically depressed,' we call you 'chronically sensitive'?"

She loved that. And it relieved her, because she'd felt guilty about her depression.

This is a simple reframe: Alison felt bad, and the frame she had around what was wrong with her was "depressed."

We changed the word from *depressed* to *sensitive*, and that changed the meaning. Her feeling bad was now a manifestation of her sensitivity rather than of depression, and she immediately felt much better. Being *sensitive* wasn't being sick, wasn't feeling bad; there was no longer anything seriously wrong with her.

I redefined how she was describing herself, and the same symptoms (behavior) now were part of a new story, a different condition. Simple verbal reframing is like magic, when it works: In an instant, one thing is transformed into something else. Cinderella becomes a princess through the touch of the reframing wand. The ugly duckling becomes the swan.

Verbal reframing transforms the immediate effect of the problem, but it doesn't go into problem-solving in depth. To do that, you have to create an open channel of communication between your conscious and unconscious mind.

The woman I'll call Rebecca was an artist who came to see me because she had painter's block. She hadn't been able to paint in a year, she said. "I want to get rid of whatever it is that's preventing me from painting. It's suffocating me."

I talked about the concept of parts, and that each had a positive intention, including, I said, the part that stopped her from painting.

"That's poppycock," she said. "No way does this part have a positive intention. This part is horrible; I want to get rid of it."

It wasn't possible to "get rid" of a part, I explained, any more than you could get rid of a physical part of the body because it was giving you pain. The pain—or the behavior—was a symptom. It was how the part communicated with you, and the only way to deal with the problem was by understanding why it was there. This meant acknowledging the part that held her back. I urged her to try.

"No!" Rebecca was adamant. "That's plain ridiculous."

I reminded her that she'd already tried everything else she could think of; that was why she was here, after all. For a long time we were at loggerheads. Whatever I said about respecting your parts, learning to communicate with your parts, about the positive intention behind the behavior—all this sailed past her.

"I just want to kill it," she insisted.

I tried one last time. "Could you at least *pretend* that there's a positive intention?"

"Of course not."

Finally I said, "OK, I'm stuck. I can't do any more for you. But since you've already paid me for my time, would you like a cup of coffee? Would you like to have a chat about the weather or politics?"

Now she was really upset. "All right," she said, pulling her lips back and very nearly growling at me. "I'll pretend." She closed her eyes.

I said, "Ask that part that stops you from painting what it's trying to do for you. How is it trying to take care of you in a positive way?"

She was quiet for all of about 45 seconds. Then her whole face changed. Her lower jaw dropped. She opened her eyes. "I can't believe this! You know what I got?"

I'd seen this reaction before: the sudden jolt, the about-face or "magic wand" effect when suddenly the connection is made, the conscious and unconscious are speaking together, and the words tumble out like an avalanche.

She went on: "That's the part of me—" but she was so excited the words couldn't get through until she took a few deep breaths. Then she continued. "That part is my *creativity*, and it hasn't been letting me paint because I've been painting in the same style for years, doing the same kind of work, and it's time to change, go on to something new, or else I'll just *suffocate*, I'd *die* as an artist. The part that won't let me paint is the part that's motivating me to be more creative, to take risks and do things differently . . . see things in a new way, find my new style.''

It made total sense to her now that the part preventing her from painting was her creative part. Once she stopped blaming herself, and the part that was blocking her, and instead simply asked and listened to what the part was trying to say, she got the answer.

She allowed the channel of communication between her conscious and unconscious mind to be opened, and in that moment the answer sailed across.

This is reframing, a new way of seeing or experiencing something by changing the frame around it. Instead of trying to solve the problem, we redefine it. Instead of changing the response (as we did with anchoring) and getting a new response to the old stimulus, we leave the response as it is and simply change the meaning of the problem. We don't change the behavior, as we did by interrupting the stimulus∅response connection and replacing it with a new response. That kind of problem-solving is called *first-order change*: new behavior replaces the old, and the original ''problem'' is solved. (If you have a migraine headache and take a painkiller to get rid of it, you're changing the response of ''headache.'' You're doing first-order change.)

Reframing is *second-order change*. Here, we don't change the response; we change the meaning of the problem. It's not problem-solving in the old sense anymore; we're looking for the root of the problem, taking the symptom (or the behavior or the response) simply as a sign or indication of the process it represents. With reframing, we change the *meaning* of the problem (the headache). We use it as a way of communicating with a part of our unconscious self, so that we can acknowledge this part and bring it into consciousness. We ask: What is the headache trying to do for me? What is the *positive intention* of the headache?

The answer that comes back might be: Trying to get you to rest, relax, slow down, take care of yourself.

That's the positive intention, whether it's taking effect or not. But now the headache isn't simply a problem to get rid of. You understand the headache in relation to yourself, your work, your lifestyle—and the headache's meaning becomes a message about taking better care of yourself. You still might take a pill to stop the pain (or not), but in any case you've learned something important about yourself: You've recognized the source of behavior and the function it serves.

Essentially, reframing is the art of changing your perception of a problem, based on having open and effective communication with your parts.

41

Communicating with Your Unconscious

Communicating with your unconscious doesn't mean some kind of supernatural communication or ESP. It simply means connecting, permitting a free association between the conscious and unconscious mind.

It means opening the path, the channels, the bridge, and letting the communication simply happen, uncensored by the conscious mind, the intellectual logic that comes loaded with acquired assumptions, prejudices, and judgments. It means trusting in the immediate connections that the imagination brings to mind, even if the meaning isn't obvious, even if it seems silly or illogical.

Communicating with your unconscious is the first step toward understanding why you do the things you do. You need to get in touch with the part of yourself that manifests the negative or useless behavior to learn what function the part plays in your life. Only when you discover the roots of the behavior can you weed it out intelligently, replacing it with different growth.

Instead of trying to yank out the behavior of yelling at your children, for instance, you understand where (what part of you) it's coming from and recognize that the behavior is necessary for your protection (and maybe even for theirs). At that point, you can look around for other ways of fulfilling the positive intention, and you replace the undesired behavior with a fruitful one.

But first you have to prepare the soil, create a hospitable environment where your unconscious mind is comfortable and receptive—"Gardens where the soul's at ease," in the words of W. B. Yeats—where you can tap into the wisdom of the unconscious and set aside the constraints and fences of the rational (judgmental, logical) conscious mind.

To do this, you need to create the same kind of rapport with your own inner parts that you've created with other people. In Part I of this book, The Meaning of Your Communication Is the Response You Get, we talked about the rapport and trust necessary for establishing interpersonal communication. In Parts II and III, we discussed *intra*personal communication, or communication with self. This includes recognizing and anchoring your resources, being able to work with submodalities, defining an outcome, and other skills. Now we're talking about the deepest form of communication, between *parts* of yourself, some of which you don't know exist: communicating between the known and the unknown you. Here, more than anywhere else, the rapport that develops from a sense of safety and trust is essential.

The technique we use for this is the Inner Reframe. Like most techniques or "magic" tools of NLP, it relies on asking questions: What, specifically, to ask, and in what order.

INNER REFRAME: *COMMUNICATING WITH PARTS*

I. CREATING THE ENVIRONMENT (RULES)

- Maintain the assumption that there is a positive intention throughout this process.
- Speak to your parts gently and respectfully.
- Always thank the part for communicating.

- Be patient and accepting.
- Even when the alternatives offered by the part are unconscious, maintain your confidence that they will work. (In fact, they'll probably work better than the conscious ones!)

II. CHARACTERS

- Part A: Part that manifests the problem
- Part B: Creative or problem-solving part

III. PROCEDURE (IMPLEMENTATION)

1. Identify a symptom or behavior you don't like or want to change in yourself.
2. Ask Part A, "What is your positive intention?" (Keep repeating this question until you get something positive.)
3. Tell Part B what the positive intention is.
4. Ask Part B to come up with three to six alternatives (three of them *not* conscious) to the problem behavior that will also satisfy the positive intention.
5. Ask Part A to review these alternatives and choose the best one. Ask it to use this behavior instead of the problem behavior.
6. Thank the parts.

You can use the Inner Reframe on yourself or to help other people learn how to communicate with their own parts and discover the intentions behind their behaviors.

Let's go through the Inner Reframe outline together, taking a form of negative behavior that's not uncommon. We'll use Melanie as our subject. Whenever she does something really well in her work, an inner voice tells her, "That was too easy. You must have done something wrong."

As we follow her through the Inner Reframe, we can think of it as a play with dialogue. Since much of the response is bound to be nonverbal (the unconscious speaks in many ways—through images, sounds, and sensations—not necessarily in English), putting this into the structure of a play makes it possible for us to follow Melanie's inner dialogue through such devices as voice-overs and stage directions.

The "play" takes place in the mind of Melanie, both conscious and unconscious regions. The setting (creating the environment) includes the backdrop, props, and lighting; a sense of calm and safety pervades. The characters are Melanie's parts A and B. The procedure is the action, the process of communicating with the parts to discover Whodunit and for what motives and then studying the evidence to see if things can be different next time, if the motives for the "crime" can be used to come up with a happy ending.

The title is *Melanie's Problem Behavior and the Positive Intention Behind It.* (The play won't win any Tonys with this title—but then again, that's not our purpose here.)

The characters are Part A, the part responsible for Melanie's inner voice saying, "That was too easy; you must have done something wrong," and Part B, a creative, problem-solving part, not yet fully disclosed.

The Inner Reframe begins.

Voice-over: *Identify a symptom or behavior you don't like or want to be rid of in yourself.*

Melanie: *It's an inner voice telling me, "That was too easy. You must have done something wrong."*

Voice-over: Ask Part A, ''What's your positive intention?''

Melanie: Part A, part that's in charge of the inner voice, what, I respectfully ask, is your positive intention? What are you trying to do for me?

Part A: (Pause) To keep you on edge.

Voice-over: Thank the part.

Melanie: Thank you, Part A, for communicating with me.

Voice-over: Ask Part A, ''What does that do for me?''

Melanie: What does keeping me on edge do for me? What is the positive intention of that?

Part A: To keep you from getting too self-satisfied and full of yourself.

Voice-over: Thank Part A (she does) and ask again.

Melanie: What's the positive intention of keeping me from being too self-satisfied?

Part A: To make sure you continue learning and growing.

Voice-over: Thank the part.

Melanie: Your intention is for me not to become self-satisfied, and to keep me learning and growing. That's a wonderful intention. Thank you.

Note: When you talk to your parts, it's the same as when you're talking to other people. Talk to them clearly, directly. Your parts are very childlike. They take things literally. They are very sensitive to disrespect and to negative manipulation.

Voice-over: Summon up Part B, your creative part. Tell this part about the positive intention of your behavior.

Melanie: Creative Part, Part B. I'd like to talk to you for a little bit. Perhaps you're aware of the inner voice that keeps telling me, whenever I do something really well, "That was too easy. You must have done something wrong." I want you to know what the positive intention of this behavior is.

The part of me that's responsible for this message is trying to make sure I continue to learn and grow and don't become self-satisfied. I'm sure you would agree this is an important and meaningful intention.

Voice-over: Ask Part B to come up with alternatives to this behavior. Make sure that at least some of these alternatives are unconscious.

Melanie: I'd like you, my creative, problem-solving part, to do what you do so well: create alternatives, come up with new ideas, new ways of doing things. Keeping in mind what Part A's positive intention is for me, I'd like you to come up with three to six alternative behaviors to having an inner voice telling me, "That was too easy. You must have done something wrong."

Please make sure these alternatives fulfill the positive intention to keep me, Melanie, growing and learn-

ing. And let some if not all of these alternatives remain in my unconscious mind.

Note: It may be better not to let Melanie's conscious mind know about all the alternatives, so that her conscious mind can't mess around with them, find fault with them, and sabotage them.

Melanie: Take your time, Creative Part, do what you do really well, and give me some kind of signal—a word or sensation or image—when you've finished generating the alternatives. Take your time.

(Melanie waits. Suddenly her face lights up; she makes a sound something like "Ooh!" The image in her mind is the foundation of a beautiful house.)

Voice-over: When you receive a signal that your part has finished generating alternatives, thank Part B.

Melanie: Thank you for communicating with me. Thank you for coming up with creative choices. I realize that the image I've conjured up helps me build on my successes. It represents an alternative, because each time I say, "That was too easy," I'm undermining myself, undermining the foundation of who I am, of my strengths—it's like knocking the legs out from under myself. It's like trying to build my house on sand.

(Melanie's creative part has generated a number of alternatives in her unconscious mind. She's aware of a voice telling her, "Remember the future—you've got all the time you need." This makes her calm, somehow; just being aware of the future calms her. She senses the existence of other alternatives, though she isn't yet clear about what they are. She has the image of a path leading upward, toward a blue sky with bright, fast-moving clouds. She lets the unconscious remain unconscious, dwelling in images, sounds, sensations, not in cognitive language or thought.)

Voice-over: Ask Part A to review the alternatives and pick the best one for you. Ask it to use this behavior in place of the unwanted message.

Melanie: Part A, please review all the alternatives my Creative Part came up with, both the ones I'm aware of and the unconscious ones. Pick whichever you think would best fulfill your intention for me—to keep me learning and growing.

(She waits until she senses that Part A has done this.)

Now, Part A, please put the behavior you've chosen as the best one in place of the old message I kept telling myself. . . . I know you're doing what I asked because I'm starting to feel calmer, more certain—of what, I don't exactly know. And even though I'm not aware which alternative you chose, I know it was the right one.

Voice-over: Thank the parts.

Melanie: Thank you, Part A, for being willing to do this. Thank you for being in touch with me, and thanks most of all for your positive intention, for taking care of me, for recognizing how important it is for me to continue learning and growing.

And thank you, Part B, my Creative Part, for lis-

*tening to me and helping me, for being resourceful and
imaginative, for coming up with choices and possibilities. Thank you for being incredible you.*

The above dialogue actually took place fifteen years ago,
with a woman called Anné. That was me, and since that
time I've never again said to myself, "That was too easy.
You must have done something wrong." I now enjoy taking credit for my accomplishments. I'm proud of what I do
well, and I also continue to try for more, to learn and grow.
To this day, however, I don't know what the specific alternative was that my creative part generated and my problem part selected.

Another example comes from Joe (not his real name), a
salesman who was in one of my workshops. He used the
Inner Reframe in a very direct and powerful way.

I'll let him tell the story the way he told it to all of us
afterward.

I have a history of migraine headaches. Once a headache begins, there's nothing I can do, but nothing. No
medicine, no pills—nothing works. I'm laid out for
thirty-six hours, in bed suffering.

A couple of weeks after we had that reframe business in the workshop, I'm driving to one of my customers. Then what do you know but I start getting the
first inklings of a migraine and I'm going, "Oh, God,"
thinking of all the work I have to do.

So then I remember the reframe business and I say
to myself, "Might as well try it—nothing to lose."

When I get these headaches, nothing works anyway.
So I'm really thinking it's not going to work. I even
feel a little peculiar doing it, but I stop the car and do
the reframe on myself.

First, I ask the part that's responsible for the migraine what it's trying to do for me, how it's taking care of me. And, believe it, I get this answer: *To get you to rest more, take care of yourself.*

So I tell the part, "Thanks. OK, I'll do what you want, I'll rest more. But look, I've got three more customers to see. If you'll let me see those three customers, I promise I'll go right home and to bed and take the next day off and rest." And all of a sudden—no migraine. Honest to God.

I keep going, I do my work, see my customers— and then, you know how it is, being human, I forgot all about that stuff. And after my third customer, I'm sitting in my car thinking about a contractor I've been meaning to see for a long time, guy called Richard whose place is nearby. "Might as well take the opportunity," I say to myself, since I'm here anyway. . . .

And bang! the migraine comes back like a shot out of hell.

The reframing technique is also very effective in work or business situations, for interpersonal problems, like employer-employee relations.

Kevin is a department manager with about twenty people in his department. He's very good at what he does, but he's hypercritical of the people who work under him, and they feel intimidated by him and are angry. A number of them have complained.

Jeremy, who heads the department and is Kevin's boss, is very concerned. He knows that Kevin is extremely valuable to the company, an excellent and tireless worker, but he realizes that everyone working under Kevin is on edge, and the morale in the office is terrible.

Using the reframing approach to problem-solving, Jeremy doesn't simply tell Kevin, "Stop being so critical." This probably wouldn't work in any case and would only antagonize him. Jeremy understands that there must be a positive intention in Kevin's behavior, in the form of either protection or motivation. He calls Kevin to his office and asks, "When you're pointing out to the staff what they're doing wrong, what's your purpose? What are you trying to accomplish?"

Kevin replies, "I'm pointing out what's wrong because I don't want them to make those kinds of mistakes again. I want their performance to improve, I want them to be much more efficient. After all, I'm responsible—and I intend for this department to shine."

Now Jeremy has the information he's looking for. He understands that Kevin is pointing out the mistakes as a way of teaching his staff: showing what they did wrong so they can avoid it in future.

Jeremy says, "So you want your people to perform at the highest efficiency possible." (Jeremy is backtracking to make sure he understands correctly.)

"Yes, absolutely."

"I can appreciate that. But you know, sometimes if you point out what people are doing wrong, they take it as criticism." (Here Jeremy is leading Kevin toward a possible alternative behavior.)

"But I'm trying to help them," Kevin protests. "I'm setting them a high standard to motivate them."

"Fine. But since the way you're doing it isn't having the effect you want, what about thinking of another way?"

"You mean, telling them differently?"

"*Motivating* them differently. Think about it. What sort of thing gets *you* motivated? Maybe you're the kind of guy where if someone tells you you've done something wrong, you feel you've got to *show* them—and you do your best. But other people aren't always like that. Sometimes they need encouragement."

Jeremy lets it go, with the request that Kevin think about

alternatives. A few days later they meet again. Kevin is smiling.

"I want to thank you for pointing out my behavior to me," he says. "I didn't realize I was being overly critical of my staff. I actually think they're terrific, the best I've ever worked with. And you know what? When I told them precisely that at our meeting on Tuesday, they applauded. From now on, I'll make sure they know how highly I think of them. And then"—he grins—"that's when I'll *really* let them have it."

If Jeremy had simply tried to get rid of the problem by stopping the behavior, chances are Kevin would have become defensive and maybe even more critical. Certainly, the situation would have become more rigid.

By using reframing, Jeremy made the situation flexible. He told himself: Honor the purpose behind the critical behavior and *then* find alternatives to the problem. Wisely, he left it up to Kevin to discover his own alternatives.

A similar situation comes up in the travel department of a large financial corporation. The department is headed by a woman, and the women working under her feel she's much harder on them than on the men.

Elaine has been chosen by the other women employees as the designated representative to talk to the boss, Paula. Instead of pointing out what's wrong (which she knows would annoy her boss and make life in the office more hellish than it already is), Elaine starts by telling Paula all the things she does that the others admire or appreciate. After that, Elaine tries to discover the intention behind Paula's behavior, and then she points out how Paula might change her way of doing things. She finds alternatives to the behavior while honoring the purpose and intention behind it.

Elaine: All of us in the office have a lot of respect for your intelligence and your ability to work really hard. We admire the way you decide on a goal and really stick to it, really push yourself. But also, we've noticed that when we've got an important project and everybody has to pull together and work really hard, you seem a lot more demanding of the women than the men.

Paula: I want the women to shine. People always expect women to do less than men. It's important that we show them.

Elaine: So your purpose in being more demanding with us is to get us to really do our best, to really show off our capabilities?

Paula: That's right.

Elaine: To be even better than they are?

Paula: Why not? I had to be better than the men to get where I am.

Elaine: So you want us to demonstrate that we're better than the men. That's why you're so hard on us.

Paula: I want you to do your best.

Elaine: OK. But do you think the way you're driving us works?

Paula: I can see you're here to complain—so, obviously, it doesn't.

Elaine: *Not exactly. I'm interested in your objective observation. Do you think you're getting the same quality of work and creativity out of the women that you get from the men?*

Paula: *The women seem to resent having a boss who's a woman.*

Elaine: *I don't know. . . .*

Paula: *The men seem to do much better. Not because I haven't tried to push the women—*

Elaine: *I'm aware of that. As a woman I appreciate that you want us to shine and not be treated as second-class citizens. That's terrific. But it's just that, even though your intention is for us to be the best we can be, maybe demanding so much, being so hard on us, isn't working as well as something else might. I'm not saying settle for less. I wouldn't want to do that myself, and I wouldn't want you to.*

Paula: *You probably all want a male boss.*

Elaine: *Maybe it's not about that at all. Honestly, I don't think that would matter. It's that sometimes you're easier on the men, you cut them some slack, and you're sort of more relaxed with them—you laugh with them more, you joke around with them. You're not as "over their shoulders" all the time.*

 And I'm wondering if doing the same with us might not have a better result than what you're getting so far.

 Don't get me wrong. I'm not criticizing your intentions. I want us to do our best too. But for me, per-

sonally, it's not so much that you're a woman, it's that sometimes I don't feel recognized by you for the work I'm doing.

Paula: *Hm, that strikes a chord. I always thought that as a woman you really have to be on top even to be recognized at all.*

Elaine: *Maybe, but sometimes we just need to be cut a little slack so we can get there.*

Paula: *Not a bad idea. Maybe we should have coffee together, all of us, and talk about this.*

Elaine: *Yes, good.*

Paula: *Let's get all the women in this department together sometime soon, maybe later on this week? And I want everyone to come with suggestions!*

These are external (interpersonal) examples of dealing with positive intentions and alternative behaviors. Instead of doing it with our own parts, we can do it with partners and colleagues or with our children, friends, husbands, and wives—anyone we deal with.

Reframing behavior, your own or someone else's, means having an understanding of behavior as separate from intention. With others, it means helping them to understand that the behavior they are manifesting is not efficient or doesn't represent the intention they have. In yourself, it means an acceptance of your unconscious mind, an awareness that it's at work, whether or not you know what it's doing, and a willingness to create an internal environment that permits communication between your conscious and unconscious parts, between all the selves you are and intend to be, the inner family and the behaviors it generates.

Being locked into a destructive or unuseful behavior is like being controlled by a tyrant. Without the freedom to choose, your life doesn't feel like your own. But when you understand that the tyrant is really acting out of benevolent impulses—that this behavior comes from a part of you that means well but has chosen a destructive way of expressing its intention—you can transform the negative behavior into other forms that accomplish the purpose.

The frog who becomes a prince, Beauty and the Beast—these fairy tales and legends correspond to the transformations we can make within ourselves. The ugly frog (the scowling boss) turns into a prince through love (or through appreciation by his employees). The Beast is ravaged by loneliness—but when he is able to care for another person, to move out of his private hell, he becomes gentle and handsome, capable of loving and being loved. The Beast is a creature who lives inside many of us, in one form or another, bearing either that name or some other. But when we recognize that the Beast isn't what he seems, that the intentions of the Beast are kind and good, we can transform even our most destructive behaviors into new and constructive ways of expression.

The mind is an amazing place, capable of performing the unthinkable. Here is where the Beast can be exchanged for Beauty, where intention can transform behavior, and we can become what we mean to be.

◆

REFRAME EXERCISE

1. Select a quiet place where you'll be undisturbed for about half an hour. Get away from phones and doorbell. Let yourself become comfortable. Breathe

deeply, relax. Remember this is an exploration, not a performance.

2. Do the Inner Reframe with yourself (see page 284). Follow the steps.

   - Identify a symptom or behavior you don't like or want to change in yourself.
   - Ask Part A, "What is your positive intention?" (Keep repeating this question until you get something positive.)
   - Tell Part B what the positive intention is.
   - Ask Part B to come up with three to six alternatives (three of them *not* conscious) to the problem behavior that will also satisfy the positive intention.
   - Ask Part A to review these alternatives and choose the best one. Ask it to use this behavior instead of the problem behavior.
   - Thank the parts.

3. Repeat the exercise several times, using the same problem behavior, until the process itself becomes easy and you're more comfortable in trusting your unconscious and allowing the spontaneous flow—the free association—to happen.

❖ ❖ ❖

THE PRINCE'S WIFE

There once was a king who had three sons, all of whom were of an age to be married. He gathered them to him and told them to go deep into the forest, shoot an arrow as far as possible, follow after it, and whoever was closest to where the arrow landed, that was who the prince was to marry.

The two eldest sons did as their father bade them and soon were married to two very beautiful women. The third son, too, set out to obey his father's wishes, but when he followed his arrow into the forest, he came upon a large lake and a huge, slimy, disgusting frog climbing out of it with the arrow in its mouth. Being a dutiful son, he married the frog. People laughed and made fun of him, but what no one knew was that at night, when they were alone together, the frog became a beautiful, smart, and talented woman. She spoke many languages, played several instruments, and was knowledgeable about all sorts of interesting subjects. The prince loved her very much. However, his two brothers teased him mercilessly. "Look at our beautiful wives while you—you poor stupid fool—are married to an ugly frog!"

Every year, the king gave a great banquet to which everyone in the kingdom came. The youngest prince begged his wife to come as her true self—since the banquet was at night, after the sun had set, she was able to do it—and because she loved her husband so much, she agreed.

On the night of the banquet she accompanied her husband as her beautiful self, and everyone fell in love with her grace, wit, charm, and intelligence. As the night was drawing to a close, the beautiful woman hurried to find the young prince, for she had to be back in their rooms and in her froggy skin before the sun rose or else she would be destroyed. When she couldn't find him, she returned alone and reached their home just before sunrise. She searched everywhere for her froggy skin but nowhere was it to be found. And then finally she saw it, but it was just the remains of her froggy skin, lying in a pile of ashes, for her husband had burned it.

She waited for him to return from the banquet and then

said to him with tears in her eyes, "My lord, I have loved you very much, but I must leave you now, for you did not love me enough to love my froggy part." And with that, she disappeared.

The prince was so devastated by what he had done that he left his kingdom and wandered for many years through unknown lands. One day, as he rested on a forest path, a hooded bandit came upon him by surprise. He took the prince's money, jewels, and fine clothing and was about to kill him when the prince pleaded for mercy. "Please spare me!" he begged.

The hooded bandit was in a wicked mood and laughed. "I will spare you only if you can tell me the answer to this riddle: What do all women want?"

"Surely," said the prince, "I can answer that, but I will need some time."

"You have the time to walk to that oak tree and back, that's all!" said the bandit, pointing to a tree no more than fifteen feet away.

The prince walked slowly to the tree. As he reached it, a humpbacked straggly-haired witch with warts covering her nose gestured to him from behind a branch. "Psst!" she called, "I know the answer. Marry me and I will tell you."

The prince gasped, seeing how ugly she was, but the bandit was shouting for him to come back or he would be murdered immediately, answer or no answer. "Yes," said the prince to the ugly witch, "I will. But first tell me the answer to the riddle!"

The witch whispered, "Sovereignty."

The prince returned to the bandit. "Sovereignty," he said, and the bandit vanished in a puff of smoke.

The prince was so relieved he forgot the ugly witch, but soon enough she was beside him, pulling at his arm. "Kiss me and our marriage will be sealed," she hissed at him.

As the prince was an honorable man, he leaned down and kissed her. In that moment, the witch was transformed into a stunning woman. "My love," she told him, "I can be beautiful for you when we are alone and be a witch when we are with others, or I can be beautiful with others and be a witch when we are alone. Which do you choose?"

"My lady," he said, "it is your choice."

From that moment, she was beautiful all the time.

◆ ◆ ◆

PART SEVEN

There Are Always More Choices

42

Defining Choices

Choices. Everybody has them. Everybody has more of them than they realize, sometimes more than they can handle.

You have choices because you're a process, and because of time. Life is an ongoing, dynamic process; everything's changing, and with change there are always more choices. It's part of the definition of being alive; not to change is death.

Change is flexibility, which is the capacity for creating choices. Flexibility means you can bend and not break. You can weather a storm, you can survive in different environments. To the yogis of India, a person is as old (or young) as his spine—a way of saying that you can remain young by remaining supple, flexible.

In evolution, the species that are able to adapt to the greatest number of environments and conditions prevail; the species with rigid demands on resources or with very specialized structures and behaviors die away when the resources aren't forthcoming or conditions change.

Having choices (flexibility) is being able to do, think, see, or feel in a new way. It's the ability to come up with a different response to an old situation, to break out of a rut or mold and to change the patterns of what you habitually do.

"There are always more choices" means you have a

choice about getting angry, about feeling dejected or overwhelmed, about saying destructive things to yourself, about
being intimidated by another person. Choice is a response
you've selected out of available alternatives. This doesn't
mean the toss of a coin, yes or no, either/or. (Remember:
one choice is no choice; two choices is a dilemma; three
choices—only now do you actively have choice.)

Nor is this the kind of choice that's involved in the
decision-making process of mediation boards and judicial
reviews. The choices that create changes in your internal
and external behavior are not part of an intellectual decision. Choice is easy, immediately available, effective and
automatic; something that has become unconscious.

During the reading of this book—particularly if you're
doing the exercises—you'll discover that you're making
little changes: in the way you think about some things, in
the way you picture them, the words you use, the feelings
you get. You've been learning to glide between your conscious and unconscious mind, carrying small changes—the
result of choices—from one to the other.

These changes lead to new choices, conscious or not, and
they in turn lead to new behaviors, which become automatic. The loop continues; what you do becomes how you
do it, which leads to new ways of doing it, which leads to
new behavior, thought, perception.

This is what everybody does most of the time—unless
you're feeling down or discouraged. And again, it's an interdependent cycle: Not having choices makes you feel discouraged so you don't make yourself available to new
choices, which in turn makes you feel bad, sad, or depressed.

Moving into uptime, becoming aware that there is *always*
another choice, more choices, means allowing yourself to
participate in the cycle of choice and change, of flexibility
and understanding.

How do you do that? What skills can you pull out of the magic toolbox that will allow you to expand beyond your usual way and patterns of doing and thinking and give you more choice?

I like to use an analogy.

You're riding down a road in a cart with wooden wheels. You've ridden down this road a lot, so that the wooden wheels have created deep ruts. You come to a fork. One road goes left, one road goes right. You've always gone left when you came to this point, so the left fork has deep ruts worn in it too.

But one day you come to the fork and think, I wonder what it's like to go right? You decide to try it out and see what happens.

Now, the only way you can get your wheels to go right is by getting out of the cart, lifting the cart out of the rut, and placing it in position on the right fork. So you do this.

The next time you come to the fork and want to go right, it's the same thing. You have to *think* about doing it, and you have to get out and lift your cart. Not until the rut is as deep on the right fork as it is on the left will you have choice. Only then can you come to the fork and go left or right with the same ease: only then do you have real choice.

That's what I mean when I say a choice has to be automatic. It has to be something you can do, think, or feel unconsciously. You don't have to "think" about a great tennis serve or swimming the backstroke or putting together a gorgeous outfit or responding to an audience or whatever it is you're really good at. You're good at it because it's built into your unconscious.

A choice isn't something you intellectually decide would be a good idea. That doesn't work. That's not a choice, that's intellectual awareness—which is a wonderful quality to have at your command, but it isn't real choice.

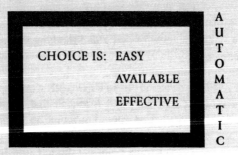

CHOICE IS: EASY

AVAILABLE

EFFECTIVE

A
U
T
O
M
A
T
I
C

Remember Pavlov's salivating dogs, changing the familiar Stimulus → Response? Choice comes when I break the old association of S—/→R and create a new association, a new response to the familiar stimulus. That means I have to dig the ruts, and run my wooden wheels over the ground until I can turn in either direction with equal effort. At that point I have choice—and when I come to the fork I can go left or right.

If Paula, the woman boss in chapter 41, starts treating her male and female employees equally, she has a *choice* at any given time whether to treat all her employees equally or to discriminate among them. If Felix, in chapter 8, whose cognitive pattern is noticing difference, now trains himself to notice sameness, he has provided himself with the *choice* of what he will notice the next time he enters a room.

Intellectual awareness, as I said, isn't choice—though before you can have choice you have to realize that it's possible to substitute other forms of behavior for your customary response.

You have to become aware that what you do is a habit, part of your routine, a dependency, or an addiction: The nature of it is that *you don't have a choice*. You set your alarm for the same time every morning; you have your own inflexible getting-up routine; you brush your teeth in a certain way; you take a coffee break at the same time every day; you always reach for the same brands of shaving cream, deodorant, mouthwash; you call your mother—or expect a call—on Sunday before noon; you play a computer game before you get started on the day's work; you wear a specific pair of shoes with a specific suit; you hear the same words going round in your head every time the boss calls you into his office; you make the same pictures in your mind before you visit your cousins; you have a sensation of pressure in the center of your chest whenever the phone rings early in the morning.

Any of these patterns can be changed or expanded to allow choice. But first you have to realize that this pattern of behavior, this way of thinking or doing something, *is* a habit or fixed pattern and can be changed—if you want it changed—to a behavior that's more useful to you. At that point you're able to intervene and substitute a new behavior. Then you install the change—the substitute behavior— on an unconscious level. Only then does it become automatic.

At this point it becomes a choice: easy, available, effective.

43

Your Model of the World

Each of us has our own model of the world, though we're usually not aware of it. It's something we take for granted, like the way we think.

Our model of the world is our personal way of perceiving and assimilating experience, made up of everything we've done, thought, and experienced. Our private history, beliefs, and values, and the way we bring them all together, give us our model. It's unique with each of us, and yet most people think that his or her model of the world is the best.

At least, most of us usually think our model of the world is *true* in a way that someone else's isn't—and "true" usually has a way of turning into "better."

If I experience the world visually and you experience it kinesthetically, I'll think you don't really *see* the world as it is—and you probably think I have no *gut* connection with reality. The point is, we are who we are, we think as we think, and we take this for granted as the only way to be, the only way to go. We're prisoners (or guardians) of our habitual patterns of thought and behavior. Our "limited thinking" makes it possible to focus, to concentrate; without it, our thoughts would sprawl all over the place and we'd never reach the end of them. Limits give shape to what we do, though they also narrow our choices.

Nobody can get out of his or her model of the world;

that's like trying to get out of your own skin. Your model, or paradigm, is everything you believe to be true. One plus one equals two. Water runs down, not up. If it didn't, nothing would make sense anymore. You have to spend all your available energy on figuring out how to get a drink of water when you're thirsty.

The best you can do is to be aware that you're inside your own system or set of perceptions ("truths"), realize that it's your model of the world speaking, and that somebody else has a different take on things. You can become aware that much of what you do is automatic, that you're inside a rut—and you can choose to peer out over this rut, over the edge of your usual limits, and expand your model of the world. You can choose to increase your own possibilities.

Ordinarily, your model of the world limits the choices you make. You're caught within your own ruts and you travel along well-worn tracks. But what if you do peek over the edge and ask, "How could I do this differently? How would someone else do it?"

That means getting into another person's model of the world, putting yourself in someone else's shoes. Being able to experience something as visual, for instance, when you habitually experience it as tactile. Another model of the world is another way of perceiving things: seeing them from someone else's point of view, hearing your own words as if another person were saying them. It's changing your perspective, getting a different handle on things.

In chapter 40, we saw that reframing brings greater flexibility in dealing with a destructive situation or pattern. Instead of trying to get rid of the problem, we looked for alternatives to the undesired behavior that satisfied the basic intent or purpose of the (negative) behavior but in a positive or nurturing way.

Realizing that alternative behavior is possible leads to

choice among the alternatives. If there's no alternative, we're stuck: We remain in the rut, the same awful words repeat themselves inside our heads, the same feelings of choking happen each time we visit a particular person, the same images come up again and again, and we're caught in an endless round of repetition. In fact, that's how we define the feeling of being stuck or frustrated or powerless: having no alternative, no way out.

With the possibility of choice, we're able to perceive a problem differently and to search for other or different kinds of solutions. This is flexibility: new choices opening up new possibilities, leading to creativity and change.

But how, specifically, do we do this? When a situation seems hopeless, how can we even begin to think in terms of choice? How does someone initiate the move out of negative or limiting situations? What can you actually do to get yourself up out of the rut and onto the wide road of possibilities? How do you expand your choices? How do you even become aware that they exist?

The magic toolbox of your mind contains many techniques for changing lack of choice into a large assortment of possibilities. Each of these techniques is a different way of using the master tool, imagination.

Imagination, which takes much of its power from the unconscious (through what we sometimes call "intuition" or the "creative process"), permits you to experience *things as they aren't*. You take the limiting situation or emotion or memory and change it around in some way that permits you to see, hear, or feel it differently, which in turn changes the meaning or effect that this situation, emotion, or memory has on you.

Think of eggs. Think of milk. Think of flour. Now think of cake—chocolate, strawberry, coconut, mocha, or any kind you like. The same three ingredients go into all of them. You just have to know what to do with the ingredients, how to put them together.

Choices—the fact that you have them and the ability to make use of them—are like the simple eggs, milk, and flour of a cake when used with a recipe. And the specific techniques or processes to use in situations where you are stuck I call recipes for choice.

These are step-by-step instructions or "how-tos" (like the blueprint for success), to use as you would a recipe when you're cooking or baking—first to learn the technique and after that whenever you need a reminder or refresher. You can make your own adaptations, putting in your own ingredients (in the form of your particular problem or situation), and you can share the recipe with friends.

All these recipes are ways of increasing choices and flexibility when you're stuck. Non-Polar Thinking is the one to use with negative memories. Shifting Perspectives is for negative interactions. Dissolving Negative Emotions is, as the name implies, for negative emotions, and the submodality recipe called Pop-It! is what you need for negative thoughts.

Each recipe works in a different way. Non-Polar Thinking projects the memory through different sensory perceptions; Shifting Perspectives lets you experience the same situation from three distinct points of view; Dissolving Negative Emotions relies on your own resources to mitigate unpleasant emotions; and Pop-It! is a radical technique to switch instantly from negative to positive thoughts. Each of these four recipes is printed at the end of the upcoming chapter that illustrates how and when to use it.

44

Non-Polar Thinking

Non-Polar Thinking is the opposite of polar thinking, and to understand what it is we have to look at what it is not.

Polar thinking is oppositional, thinking in extremes and opposing one to the other like poles at opposite sides of the playing field or at the ends of the earth. It's either-or, right-wrong, good-bad, wonderful or terrible, yes or no, north or south, with nothing in between. It deals in polarities, and is always rigid.

Polar thinking is judgmental—you *must*, you *shouldn't*—and though there are certain situations when polar thinking might be helpful (when you're teaching a child about *not* crossing streets alone, for instance), it's important to be aware when you're doing polar thinking so that you can have a choice about it.

Polar thinking can be useful, even necessary, in establishing laws or moral principles (murder is wrong, rape is wrong, stealing is wrong). Parents of young children might want to set down absolute values (God is good; we love Grandma) that don't permit shadings. But on the whole it's more useful to do non-polar thinking, which offers alternatives to either-or and leads to more flexibility, creativity, and choice.

It's one thing to tell your kids, "Rape is absolutely wrong"; it's something very different to say to them, "It's never OK to have sex before marriage."

Of course, if your religion and/or morality stipulate this, you're going to say exactly that. But since most kids are probably going to experiment in some way or other (or spend an enormous amount of time thinking about it), it's certainly more useful (and more helpful to them) if you do some non-polar thinking about sex: When (under what conditions) is having sex not acceptable at all? What are the conditions that make it more acceptable or make it safer to have sex? Not just safer from a medical point of view but safer emotionally, mentally?

You might tell your children that it's essential to care about the person you're going to have sex with, not necessarily to be in love, but at least to have respect for the person as a human being. That it's important to have sex when *you* want it, not when somebody else wants you to or because everyone else is doing it.

Whatever values you might want to instill in your children, only if you're open to different points of view can you and they actually discuss the subject, and you'll have far more influence than if you put a wall between the two of you in the form of polar thinking: My way is right, your way is wrong. Once the wall is up, it's very hard to bring it down again.

Polar thinking uses "always" and "never." I don't want to give the impression that I'm doing it just by saying you must *never* do polar thinking or that it's *always* good to do non-polar thinking. That would be ridiculous. What I *am* saying is, be aware if you're doing it. Polar thinking might be a part of your model of the world. It can lead to prejudice.

"All red-haired people are angry."

"Everybody who drinks alcohol is an alcoholic."

Or even "Always respect your elders"—usually a fine sentiment, but what do you do if one of your elders is abusing you?

Polarities help to hold up institutions like law and religion, which may be necessary for the workings of society in general, but as individuals we need to get in between the good-bad, either-or, so that we can expand our model of the world and, by enlarging our understanding, increase our choices.

We do this by switching from polar to non-polar thinking.

Non-polar thinking is observational or, as I call it, "optional" thinking, because it allows options, it lets you make any number of distinctions between extremes of good and bad. It's also observational, the opposite of judgmental, relying on what you see, hear, and feel.

To get to non-polar thinking about something from the past that continues to control some present behavior and prevents you from changing it, you start by calling up this limiting memory about which you seem to have no choice. Then you go through the experience, reliving it along different sensory routes. You use observational thinking to get more information about everything that was going on at the time or place. What you learn enables you to take a new perspective about that experience and changes the way the memory affects you.

I'll illustrate with a woman who came to see me just after Thanksgiving. Bernice (not her real name) is a young-looking forty, with close-cropped hair and the kind of skin you can practically see through. She speaks quickly, as if tossing out parcels of words at a time. Her hands fly up to her face when something bothers her particularly, and her fingers drum rapidly along her jawbone.

Bernice gets very anxious every year as Christmas approaches. When she was a young girl, her father, who was not ordinarily an alcoholic, would go to Christmas office parties and come back drunk, then would fight with her mother, in a way that terrified Bernice.

Now, as an adult, when Christmas approaches Bernice feels a desperation to make it wonderful and at the same time fears it will be terrible. This has become a kind of self-fulfilling prophecy. If somebody does anything the slightest bit unpredictable, she blows it out of proportion. Christmas is either-or, fairy tale or disaster. It has to be terrible or wonderful, with nothing in between.

This is where Bernice is stuck. We do the non-polar thinking exercise to soften the extremes and permit her to have choice.

First, I ask her to remember just one of the times when her father came home drunk and verbally abused her mother.

Go through that memory as though it's a movie. Watch the whole story, from the beginning, through the middle, to the end. See yourself in it. Watch yourself in the memory.

When I'm satisfied that she's done this, I say:

OK. Take a deep breath. Change your posture. Sit up. Lift your rib cage.
Keep your head up. Take a few more deep breaths.

That's the first ''screening'' of the memory. Now I ask her to go through it again, but in a different way. I'm asking her to enter into the movie and direct her consciousness toward what she *sees*, focusing on *visual* information only.

Now step into this memory and go through it again from beginning to end. Focus on everything you see. Fill your consciousness as best you can with the visual memory. Don't bother about what you might hear or what you might feel in your body, just concentrate on

*seeing everything. Look around the room: What colors
are the walls? The furniture? Any patterns in the up-
holstery? Are there pictures? Can you see a pattern
in the carpet?*

*Now look at your mother. Look at your father. What
is your mother wearing? Does she have a dress on?
Skirt or pants? Blouse, sweater? What colors can you
see in the outfit? Notice how her hair is styled. Is it
short or long? Any gray in it? What is your father
wearing? If he has on a shirt, is it open at the neck?
Buttoned? Is he wearing a tie? How close are your
mother and father to each other? Standing, sitting?
What expressions do you see on their faces? Can you
notice any gestures they make?*

*Go through this memory and fill your consciousness
with visual information, everything you can possibly
see about this experience—colors, light, design: the
shapes of things, their size, the sizes of things in relation to each other; the quality and source of the
light.*

When she gets to the end of that memory I ask her to
erase it or, as actors say, "break state." I ask her again to
sit up, change her posture, relax her neck and shoulders,
and take a couple of deep breaths.

Then I tell her to go through the memory again, this time
paying close attention to what she can *hear*, to fill her consciousness as best she can with all the *auditory* information
she can extract from the memory.

*Go back to the beginning of the memory. Listen to the
sounds in the room, the sounds coming in from outside. If you want to, close your eyes. [This is usually
helpful.]*

Listen to your mother's voice, your father's voice.

Not just what they're saying, hear the difference in the pitch of their voices. Are they speaking in whispers? If they're shouting, what's the difference in voice level, in volume? How quickly are they speaking? Are their voices of equal tempo?

What surrounding sounds or noises can you hear? Music from anywhere? Is the wind blowing? Rain or sleet falling on the windowpane? The hush of new snow? Is the dog panting, snoring? Can you hear the cat scratching at the door? A rustling of papers? The whistle of a boiling kettle? Birds outside? Cars going by?

Most important, make sure you listen to the quality of the voices in the room.

Again, she breaks state: takes another deep breath, moves her shoulders, changes her posture, relaxes.

For the final rerun I ask her to go through the memory again. This time she is to pay as much attention as possible to the sensations in her body. *Sensations*, I repeat—pressure, contractions, expansions, temperature, vibrations—*not* emotions. Emotions are the result of judgment and interpretation, a decision that something is good or bad. What we want here is *observation*: gathering information about the body's senses and sensations. I now tell her:

Go through the memory. Fill your consciousness with everything that's happening in your body. Your arms and legs, hands and feet—how do they feel? Are your feet numb? Do you have vibrations in them? Is the lower part of your body colder or warmer than the upper part? Your diaphragm, chest—

"I feel I'm choking," she says. "I can't breathe."

That's not observation, it's interpretation. I ask her to be specific, as a way of leading her into observational thinking.

Where exactly do you have this sensation? At the base of your throat? Your chest?

"*Yes,*" she says, "*there.*" She points to it.

OK, your chest. You're feeling pressure there. Does it radiate out? How far does it radiate? Does the pressure extend all the way across to your shoulders? Does it go down to your diaphragm? Is the pressure more intense at the center, becoming less intense the farther out it extends? Is there a different temperature at the center of where you feel the choking or the not-breathing?

What other body signals are you picking up? Do you feel your fingertips, your scalp? Are your ears burning? . . .

When she gets to the end of the memory she takes a deep breath, relaxes, moves her shoulders, looks around the room.

I ask her to think of the original memory, the original version of the movie she's been playing in her head. What does she think about it? What does she feel about it?

"Easier," she says. Bernice hadn't remembered until we went through the exercise that her aunt and uncle were also present—they always came to visit at Christmastime—and that her aunt was cooking. (Bernice heard the sounds from the kitchen when I mentioned the whistle of the kettle.) Noticing that there were other people in the house opened up the memory for her and she realized that the "bad part" lasted a much shorter time than she had remembered.

"This gives me a lot more information," she tells me. "It makes [the memory] easier to look back on. It makes me realize it was just unpleasant, nothing really terrible—and that after a while things settled down to more or less "normal," or at least bearable anyway, and we had our Christmas dinner and sang carols and we didn't have such a bad time after all."

This is a typical response. People who go through this exercise usually say that they've gained a better understanding by the end of it, more information about what happened, and that the dread or unpleasantness surrounding the memory seems to fade away.

Note: This exercise is not appropriate for deeply traumatic memories. In such cases, the person usually needs to consult with a professional.

You can also do a Non-Polar Thinking exercise with a future goal, using a "memory" in the future.

Trudi Ann, as I'll call her, is a young architect who has a terrible time with job interviews—"I *never* do well at them," she assures me—and the "never" signals to me that she's thinking in polarities.

What she says next clinches it.

I'm very proud of my designs. But I can never *seem to put them over. I go into someone's office, and—I'm my own* worst *enemy. I* always *antagonize the guy because I* absolutely *don't know the* right *way to respond.*

She's been asked to present her design for a clinic to an important group of investors.

It's the best design I've ever made. I really want to do it. But I'll never be able to convince anyone of its value.

We do the non-polar exercise. Trudi Ann recalls the last time she failed to get a job. She goes through the memory as if it were a movie, doing the triple descriptions—*visual, auditory*, and *kinesthetic*—with a break between each, just as Bernice did. When she's completed the last reenactment of the memory, I ask what she's learned.

> *Hey, you know—it's amazing I never realized it be-fore—I was mixing up these two things. See, since I look like this* [Trudi Ann was a model for a while and still looks like one] *I come in, there's a man sitting there, and I'm on the defensive. I'm watching myself in that memory, walking in too fast. I start talking to him very fast, don't let him get a word in edgewise. When he's talking to me, I jump in, cut him off.*
>
> *I didn't even give him a chance to look at the design I was presenting him.*

She realized she was talking too quickly by listening to her own voice—tempo, volume—and to the voice of the person who was interviewing her. She realized she was moving too fast, felt herself out of breath, her breathing shallow.

> *I figured he was sizing me up as a woman. But I wasn't aware of that—I mean, thinking like that—until just now doing this exercise. There I am, behaving as though this guy was coming on to me, when in reality he probably could care less and the reason I was there was to show him what I could do, my work.*

Consciously, she wanted to make a good impression. Un-consciously, a lot was going on that came out in her be-havior: fast movements, nonstop talking.

*And when you told me to pay attention to my body—
mainly, my hands were moving so fast it could
make anybody nervous. I don't think I gave the guy a
chance to really evaluate my design because in some
way I was telling him to evaluate me, or else that's what
I was scared he was doing. Something like that. But I
sure didn't give him a chance to look at the design.*

What Trudi Ann learned from this made it possible for
her to have choice, to take control of the future situation,
and to change her behavior. From failure to feedback. From
choice to control to change.

◆

RECIPE FOR CHOICE I
Non-Polar Thinking

Non-polar thinking is a release from the rigidity of a disturbing or limiting memory. New information provides
choice in how to think about the memory.

1. Identify a limiting or disturbing memory that continues to bother you.
2. Turn this memory into a movie and watch yourself in
   it.
3. Go back to the beginning and step inside yourself.
   Redo the movie from this perspective.
   Concentrate on what you *see*: colors, shapes, light,
   patterns, the size of things. Turn off all other sensory
   perceptions and fill your consciousness with visual information only.
4. Redo the movie from the beginning, concentrating on
   what you hear.

Listen to sounds, voices, words, tonality, tempo. Turn off all other sensory perceptions and fill your consciousness with auditory information only.

5. Redo the movie from the beginning, concentrating on your physical sensations.

   Pay attention to temperature, movement, texture, pressure, and expansion—and to the way these variables shift and change. Turn off all other sensory perceptions and fill your consciousness with what you feel in your body.

6. Call up the original memory.

   You will have gained new information about the experience that will change the way you think about the memory and make the memory less disturbing.

45

Shifting Perspectives

The ideas of Neuro Linguistic Programming spring from different sources that join together in a unified approach to communication and change. One of these sources is the work of anthropologist Gregory Bateson, whose concept of ''triple description''—the perception that all experiences can be described in at least three different ways—is at the heart of Shifting Perspectives.

Basically, it means that the way you look at things determines what you see. An apple to a hungry person is something to eat; to Cézanne, it's the subject of a painting or series of paintings; to a biblical scholar, it's the embodiment of man's disobedience, the reason for our loss of Eden. Your model of the world, the place you're coming from, your presuppositions: All these determine how you interpret experience.

But when an experience becomes static or painful, like a recurring interaction that leaves you frustrated, you want to be able to change the way you view it, so that you can open it up to choice.

The technique of shifting perspectives lets you move between three perceptual positions—Self, Observer, Other— to look at the interaction from different angles, points of view, or models of the world and then return to your own perspective with new information that allows you to evaluate your interaction from a fresh perspective. You expand your choices by changing the way you look at something.

You peer out over the edge of your model of the world to see what else might be available, taking any one of the three perceptual positions and moving between them.

The position of Self means seeing through your eyes, hearing through your ears, feeling your sensations and emotions. This is the starting position, home, where your model of the world comes from.

Or you can take the position of (dissociated) Observer: watching yourself and the other person, listening to yourself and the other, observing your feelings. You're like a camera, an onlooker, a spectator: one step removed.

The third position is Other. It's the ability to identify with and through another person. You see the world through someone else's eyes, hear what they're hearing, start to get a sense of what it *is* actually *to be* someone other than who you are. This allows you to have a sense of what the other person could be feeling.

Of course there's no guarantee you're going to be absolutely correct. But even starting to get in touch with how someone else approaches experience can be very useful. It's part of empathy: the capacity to identify with another person. It can enormously broaden your model of the world, opening up a completely new set of choices.

You do this position the way an actor does a role: by imagining you can literally step into the character or persona of someone else. You act *as if*; you pretend to be someone else; you adopt the person's posture; you allow yourself to begin to have his or her feelings. From this position, you can look at yourself and the situation or interaction in a new way. The shift in point of view increases your awareness, gives you new information, and makes you more flexible, which means a much wider range of choices.

Let's go over the recipe for shifting perspectives with

Claudette, a recently divorced woman with two young children. Formerly a computer programmer and now without a job, Claudette lives close to her mother, who helps take care of the children while Claudette goes back to school.

Claudette loves her mother in a traditional way but doesn't like her very much. She feels her mother doesn't really acknowledge her, doesn't recognize who she is as an independent person, doesn't respect her or approve of her. In most interactions with her mother, Claudette says,

I let her have her own way. I go along with whatever she says, whatever she wants to do, just to avoid a big hassle. I resent it, though, and if I could I wouldn't have much to do with my mother, at least not now, when I have all these other things to deal with—but I don't have any choice because of the kids.

There are three chairs in the room, each representing one of the perceptual positions. When Claudette goes to Chair No. 1, the position of Self, she sees her mother frowning at her, her mouth pinched and disapproving; she hears her mother's loud voice asking the same questions over and over:

Are you sure that what you're studying is going to help you earn a better living? Are you sure it's worth investing all this time in your new training? How do you know this is going to pay off? Are you thinking about the children's future? Are you being sensible?

In this position, Claudette feels small, unimportant, as if she's of no account; as if her knowledge, skills, opinions aren't worth anything.

Now she goes to Chair No. 2, the Observer position, and becomes a neutral audience, stepping back from the confrontation. She's not invested in either Claudette or Mother's being right or wrong, she's just watching and listening to them, observing, not judging or interpreting.

She sees Mother standing very close to Claudette, hovering over her. Mother is looking directly at Claudette and seems to be trying to reach out to her with her hands, but keeps pulling them back before she can touch her daughter, who stands with her head down, her body turned away.

Remaining in Observer position, Claudette listens to the two of them: Mother's loud insistent voice repeating the same things over and over and Claudette's own barely audible responses, short phrases, sometimes monosyllables, spoken in a low monotone: "No . . . Yes . . . I don't know . . . You're probably right" and then "I have to go now."

In Chair No. 3, the Other position, Claudette reluctantly becomes Mother—and suddenly gasps as she enters the experience from this perspective, seeing and hearing the interaction through Mother's eyes and ears. This is how she describes it as Mother:

> *I'm trying to reach Claudette, but she won't respond to me; it's as though I'm not there. I see someone who's so sad and lonely and closed off, I'm very worried about her. I miss her; I wish she'd see me—even if she yelled at me, I'd feel as though at least she knew I was there.*

When Claudette returned to her Self position, she brought with her the recognition that her relationship with her mother was not unilateral, not a one-way street. She realized she controlled it as much as her mother did.

By seeing the interaction from her mother's position, Claudette now recognized the possibility that her mother could feel as ignored or unacknowledged by her as she did by her mother. "Amazing!" she said. She could hardly believe it—and for a moment she tossed her head back and forth as if shaking off the remains of a dream.

Claudette began to have a different perception of the interaction between them. She realized that her mother cared about her and worried about her and wanted to have a connection with her. Claudette decided to change her behavior when she was with her mother—to look at her when she was speaking, to disagree when she felt like it, and to tell her mother what she was feeling and thinking. It was like a whole new beginning, she told me later. A small shift, and everything seemed to change for the better.

With Claudette, the shift in perceptual positions worked like a charm. It was as if a clasp had been suddenly opened and she was able to see both sides of the locket.

But this technique isn't about "fixing." The situation you start with doesn't suddenly disappear. It's simply that by changing the point of view you get out of your traditional or habitual ruts, you can think about things in a different way, and the fresh approach brings on new possibilities.

The skill we call shifting perspectives means taking up the three positions in turn and acting them out like separate characters or like puppets—observing, on the one hand, self; on the other, other.

Milton Erickson, a major contributor to the rich network of ideas that form the outlook and methodology of NLP, said that change depends on the ability to alter our perspective, to have a sense of the future and a sense of humor about ourselves.

Having a sense of humor about yourself stems from the ability to be an observer. It means I can step back and laugh at myself, not in a negative way that makes me feel foolish or clumsy, but in a way that lets me be part of the fun, aware of absurdity. Laughter gives a sense of proportion: How important actually is this problem in the scheme of things? By comparison to the problems of the world? To other problems in my life? In relation to someone else's problem?

Every actor knows about stepping in and out of character, and every writer (and reader) knows about changing points of view to make a story more interesting or to give it greater breadth. The "I" doesn't have to be the actual author.

Moby Dick opens with "Call me Ishmael," but nobody thinks Herman Melville is announcing a name change. What he's doing is telling the story from the point of view (perspective) of Ishmael, the narrator (the observer).

And even if the story is by you and about you, it's a good idea to shift perspectives, to step back and be the Observer or to go forward with compassion and try to get an understanding of what it is to be someone other than the person you usually are. These forays into perspectives other than your own bring you back to your self extraordinarily enriched, with your model of the world expanded by your experience from different points of view.

Now let's try an experiment. Let's assume that all the world's a stage: that includes this book and you, wherever you're reading it. Let these pages be our scenery; you are playing the leading role and I'm your director and stage manager. Instead of using someone else as an example to show how this technique actually works, we'll use you. I'll give the stage directions, tell you what props you need, and give you the cue lines so you know when to start. We'll call it *Triple Play*; or, *Shifting Perspectives in Three Parts*.

Arrange three chairs in a kind of ring or triangle. That is, there will always be one chair to the side of you and another chair opposite you. Each chair is equidistant from the other two. Label the chairs as 1, 2, and 3.

#2

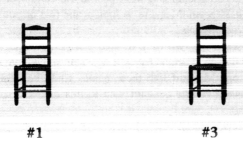

#1   #3

Part I of the exercise is to define the problem or situation. Think of an interaction that limits you, a relationship you feel stuck in or dissatisfied with. (Remember: nothing traumatic or overwhelming.) Now sit in Chair No. 1, the Self position. In the first chair you take the role of Actor 1, Self, the person who uses the pronoun "I." Call up the interaction. See it with your eyes, hear it with your ears, feel in your body whatever sensations or emotions this experience brings you. And as you remember this experience, describe it.

Describe the interaction from the point of view of Self— always using "I"—seeing, hearing, feeling the situation from your own (usual) perspective.

In Part II of the exercise, you get out of the position of Self and into the position of Observer. Now you're going to be changing your seat (a lot of action in this play!). Go and sit in chair No. 2. Do it. Literally do it. Take your book along with you. In the second chair you take the role of Actor 2, Observer, who uses the pronouns "she," "he," "them," or "they."

You've moved to the Observer position (chair No. 2) so that you can imagine looking and listening to yourself and the other person from this place outside yourself. It's as though you got up and went behind the curtain of an old-fashioned portrait camera to look at the two of you from a different position.

Observe the two of you. Use your own name and the other person's actual name. Let's call you Chris and the other one Marty. (Both these names could be either male or female; gender isn't relevant to this model of an interaction.)

Describe what both of you look like at this moment. What is Chris wearing? Describe Chris's facial expressions and posture: Shoulders slumped? Rib cage up or down? Do the same for Marty. How are the two sitting—or standing? Do you see any pinched lines on the faces? Furrows on the forehead? Wrinkles between the eyebrows? Any unusual color or splotches of color?

Watch the breathing: Is it shallow or deep? Fast or slow? How do the voices differ? Listen to volume and tempo, the varying pitches of the voices. Listen to how the two are talking, to the words and tonality.

What do you notice about the setting where this is taking place, the actual room or surroundings? Indoors or out? Windows, walls? Grass, concrete? Is the light bright or faint? What time of day is it? What sounds surround them? Do you hear background noises?

Describe the feelings you're having as the observer: about the interaction, about Chris and Marty.

In Part III of the exercise, you see yourself from the perspective of the Other.

Get up and move to chair No. 3, the position of the person you are interacting with in this difficult situation. In the third chair you take the role of Actor 3, Other (in this instance Marty), who uses the pronouns "I," "her," or "him."

You are now this other person—this Marty—probably someone you know well, a friend, lover, colleague, boss, member of your family.

Imagine you can step inside Marty's shoes, as literally as possible. You know Marty's posture; take on that posture.

Good. You are now inside looking out through Marty's eyes, hearing through Marty's ears. Allow yourself to begin to have Marty's feelings.

In this position, look at Self (Chris) in chair No. 1. I'd like you, Marty, to describe Chris and the interaction. What do you see *specifically*? What do you hear? You've listened to Chris and yourself. How do you think the two of you are dealing with this situation?

Rehearse this exercise as often as you need to—as long as you feel there's more information to be mined from it. Relive the experience from beginning to end in each fully enacted position, making sure the input from your three major sensory systems—visual, auditory, and kinesthetic—is coming only from that perceptual position. Be sure not to mix up sensory input, like seeing yourself or having the other's feelings when you're in the Self position.

Start making the move from one chair to another more quickly each time until you are fully comfortable in each position, in each role you take on.

When you're secure in all three positions, forget about acting. Go back to the original limiting interaction. Ask yourself what you know now that you didn't before.

Imagine how you'll be different the next time you interact with this person.

◆

RECIPE FOR CHOICE II
Shifting Perspectives

Shifting Perspectives is for use with unproductive interactions with others, relationships or situations where you get stuck. It allows you to be in the other person's shoes as well as your own, and also to observe both of you from a dissociated position. This exercise encourages empathy as well as dispassionate observation and increases choice by changing the angle of perception or point of view of the interaction.

1. Think of an interaction with a particular person that is troublesome for you, that makes you feel bad about yourself.
2. Set up three positions (chairs) that you can alternate between as Self, Observer, and Other.
3. Go to the Self position.
   Recall and participate in the interaction between yourself and the other person through your own eyes and ears, allowing yourself to have the emotions of the experience contained within the situation.
4. Go to the Observer position.
   You are now dissociated. See yourself and the other person, watch and listen to the two of you. Your emotions will be about what you observe.
5. Go to the Other position.
   Be the other person, seeing through his or her eyes, hearing through his or her ears, allowing yourself to feel his or her emotions.

6. After having lived through the interaction from each of the three positions, review the new insights and information you've gained. Then repeat the exercise, adding new information with each repetition.

◆

46

Dissolving Negative Emotions

Emotions can be like a tidal wave, rising up and threatening to overpower you. Sometimes even when you can see the emotion about to come crashing down, it seems there's nothing you can do. You can't run, can't hide—you just stand there and let it break over you.

Emotions don't listen to reason. Emotions are usually not "sensible," and they're often not appropriate for the situation you're in.

Let me explain what I mean by the "appropriateness" of emotions. Remember that an emotion is simply the label we give to a thought or an idea that's accompanied by a body sensation. Emotions can be painful, uncomfortable, pleasurable, but they're not "good" or "bad." *Appropriate* means that the emotion fits the situation. If I lose my job, I feel discouraged. If a friend dies, I'm sad. When I'm learning something new, I sometimes get confused. These emotions suit the circumstances and are therefore appropriate. However, if I'm learning something new and get in a panic, or if the toaster breaks and I become enraged, or if a client cancels an appointment and I'm deeply depressed, my emotions are not appropriate to the situation. It's not healthy to change appropriate emotions—emotions are an important means of expression in our lives—but it's certainly helpful to be able to change emotions when they're inappropriate.

The grip of emotion can feel like a vise. It can be thrilling—passionate love, terror on a roller coaster, a sense of awe among glaciers or when watching a brilliant sunset—or it can be very limiting. You become like a child, a baby, helpless in the grip of an emotion from which you can't escape. Like a small boat bobbing in a thunderstorm, you're rocked on that emotion. All you want is for it to *stop*.

In chapter 15 we talked about creating anchors. We're going to use them again here, to keep us safe, hold us in place when an emotional storm threatens.

Anchors, as you'll remember, are ways of intervening between stimulus and response, creating a pause between the two parts of an automatic reaction (stimulus→response) to provide a possibility for a new response to become attached to the old stimulus.

In other words, we "teach" our unconscious to make new choices available. When the new emotion becomes automatic, it can stand in for the old. It becomes an alternative, and the familiar pattern can now be interrupted by a new response.

Basically, what we're doing is reprogramming our responses. Neuro Linguistic Programming, as its name implies, is based on the way experience is programmed. To change experience, or to change the impact an experience has on us, we have to change the programming; and we do this by interrupting the automatic connection of stimulus and response.

WE INTERRUPT
THIS PROGRAM

to stop the behaviors, habits, thoughts, memories that are destructive or wasteful. We replace the undesired response with a desired one, and then

WE RETURN

to the situation or memory but with a new response, which is installed in place of the old one, giving us immediate and automatic access to a new emotion.

We do this through anchoring, a technique for securing our resources so that we can use them to change emotions. In chapter 16, Future Conditioning, we used anchoring to *replace* an undesired response with a more positive or useful one. We can also use the technique of anchoring to *neutralize* a negative emotion.

Dissolving negative emotions doesn't mean going from sad to glad, bad to good. As with the other techniques, this isn't about "fixing." It's creating options to the feeling of being stuck, becoming able to hold your own when negative feelings threaten to limit you.

This is how you do it.

Think of a time when you experienced the emotion you want to have more choice about. Go into the experience, seeing, hearing, and feeling it through your own body, and as you're doing this hold on to an anchor, such as touching thumb and forefinger together or putting pressure on a specific place on wrist or knee or elbow. Hold the anchor for ten seconds. Then "break state," take a deep breath, and relax.

Now think of the *opposite* emotion to the one that limits you. This is not the same as the one you want to have. Remember a time when you experienced this opposite emotion and relive it, while holding on to a different and opposite anchor (thumb and forefinger of the *other* hand, for example; pressure on the *opposite* wrist or knee). Again, hold the anchor for ten seconds. Then break state, take a deep breath, and relax.

Now hold both anchors at the same time. When you do this, both emotions start rushing at each other. The first (negative) emotion washes over you; then its opposite comes at you—they volley back and forth, pitching you from side to side in an emotional rocker. And then—calm. The seas of emotion will subside. You sail through.

Now think of the original memory. It's much easier to take, isn't it?

Think of a time in the future when the old emotions might have threatened to limit you. It's not so threatening now. It all seems possible; you can get through the storm and out, safe and calm.

Tanya (not her real name) is a law student, usually independent and self-sufficient. But whenever Justin, her boyfriend of three years, goes away, she feels "disconnected . . . alone." She has trouble concentrating; she gets nervous: "It interferes with the rest of my life," she says, adding, "I don't mean I can't function *at all*. It's not as bad as that, not a trauma. But I have this feeling of separation, and it ties me in knots. I brood. Look, I know he's got to do this, it's his profession. I don't want to be a drag on him— or on myself either."

Tanya wants more choice about the feelings that come over her whenever Justin leaves. These feelings interfere, as she says, with her life in general—and in particular, now that she's about to take the bar exam and needs to use every possible moment to prepare.

"I don't try to stop him from going; that would be ridiculous, and impossible besides. This is his *work*. It's up to me to overcome my feelings about it, I know that. But whenever he leaves I get fearful. I'm afraid he's gone forever. The separation makes me feel as if he isn't there anymore—in my life, I mean."

Here is where the Dissolving Negative Emotions recipe can come to Tanya's rescue. She can do it herself, without input from me, trying it out like the reader of this book.

Let's assume Tanya knows what a self-anchor is (that

she's read Part II, You Have All the Resources You Need), and knows the importance of anchoring in precisely the same way each time—the same gesture, the same amount of pressure—so the anchor will be effective.

She chooses a comfortable chair, switches the ringer of her telephone to OFF, closes her eyes, places her feet squarely on the ground, and begins the exercise.

> *Remember one of the times when Justin went away and you felt awful: separated, alone. Slip into the experience. See it as you saw it then, when he went to Boston, the colors. . . . He's wearing the green shirt I gave him, packing his clothes, the suitcase on the bed. Now I can see him closing his bags, walking to the door; I can hear the door closing, the way he says, "Love ya, Peachy," with that little catch in his voice, the song on the radio; and I feel the quick squeeze of his hand on my shoulder before he's out the door and then the weight coming down, the sense of pressure in my chest: the heat, then the cold.*
>
> *Now, as you're reexperiencing the memory, reach up with your left hand and hold your left earlobe. Continue to hold it for ten seconds as you go on reliving the memory.*
>
> *Release the anchor, open your eyes. Look around you, take a deep breath. Another one. Stand up. Stretch. Sit down again.*
>
> *Now identify the opposite emotion. Not feeling alone, not separated. (This isn't what you want necessarily, it's the opposite of what you don't want.) What's the opposite of being separated? Being together, togetherness.*
>
> *Remember a time when you felt "togetherness." Use someone else, not Justin—a different situation, a different experience of togetherness. Choose another*

anchor; this time hold your right earlobe.

.   *Close your eyes. Step inside that memory and relive it as though it's happening now. See the other person. It's Fran, she's wearing her pink bikini, we're on the beach, the sun burning down, the wind starting up, waves crashing. She's telling me she's going to marry Ted, she's going to be my sister, and I'm feeling so light, so buoyant, as if I could float up into the sky; I feel there's no weight to my body, the light can shine through me, I'm all light and warmth and bounce.*

  Relive the memory on the beach. Release your right earlobe, look around, take a deep breath, stand up, take another deep breath. Another.

Tanya sits down again. She has established both anchors. With her eyes closed, she reaches up with her left hand and with her right, taking hold of both earlobes simultaneously. While she holds both earlobes, her emotions sweep across her face. The color of her skin changes: pale, then flushed; her breathing is heavy, then light; she is rocked by her two opposing emotions—separation, togetherness; separation, togetherness—the emotions pitching and shifting over her features. And then, nearly half a minute into holding both anchors, she assumes a new expression. The volleying emotions stabilize. Her features become calm.

She releases the anchors, brings her hands down, and opens her eyes. She describes how it felt to have both emotions coursing through her at the same time. "There was a lot of confusion—almost as if I were spinning, as if a wave caught me up—and then I got quiet."

She recalls the original memory, of Justin leaving, and says, "The feeling's different now, not so overpowering."

She thinks of a time in the future—a week from Wednesday—when he will have to leave again on business, and she goes through it in her mind as if it were happening now, "recalling" the future as though she were looking back on it as a memory.

What she feels is, "It's OK. It's—well, almost as if I'm still connected to him, even though he's away. I mean, I know we're separated, we're apart, but I'm not feeling that negative rush anymore. It's sad that I'm not with him, of course, but it isn't terrifying. There's no pleasure in him being away, but it's not horrible either."

By neutralizing the limiting emotions of separation, of being alone, Tanya gets to where she has choice. She still won't be happy when Justin goes away, she won't look forward to it, but she'll be able to remain calm, doing her own work, preparing for her bar exam, and knowing that she and Justin will be together again soon. The separation is bearable; it becomes part of their relationship, and Tanya can use the time when they're apart in a constructive way, doing what she wants or needs to do, having control over her life and not being swept away in a wash of limiting and inappropriate emotions.

❖

RECIPE FOR CHOICE III
Dissolving Negative Emotions

1. Identify a recurring and limiting emotion. (Please do not use a trauma or phobia here; no overwhelmingly painful emotions.)

2. Think of an experience of this emotion. Relive it and anchor it, holding your left earlobe with your left hand for 10 seconds. (For instructions on self-anchoring, see chapter 15.)

   Repeat the anchoring several times until you're able

to hold your left earlobe and the emotion comes flooding back.

3. Identify the opposite emotion to the limiting one. Remember, this is not the emotion you *want* to have. Think of an experience of this (opposite) emotion, relive it, and anchor it by holding your right earlobe with your right hand for 10 seconds.

    Repeat the anchoring several times, until you're able to hold your right earlobe and the emotion comes flooding back.

4. You now have two self-anchors. Simultaneously, hold both anchors for 30 seconds or until your emotions stabilize.

    The emotions will play from one anchor to the other before they "settle"; the amount of time varies among individuals. Hold both anchors until your experience stabilizes; then release both anchors, take a deep breath, look around for about a minute.

5. Hold the first anchor. How does the limiting emotion feel?

    It will be neutralized, giving you more choice. (*Note*: Once you've neutralized the limiting emotion, you can self-anchor the desired emotion and use it in situations where previously you would have felt the limiting emotion.)

6. Think of a future situation in which you would have felt this limiting emotion before doing this exercise. How is it different now?

◆

47

Pop-It!

Of all the techniques we've used to expand choices, clarify communication, and implement changes, this last one—Pop-It!—is probably the most magical. It's certainly the most dramatic, like the swish of the cape as Clark Kent turns into his super self.

And that's what Pop-It! is, an instantaneous change from one to the other, the moment when the butterfly emerges from its chrysalis, wings dripping, the dry shell discarded. It's the instant when sunlight takes over a room after the shade is raised. It's the image that suddenly swims into view on photographic paper in developing fluid.

Pop-It! capitalizes on the mind's ability to switch in an instant. We've all had moments of tumbling from joy to despair, from feeling that everything is lost to a sudden discovery that it's found.

The mind, after all, is filled with circuits. They can be switched—ON, OFF, OFF, ON—or they can veer suddenly. "The mind," as Milton said, "is its own place." Within it, incredible transformations take place in an instant. The mind moves from one thing to the next along many routes. Think of imagination, of fantasy, of sudden inspiration, of the creative moment. How do these things happen?

The mind is a magic place. But magic, as we begin to learn even in childhood, is based on illusion. Illusion means seeing things in a strange or new way. Something ordinary becomes mysterious. What we see is the sum of many steps, though the steps themselves remain invisible.

A word, a name, pops into your head. How? You see a perfectly detailed picture of yourself with your grandmother forty years ago, the sun as bright as it was then, the faint smell of autumn bonfires in the air. How is this possible?

Magic is the end product, the consciously realized summation of all the tiny steps that went before. Newton didn't discover gravity at the exact instant when he saw the apple fall. That was simply the moment when all his knowledge and study, his hunches and imagination, came roaring together in a burst of perception. But a lifetime of preparation had gone before.

In the Pop-It! exercise, you take an image that arouses negative emotions or behavior and flip it to a positive image. You do it instantaneously, like snapping your fingers or switching a dial. From dark to light, negative to positive: from something that oppresses (limits) you to something you have control over. This may seem complicated to your conscious mind. However, your unconscious mind knows exactly how to do this; it has done it many, many times before. The only difference now is that you are directing the action instead of letting it happen at random. All you have to do is set up the two images, the limiting one and the more resourceful one you want to replace it with. Then give your mind the instructions and get out of the way. Have trust that your mind can do this.

The Pop-It! exercise is based on submodalities. Let's just review them for a moment.

In Part I, The Meaning of Your Communication Is the Response You Get, we discovered that thinking is sensory-based, meaning not only that we take in experience through our senses, we also represent our memories and knowledge through our sensory systems. Each of us has a primary filter, or modality, through which we customarily process information. The basic or most-used modalities of our thinking are visual, auditory, and kinesthetic.

In Part II, You Have All the Resources You Need, we took this one step further to submodalities, which are the smaller, more specific aspects of the larger modalities.

To imagine them clearly, we used the analogy of a TV or VCR: The pictures, sounds, and movements are being sent out in the same way to all receivers, but each of us picks up this information differently. We can turn up the sound, increase the bass, make the picture less blurred, intensify the reds or blues, change the speed. (And of course we can change channels.)

This is analogous to what we do within our own brains. The mind's projector and amplifier and speed control are all transmitting our memories, thoughts, ideas, and dreams onto our mental screen by means of tiny units, fragments of perception that we call submodalities. They are the atoms of thought that make up the mind's code, the brain's bits of information. Submodalities code our experience. Submodalities are the way we perceive experience; *how* we interpret it. Submodalities provide meaning.

If you want to change the meaning of an experience, making changes in a submodality is a lot easier than trying to change the whole experience.

Through changing submodalities you can take a memory that's limiting you, or keeping you stuck in a situation, and simply flip it to another dimension.

Submodalities change—pop!—like a jack-in-the-box; they happen in a flash!; they come to you *like that!* (snap your fingers).

Submodality changes are the *Eureka!* type of thinking, the sudden inspiration, the scales falling from your eyes, showing you things in a new way, giving instantaneous understanding. They work below the level of consciousness, darting along the neural wires to find brand-new connections that change your perspective and lead to new interpretations of experience. That means more choices.

Any kind of submodality change can be extremely powerful.

I think of Julie (not her real name), a woman in her fifties who was romantically interested in a man a dozen or so years younger. But whenever she was with him she felt insecure. She lost her usual confidence and sparkle. A voice kept telling her, *You're too old, you're too old. . . .*

The voice Julie kept hearing (her own), was coming from *inside* her head, from the *left* side. With auditory submodalities, the direction the words or message is coming from can be crucial. When I asked her to move the voice *outside* her head and place it at the *back*, she listened for a moment and then giggled.

"Really silly," she said. "It sounds squeaky, like a rubber ducky. It's ridiculous!" She was laughing with relief.

A single change in the location of this auditory message transformed a very unpleasant utterance into something funny.

Submodalities are extremely powerful. "Submodalities," as a student in my workshop said, "are *awesome.*"

By changing submodalities we change the impact of an experience, and therefore its meaning. Pop-It! is a very simple exercise in changing submodalities, very direct and extremely powerful.

Jeff (not his real name) is a resident neurosurgeon in a Boston hospital, fascinated by his work and completely engrossed in every aspect of it, but whenever one of the staff surgeons looks at him in what he calls an "intense" way, Jeff gets nervous. He starts talking too fast, loses his concentration, and gets defensive. This annoys the surgeons, who don't want him on their team.

The expression—piercing eyes and a slight frown—that so upsets Jeff is not uncommon among busy preoccupied surgeons. But whenever Jeff sees that expression, he instantly connects it with an image of his father, the way he looked when Jeff displeased him: when Jeff didn't try out for Little League, or didn't apply to the college his father wanted him to go to, or brought in one of the injured animals he was always finding throughout his boyhood. Jeff sees in the surgeon's expression the face of his father and connects the expression with disapproval and fault-finding, with the sense that he's not good enough, he's doing something wrong or inappropriate.

To change the negative thought—in the form of his father's face—I suggest to Jeff, "Make a big bright picture in your mind of your father scowling at you."

Jeff becomes visibly agitated. He squirms in his chair, squeezes his eyes shut, leans far forward, then all the way back. He's in a lot of discomfort.

In the bottom left-hand corner of this image of your father, looking at you with that "intense" expression, I'd like you to make a small, dark image of you the way you want to be. An image of you being the way you want to be when anyone in authority looks at you "intensely." Got it?

Jeff nods. "Right," he says. "Got that image."

Good. So you have a big bright image of your father looking at you with that intense expression, and in the bottom left-hand corner a small dark picture of you the way you want to be. Now let the small dark image become big and bright as the big bright image becomes small and dark and disappears. You're going to do this quickly. Your mind can do it quicker than you can say Pop-It! It happens in a flash.

When I say Pop-It! to you, you'll let the small dark picture of you become big and bright as the big, bright picture of your father gets small and dark and disappears, so you're left with a big bright picture of you the way you want to be.

Pop-It!

I say the words quickly in a loud, clear voice. Jeff seems to jump a little. He opens his eyes.

We do it again. We do it four times. Each time I tell Jeff that he will take the small dark picture of himself and make it big and bright while the big bright picture of his father gets small and dark and disappears. This will happen very quickly, I tell him, whenever I say "Pop-It!"

At the end of each try, Jeff opens his eyes, looks around, takes a few deep breaths.

After the fifth time, Jeff says, "It's happened. I can't even get an image of my father anymore. Every time I try to think of him looking at me in that way, all I get is a picture of me looking confident and very busy."

I ask him to make an image of one of the surgeons at the hospital wearing that "intense" expression.

"Same thing," Jeff says. "It's still me, cheerful and busy."

He has new choices now; the rut has been created in a new direction. Jeff is no longer nervous and defensive when a surgeon looks at him in that way. He can separate himself from what was an automatic response. He's placed a new "thought," in the form of an image of himself as he wants to be, between the surgeon's facial expression and his old habit of response.

There's always another way of doing things, another way of thinking, another way of feeling. There are always more choices. And that's what freedom means: the ability to choose.

In chapter 43, we defined choice as flexibility. And what is flexibility except freedom?

Freedom, whether for an individual or a group or a country, means the opportunity for choice. Personal freedom; political freedom; economic, religious, any kind of freedom: It's all based on having the right to choose, on being able to make choices. In a "free" society we can vote, make up our own minds about any number of things, express our opinions and lifestyles in thousands of ways. We choose among competing goods, politicians, ideas, partners, beliefs. We're free as citizens and as individuals because we have choices.

"There are more things in heaven and earth, Horatio, than are dreamt of in your philosophy," Hamlet tells his friend. Within ourselves, there are more possible choices than we can imagine: numberless ways to represent our thoughts, infinite distinctions and shades of meaning, unlimited forms of behavior.

Having choices gives us freedom and provides a moral dimension to our lives. People who refuse to exercise their power and ability to make choices aren't people we look up to or honor. People who don't want to have choices are denying themselves a part of their humanity because they're refusing to grow. They're not in charge of their own lives because they refuse to be responsible; unwilling or unable to change anything, they become "victims" to their own fears or habits, memories, or thoughts.

We don't have to be victims of our own lives, of past or present, of our jobs, relationships, self-image, failures, or omissions. There are always more choices. Everything that lives changes; each new moment represents more possibilities, another choice. Choice means freedom; freedom brings responsibility; and responsibility means that you're in charge, you have the power to choose.

By learning how to communicate with yourself and others, and especially within yourself, between your conscious and unconscious mind, you gain access to your resources, get in touch with the strengths and talents you already have, and are then able to use them when and where you choose. You take control of your life, as you take over the controls, the invisible knobs and handles and anchors and words; the images, sounds, sensations, and emotions that are constantly informing you about the world while providing you with the means to act upon it.

The power of choice puts you in the driver's seat, giving you the freedom to go just about anywhere you want, at the pace you choose, making changes along the way whenever you want to or need to, on the road to the place where everything is possible.

◆

RECIPE FOR CHOICE IV
Pop-It!

1. Identify a recurring negative image that limits you; something that stops you from having choices about your behavior (this includes thoughts and feelings).

2. In your mind's eye, make the image big and bright, put it in a frame, and place it directly in front of you, neither too far nor too close—at a comfortable reading distance.

3. In the bottom left-hand corner of this image put a small dark image of yourself the way you want to be in the situation where you get that limiting image,

responding the way you'd like to respond.

4. Practice this: At the same time, make the small dark image of yourself become big and bright, and the original big bright image small and dark, until it disappears. The image of you the way you want to be completely replaces the original big, bright, limiting image. This must be done in the blink of an eye: a sudden flip.

5. At the signal "Pop-It!" make the switch. The small dark image of yourself becomes big and bright as the original image becomes small and dark and disappears. This happens instantaneously, flipping one image for the other, the positive for the negative. Break state. Open your eyes. Take a deep breath. Do this three times.

6. After the last flip, open your eyes and take a breath. Think of the original negative image. If you automatically see a big bright image of yourself the way you want to be instead of the negative image you started with, you've done it!

NOTE: *If it doesn't happen instantaneously, practice the Pop-It! exercise several times more until it happens automatically: Your unconscious mind takes over the magic and all you can see is yourself, big and bright.*

◆ ◆ ◆

JAKE O'SHAUNESSEY

Once on the west coast of Ireland there lived a seagull whose name was Jake O'Shaunessey. Jake was a healthy, handsome, and intelligent seagull, but he was not able to fly.

When he was just a wee bird, Jake's parents and siblings had been lost in a severe storm and he'd had no one to teach him.

He grew older and decided to try to learn by himself. He watched other seagulls and imitated them. He ran along the ground and flapped his wings and hopped up and down, trying to get into the air, but nothing would happen, and the young seagulls laughed at him because Jake looked so funny.

Some of the older seagulls tried to teach him, but each one told Jake a different way of learning to fly, and Jake tried to think of all the ways each of the seagulls had told him: "Flap your wings more, get your feet back, head straight," and all the other instructions. He was thinking so hard about what everyone told him that he wasn't able to get off the ground. He began to believe something was wrong with him, that he would never fly.

He tried going to the top of a cliff and jumping off, but he simply fell to the bottom. He went to a higher cliff, over the sea, closed his eyes, and jumped. Again, he fell. Other seagulls took pity on Jake and tried to take care of him. But this made him feel more discouraged than ever. He felt like a cripple.

One day a very old and wise seagull flew in to the western coast where Jake lived. He listened to Jake's problem and told him to climb to the top of a special cliff, the highest and steepest one. On the top of this cliff he would find a large boulder, and on this boulder was written a secret message. This was the message Jake needed in order to fly, the wise bird told him.

No seagull had ever climbed such a steep cliff before. Jake had to tie starfish to his feet to help him with the suction. He climbed slowly, painfully, and finally reached *the top. He saw the large boulder. On it was written,* What you believe, you can do.

Jake looked down from the dizzying cliff and was terri-fied, but he closed his eyes and jumped. He started to drop, and as he did he remembered to say to himself, "I believe I can fly, I believe I can fly." He was so busy saying it that he forgot to doubt himself. Instead of paying attention to all the different things he'd been told to do, he just did it. And he found himself flying—flying like any other seagull, with wings outstretched, gliding on the winds. It was the most wonderful moment of his life. He flew and dipped and never once wondered if he was doing it right. Far below on the sand, the other seagulls, who were watching him, heard him sing out, "I can fly! I believe!"

◆ ◆ ◆